Two or Three Things
I Know about Her

HARVARD FILM STUDIES

Two or Three Things I Know about Her

Alfred Guzzetti

ANALYSIS OF A FILM BY GODARD

HARVARD UNIVERSITY PRESS
Cambridge, Massachusetts, and
London, England
1981

Printed in the United States of America

Publication of this book has been aided by a grant from the Andrew W. Mellon Foundation

Library of Congress Cataloging in Publication Data

Guzzetti, Alfred, 1942–

   Two or three things I know about her.

   Includes the French script of Godard's 2 ou 3 choses
que je sais d'elle, with English translation.

   1.   2 [i.e. Deux] ou 3 [i.e. trois] choses que je
sais d'elle. [Motion picture]   I.   Godard, Jean Luc,
1930–   2 [i.e. Deux] ou 3 [i.e. trois] choses
que je sais d'elle. English & French.

II.   2 [i.e. Deux] ou 3 [i.e. trois] choses que je
sais d'elle. [Motion picture]   III.   Title.

PN1997.D45573G8   791.43'72   80-15832

ISBN 0-674-91500-3

Book design by Edith Allard

To my mother and father

Contents

Preface

I first saw Jean-Luc Godard's *2 ou 3 choses que je sais d'elle* with my friend Joel Haycock shortly after its American premiere at the New Yorker Theater on April 30, 1970. The following autumn we saw the film again, this time as part of a Godard retrospective mounted by the Orson Welles Cinema here in Cambridge. By then Haycock was at work, nominally under my supervision, on a Harvard College honors thesis entitled "Radical Ideology in the Cinema" in which he discussed *2 ou 3 choses* in relation to the films Godard had made immediately before it. This project stimulated my interest in the film further, and in the fall of 1971 I persuaded several Harvard departments to contribute to the purchase of a 16mm print. Interest spread to a number of faculty members concerned either centrally or peripherally with film; in a short time a study group had formed, which included as regular members Stanley Cavell from the philosophy department, Michael Fried from art history, Ruth Fried from the history of science, Roy Glauber from physics, Barbara Herman from philosophy, Brooke Hopkins from English, Soren Kjørup, a Danish Fulbright scholar in philosophy, Janet Mendelsohn from visual and environmental studies, Laurence Wylie from French civilization, and myself. We met in Harvard's Carpenter Center for the Visual Arts every Tuesday evening during the academic year 1971–72, devoting one and sometimes two sessions to the screening and discussion of each sequence.

Meanwhile, the curricular study of film at Harvard was beginning in earnest. In 1972 the university received a grant from the Luce Foundation for a visiting professorship in film history. The following year we joined with New York University and the State University of New York at Buffalo, where ventures into this field were also in the initial stages, for a three-year series of seminars on the problems of film scholarship and teaching. In the spring of 1975 Vlada Petric, then the Luce Professor, asked me for a paper on *2 ou 3 choses* for an upcoming seminar meeting. I agreed, thinking only to write up the notes I had made during our study-group discussions of the opening sequence, but in the last, very hot weeks of that summer I yielded to the temptation to go beyond the first sequence and further than the content of my notes. The long paper that emerged was—as the present commentary is—a mixture of my own ideas and my memory of what others in the group had said, for by then I could no longer be sure which was which.

After the seminar meeting I assumed that my work on *2 ou 3 choses* had ended. But in the spring of 1977, when plans for the Harvard Film Studies series were laid, Cavell proposed that my paper, slightly revised, be one of the initial volumes. William Rothman, who had led the seminar discussion, gave it a second reading, making meticulous, detailed, and lengthy criticisms. With his comments in mind I rewrote, expanded, and revised the text, and devised a scheme for relating it to a systematic rendering of the film. The result is the book in its present form.

This brief history will suffice to indicate how much this project owes to my colleagues and friends. Among these debts perhaps the deepest is to Joel Haycock, who in the course of the past ten years has indelibly influenced my thinking not only about Godard but about the broader problems of relating politics and film. I believe that his analysis of these problems, once it is completed and published, will be seen as providing a necessary complement to much of what I have written here.

I wish to extend my thanks to New Yorker Films and Argos Films for permission to include frame enlargements from *2 ou 3 choses;* to *L'avant-scène du cinéma* for permission to reproduce the French dialogue: and to Lorrimer and Seymour, Ltd., for allowing me to publish an English translation. Jacqueline Martin checked the transcription and translation of the French, and Vlada Petric transcribed and translated the Serbo-Croatian lines in Sequence 4. The resources of the Harvard Film Archive and the Carpenter Center for the Visual Arts allowed me to study the film at length, and grants from the Harvard Graduate Society enabled me to obtain professional-quality negatives for the frame enlargements. New Yorker Films kindly lent me a 35 mm print from which to make these enlargements; Film Opticals, Inc., made the negatives, and David Saul printed them. Ellen Weise furnished the advertisement on page 347, and Bertrand Sauzier suggested the important connection between *2 ou 3 choses* and Cocteau's *Orphée.*

Quotations from *The New Wave* (edited by Peter Graham) appear by permission of Martin Secker and Warburg; and those from *Godard on Godard* (edited by Jean Narboni and Tom Milne), by permission of Martin Secker and Warburg and the Viking Press. Selections from *Brecht on Theatre* (edited and translated by John Willett, copyright 1957, 1963, and 1964 by Suhrkamp Verlag, Frankfurt am Main, translation and notes copyright 1964 by John Willett) are reprinted by permission of Farrar, Straus and Giroux, Inc. The cartoon on p. 47 is copyright 1966 by Jules Feiffer and appears by his consent. A few paragraphs in the discussion of Sequence 12, adapted from my article "Narrative and the Film Image," are reprinted by permission of *New Literary History.*

I should also like to acknowledge the special contributions of Vivian Wheeler, who edited the manuscript with such care, and Edith Allard, who devised elegant solutions to the unusually difficult design problems it presented.

As a student, it was my good fortune to have four extraordinary teachers—William Alfred, the late Reuben Brower, Anne Ferry, and Richard Poirier. I hope their influence is evident in the pages that follow.

Two or Three Things
I Know about Her

Introduction

Jean-Luc Godard came to film as a critic. In 1950, while nominally a student of ethnology at the Sorbonne, he began writing about films, at first for a magazine he had helped found, then chiefly for the recently launched *Cahiers du cinéma.* Like his colleagues at *Cahiers*—François Truffaut, Eric Rohmer, Jacques Rivette—he thought of criticism as a preparation for filmmaking and during the fifties directed four shorts. In 1959, at the age of twenty-eight, he shot his first feature, *Breathless,* which established his reputation and associated him with what a journalist had dubbed the "New Wave" of French filmmakers.

The success of *Breathless* enabled Godard to follow his inclination to work rapidly. In 1960 he shot *Le petit soldat,* a story of political intrigue set in Geneva; in 1961 *A Woman Is a Woman,* a musical of sorts; and in 1962 *Vivre sa vie,* a tale of prostitution. In a December 1962 interview quoted in *Godard on Godard* (ed. Jean Narboni and Tom Milne, New York: Viking, 1972, p. 181), he looked back over these first four features in the following terms:

Cinema, Truffaut said, is spectacle—[Georges] Méliès—and research—[Louis] Lumière. If I analyse myself today, I see that I have always wanted, basically, to make a research film in the form of a spectacle. The documentary side is: a man in a particular situation. The spectacle comes when one makes this man a gangster or a secret agent. In *Une Femme est une Femme* the spectacle comes from the fact that the woman is an actress; in *Vivre sa Vie,* a prostitute.

The mixture of what Godard calls "research" and "spectacle" persists in the films he made in the five years following. *Band of Outsiders* (1964) and *Made in U.S.A.* (1966) are, like *Breathless,* gangster movies. *Alphaville* (1965) and *Pierrot le fou* (1965), like *Le petit soldat,* are stories of secret agents. The protagonists of these films are, as Godard puts it, people who have an idea and go to the end of that idea. This act, with its existential overtones, is the mainspring of the fiction, the spectacle.

As for the element of research, it results from Godard's predilection for what he calls "the documentary side" of the cinema. *Vivre sa vie* is indebted for its plot and for many of its details to a sociological study of prostitution and includes a four-minute sequence in the style of the voice-over documentary. *Les carabiniers* (1963), a war fable, derives a number of its texts verbatim from historical documents and reproduces in its imagery the quality of battle footage. *Une femme mariée* (1964) goes a step farther in this direction, relinquishing spectacle in the pursuit of a sociologically defined subject, the married woman. This line of development culminates in *Masculine Feminine* (1966), a film that evokes the world of documentaries not only through its use of available light, hand-held shots, coarse-grained black-and-white imagery, interview footage, and candid street scenes, but through the frankly sociological character of its subject— youth culture.

As this account suggests, the films Godard made before 1967 can be divided into two groups: those that emphasize research and those that emphasize spectacle. How- ever, neither emphasis develops at the expense of the other: *Masculine Feminine,* which epitomizes the first group, was shot within months of *Pierrot le fou,* which epitomizes the second. Indeed, even the most spectacular of Godard's films reveal a passion for the factual, the speculative, and the intellectual. *Pierrot*—for all its chases, murders, intrigues, and gun battles—finds moments for striking reflections on painting, writing, and photography. Conversely, *Masculine Feminine* ends with an arbitrary death of the sort more logically associated with the spectacles of *Pierrot, Vivre sa vie,* and *Contempt.*

The mixture of spectacle and research goes far toward defining Godard's style, a style that also mixes the popular with the intellectual, the serious with the comic, the composed with the accidental, the romantic with the witty. The freedom with which Godard combines these opposites points to a central characteristic of his work: a refusal to allow the narrative to determine all of the elements of the film. This attitude mani- fests itself in complementary ways. On the one hand, the action of the films is fre- quently interrupted by passages extraneous to the story—characters' remarks to the camera, songs, dances, philosophical discourses, interviews, vaudeville routines, and, in one instance, a recapitulation of the plot for latecomers. On the other, the audience is repeatedly confronted with the formal properties of the sound and image and made to reflect on the mechanisms and processes of the cinema.

Indeed, for many spectators the preoccupation with the cinema is Godard's trademark. His characters go to the movies, talk about them, quote them, and live in an environment of movie posters. Actors, actresses, and directors appear in cameo roles: Jeanne Moreau in *A Woman Is a Woman,* Brigitte Bardot in *Masculine Feminine,* Samuel Fuller in *Pierrot,* and Fritz Lang in *Contempt.* Many of the films are modeled to one de- gree or another on films of other directors—*Breathless* on *Scarface, A Woman Is a Woman* on Lubitsch, *Vivre sa vie* on Dreyer's *Joan of Arc, Contempt* on Rossellini's *Viag- gio in Italia, Pierrot* on Lang's *You Only Live Once,* and *Made in U.S.A.* on *The Big Sleep.* *Les carabiniers* includes parodies of two films by Lumière, *Masculine Feminine* a parody of Bergman's *The Silence.* And *Contempt* is the story of the making of a film.

In the mid-1960s two tendencies emerge in Godard's work. First, beginning with *Une femme mariée,* there is a marked weakening in the role of narrative; Godard warns the audience of this in the subtitle *Fragments d'un film tourné en 1964* (*Fragments of a Film Shot in 1964*). Apropos of *Pierrot* (1965), which is adapted from an American novel, he admits: "The Americans are good at storytelling, the French are not." Indeed, the ellipses and digressions of that film end up making its plot virtually incomprehensi- ble. In *Masculine Feminine* the narrative is minimal and incompletely realized—a point underscored by the gratuitous death of the male protagonist at the end. *Made in U.S.A.* (1966), a labyrinthine political intrigue with no intelligible narrative line at all, takes to an extreme the obscurity of *Pierrot.*

Second, Godard begins to redefine his interest in the political. It is true that as early as *Le petit soldat* he produced films with political themes—notably *Les carabiniers,*

Une femme mariée, Alphaville, Pierrot, Masculine Feminine, and *Made in U.S.A.* But in *Le petit soldat* little importance is attached to the specifics of political allegiance. This attitude persists as late as *Made in U.S.A.,* which closes with a declaration that right and left constitute an "outdated equation." At the same time there is, beginning in 1965, evidence of a growing political commitment. *Pierrot* includes an attack on America's role in Vietnam, as does each of the films that follow it. The action of *Masculine Feminine* takes place between, and in relation to, the two rounds of French elections of the winter of 1965–66—a politically important moment—and two of its main characters have strong commitments to the left. Godard is openly sympathetic not only to these characters, as he is to the right-wing protagonist of *Le petit soldat,* but to their cause as well.

Godard's slackening interest in narrative and his growing absorption in the political come to a head in his thirteenth feature film, *2 ou 3 choses que je sais d'elle,* shot in the late summer of 1966 and premiered in Paris on March 17, 1967. In several crucial respects this film represents not only a development of, but a departure from, those that precede it. Perhaps most importantly, it includes a significant number of shots and texts, extending from the first sequence to the last, whose presence is not explicable in terms of the narrative. This material, unlike its counterparts in the earlier films, comprises a major element in the structure of the whole. Accordingly, the burden of the "spectacle" is shifted from the narrative to the image; the film is, as it were, built from sounds and images rather than story. Finally, the director's voice is heard throughout, reflecting on the dilemmas before him, commenting on the sociological ramifications of the action, and ruminating on politics and philosophy.

The direction marked out by these innovations is one that, as in much of Godard's work, deeply divides spectators and critics. Largely because of the de-emphasis of narrative and the abstruseness of the voice-over commentaries, audiences find *2 ou 3 choses* a difficult experience. Much of the controversy surrounding the film stems from this fact. We are, after all, accustomed to go to the movies for entertainment, and when at an entertainment we are, in general, not eager either to do work or to see it done. Godard's earlier films take care to indulge—and even to cultivate—this reluctance. With *2 ou 3 choses,* however, he turns his attention more exclusively to the demanding process of investigating the world through the agency of pictures and sounds. What emerges from this process is a work not in the sense of a task accomplished, but a task being done and *to* be done. A portion of this task falls to us.

How are we to respond? Those inclined to be hostile to Godard's project will fixate on the film's tedious stretches and complain that nothing happens in the plot, that the characters are unremarkable and unsympathetic, that they have no convincing psychology, and that there is talk and intellectualizing instead of emotion. Such objections are not to be ignored, for at their root is a quarrel of fundamental proportions. In *2 ou 3 choses* Godard attacks a society to which, as he makes clear, certain cinematic practices belong. To those practices he must, therefore, search out an alternative. Consequently, the sounds and images that constitute his film have a special, and quite contradictory, function, for they must express ideas opposed to those implicit in the world they represent. This dilemma exerts an inescapable strain on the film's style; it puts many of the conventional ways of organizing sound and image beyond Godard's reach and makes the resulting organization difficult, a "problem," for the viewer. Those least tolerant of this difficulty will be those who do not understand the ideas under attack to be ideas at all, but consider them rather the ineluctable constituents of normality, of "experience."

Thus *2 ou 3 choses* not only requires a change in our understanding of what cinema is and should be; it moves that understanding in a political direction. Compared to Godard's preceding films, it devotes much more attention to the social and economic world. Its reduced emphasis on narrative implicitly argues that the characters (unlike those, say, of *Pierrot* or *Vivre sa vie*) do not make their own destiny; they are not "responsible" in the existential sense that the heroine of *Vivre sa vie* gives to that word. Here such responsibility is, as the title phrase indicates, laid on the political entity Godard calls *"elle:* the Paris region."

To take the side of *2 ou 3 choses* is, therefore, to assent to terms that are at once political and stylistic. I mean to do precisely this by laying down the claim that *2 ou 3 choses* is the most complex and profound work of the most interesting and inventive filmmaker of our time—that it is, in other words, one of the masterpieces of the sound cinema.

Yet even those who support such a claim must acknowledge that, while *2 ou 3 choses* clearly reflects Godard's growing commitment to the left, it fails in the end to arrive at an unambiguous and coherent political position. A vexing question therefore arises: does the film owe its persuasive complexity to what is patently a crisis of ideology, of belief? I do not wish to deny that it might. But I do want to dissociate myself from the more general thesis this suggests: namely, that Godard's films—or, some would say, any films—deteriorate from the moment they take a specific political stance. The consensus of those who have followed Godard's career is, I fear, that after 1967 he squandered his enormous talent on works of monotonous political rhetoric.

The truth, it seems to me, is more complex. The political irresoluteness of *2 ou 3 choses* also informs *La chinoise* and *Weekend* (both 1967). These, the last of Godard's films to reach mass audiences (with the possible exception of the recently completed *Sauve qui peut la vie*), reflect the admission he makes in *Far from Vietnam* (also 1967) that his ideology is "a bit vague." With *Le gai savoir*—a dense and virtually plotless dialogue about images, sounds, politics, and knowing—he moves to remedy this situation; his tone becomes more defined and his political stance more militant.

Between the shooting and editing of *Le gai savoir* fell the strikes and demonstrations of May 1968, events that prompted Godard to renounce his identity as bourgeois director and ally himself openly with the left. In the period following, besides directing *One Plus One* (1968) on his own, he entered into several collaborations with militants, among them Jean-Pierre Gorin, and, as a member of the newly formed Dziga Vertov Group, engaged in a succession of projects stylistically and thematically akin to *Le gai savoir*: *Un film comme les autres* (1968), *British Sounds, Pravda, Wind from the East, Struggles in Italy* (all 1969), *Vladimir and Rosa* (1970), and *Letter to Jane* (1972). These films reflect a definite, but shifting, political line. Shot in 16mm, they were intended mainly for militant audiences and played only rarely in theaters. In 1971, the year before *Letter to Jane,* Godard and Gorin attempted a large-scale project in 35mm in an effort to recapture a mass audience. This attempt, *Tout va bien* (1972), failed, and in 1973 the Dziga Vertov Group disbanded.

It must be admitted that, apart from three stunning sequences in *British Sounds*—the automobile production line, the naked woman, and the meeting of the auto union militants—the films of the Dziga Vertov period do not achieve the standard set by Godard's best work. However, the same cannot be said of the three brilliant films that follow: *Numéro deux* (1975), *Ici et ailleurs* (1975), and *Comment ça va?* (1977).

These projects, carried out in collaboration with the militant and feminist Anne-Marie Miéville, owe their success not to any lessening of political commitment, but to the critical perspectives they develop both on themselves and on Godard's preceding films, including, in particular, those of the Dziga Vertov period. *Numéro deux* (a phrase referring to Godard's *Numéro un, Breathless*) is a rigorous reconsideration of the subject of *2 ou 3 choses*—a family living in a high-rise apartment building and the effect of politics on the family's sexual life. *Comment ça va?* (a question that pointedly retreats from the ironic confidence of the earlier answer *Tout va bien*) develops further the analysis of the mass media, and specifically of news photographs, begun in *Letter to Jane*. And *Ici et ailleurs*, the most outstanding of the group, is a complex meditation on footage from *Until Victory*, an uncompleted project of the Dziga Vertov period commissioned by the Palestine Liberation Organization. The posture of all three of these films is aptly summarized in a series of intertitles in *Ici et ailleurs:* EN/REPENSANT/A/CELA—"rethinking this."

The problems that *2 ou 3 choses* explores and that prompt me to write about it have their counterpart in the task of the writing itself. Chief among them is that, given the medium of print, one cannot quote a film as one can a text; one cannot even notate it as perfectly as music, or reproduce it as completely as a painting or drawing. Without an adequate reference mechanism, how is rigorous analysis possible? Indeed, few writers have even attempted such analyses. Accordingly, I have, in approaching this project, taken it as part of my task to devise a way of accurately rendering the film, especially those aspects of it that are most relevant to my discussion.

Of course, the scarcity of serious studies of films is not due only to technology. It is also the result of the unspoken prejudice that a film is not worth the attention customarily given to a good book or painting or musical composition. One of my purposes here is to challenge this prejudice and to undo some of the damaging effect it has had on our understanding of the medium. Underlying my efforts is the contention that, lacking a thorough and patient analysis of some films, we do not—and in fact cannot—pay full and uncompromising attention to any.

Clearly, then, this volume has as much to do with the problems of film study as it does with the work of Jean-Luc Godard. At the same time, my approach has a character that is unavoidably shaped by the film it takes for an example. Because *2 ou 3 choses* presents itself, as I have said, as built from images and sounds, it encourages and supports an analysis along the same lines. Is such an analysis transferable to films that do not resemble this one stylistically? In an article entitled "Narrative and the Film Image" (*New Literary History,* 6 [1975], 379–392), I have argued that it is; having done so, I here allow this to remain an open question.

As for the particular character of my analysis, it is shaped in part by the decision to follow in my commentary the succession of shots and sounds in the film. If I had to describe this procedure in a word, I should call it "empirical," since it begins from the organization of the seen and the heard. A critic of my method has forcefully argued that it is inherently approving of the film, that it masks precisely the value judgment I deliver explicitly in this introduction. It is true that, in interpreting what the film signifies at each moment, I accede to its terms in some very fundamental way and thus forgo a vantage point from which to articulate a more far-reaching criticism.

In spite of this, I have not hesitated to venture value judgments about many portions and aspects of the film. For example, I criticize Sequence 15 for being thin and tedious and praise Sequence 12 for its complexity and beauty. In doing so, I expose my interest as a filmmaker in the problems of constructing and organizing sound and image. From another perspective, Sequence 12 represents the artist's self-indulgent theatricalization of his own problems, while in Sequence 15 he admirably, if clumsily, attempts a self-criticism. As this example indicates, the basis of my critical remarks is the measurement of details against what I take to be the film's dominant and successful line. These issues coalesce around the judgment, which I make explicit in the section headed Digression, that what follows Sequence 12 is on the whole not so good as what precedes it. While I argue this judgment at some length—indeed, it is woven into the entire fabric of my analysis—I do not claim to justify the values on which it is based, for I believe this to be a major, separate, and largely theoretical task.

Some explanation of the book's referential apparatus is necessary. I have divided the film's 227 shots into 18 sequences. Since there is no rigorous and widely accepted definition of a sequence, this division is necessarily somewhat arbitrary but is, I think, more manageable than no division at all. Within each sequence I have numbered the shots. Thus 16.12 means the twelfth shot in Sequence 16. I refer to cuts with a slash: 16.11/16.12 indicates the cut joining shot 16.11 to shot 16.12. In the division and numbering of the voice-over commentaries I have followed the script (actually an after-the-fact transcription) published in *L'avant-scène du cinéma* and republished as a paperback by Seuil/Avant-Scène.

On the left-hand pages appears my rendering of the film. Each shot is introduced by the shot number in the left-hand margin and is illustrated by at least one (where necessary, more than one) frame enlargement, placed in proper relation to the dialogue and action. Concluding the account of the shot are two small numbers, one above the other, at the right-hand margin. The upper gives the duration of the shot; the lower, the time elapsed from the beginning of the film to the cut in question.

Godard filmed *2 ou 3 choses* in 35 mm Eastmancolor and in Techniscope, a process identical to Cinemascope at the print stage and differing only with respect to the camera apparatus. A 35 mm Techniscope or Cinemascope image, correctly projected, is 2.35 times as wide as it is high. The frame enlargements in this volume were made from the only intact 35 mm print of *2 ou 3 choses* extant in the United States. Those who see the film in 16 mm should be aware that 16 mm prints of all 'scope films are proportioned at 2.67 to 1 (an unnecessary but conventionally accepted error) and thus lose a bit of the image at the top and bottom of the frame.

In square brackets I give a description of the sound—or more precisely, the sound as it is related to the picture. A new set of brackets appears only when this relation changes. I use the word "actual" to describe sound that belongs to, or originates in, what we see in the image, whether this sound is synchronous—that is, recorded at the same moment the image is filmed—or postsynchronous—recorded afterward and coordinated with the image in the editing stage. In practice, synchronous and post-synchronous actual sounds are often impossible to distinguish. I do not try to make the distinction except where it bears on the meaning of the shot—as, for instance, in 6.3, where we hear a track that, because of the lip synchronization, must be synchronous (therefore by definition "actual") and a second track of "ambience" (that is, background sound) mixed with it.

The spoken dialogue appears in two columns, the original language—chiefly French—to the right and an English translation to the left. This translation is mine and is deliberately literal, since my discussion often enters into details of phrasing. For example, in 6.6 I translate "vous désirez?" as "do you desire?" rather than the more idiomatic "may I help you?" because in 6.8 the person to whom the question is directed cites "desire" as an impression that does "not always refer to a specific object." Connections such as this would be lost in a more idiomatic translation.

In both French and English, words spoken on camera are indicated by roman type, those off camera by italics, and voice-over by boldface. These distinctions are sometimes problematical. "On camera" applies to cases where we can see the speaker—although, as my discussion of 11.1 and 11.2 shows, even this is not unambiguous. The clearest case of "off camera" is where a speaker who has been on camera moves out of the frame or continues to talk after a cut to a shot that does not show him or her. What if this new shot does not unequivocally represent the same space—as for example, the book jacket *Introduction to Ethnology* (9.2) or the exteriors in Sequence 10? The first instance is conventionally called an "insert," since preceding and following it are shots of the same room. I have categorized the voices with this and comparable shots as "off" (though a case could be made for calling them "over"). The clearest instance of a voice "over" is that of the speaker of the commentaries, for his speech does not belong to the time or the space designated by the picture. Does the woman's voice with the exterior shots of Sequence 10 meet this criterion? Since the image track there tells us nothing about the spatial relation of the exteriors to the views of the woman speaking, the case could be argued both ways. Because the exteriors do not appear to be inserts, I have classified this as an instance of voice-over. I have done the same in the few passages in which the speaker is never seen at all, even though he or she may in fact be off camera.

In certain other matters of terminology, I have simply followed the usage of filmmakers. Thus I call the beginning of any segment of film the head and the end the tail. A shot that shows one person is a one-shot and a shot that shows two people is a two-shot. Sound that increases or decreases in level is said to fade up or down; sound that enters or disappears gradually is said to fade in or out; and sound that enters, disappears, or changes abruptly does so by means of a straight cut.

On the right-hand pages my discussion of the film appears. Although this commentary and the film rendition are nearly always of unequal length, I have tried to coordinate them so as to minimize the need for turning pages. The reader can perhaps most easily proceed by reading through the rendition of each sequence—that is, the left-hand pages—then reading the commentary on it, referring again to the film rendition as necessary.

2 ou 3 choses que je sais d'elle

Sequence 0

0.1   [Silence.]

$$\frac{3.0''}{0'03.0''}$$

0.2   [Construction noise.]

$$\frac{1.0''}{0'04.0''}$$

In shot 0.13 we read that "elle" in the title *2 ou 3 choses que je sais d'elle* is "la Région parisienne." Nearly a minute later, in shot 1.5, we hear that "elle" is Marina Vlady, "an actress," and in 1.6 that it is Juliette Janson, the character whom she plays. Since the English phrase *Two or Three Things I Know about Her* misses both the equivocation region/woman and the priority that the film gives to the former, it will not do as a statement of the film's subject.

The "je" of the title is, clearly, Jean-Luc Godard. The wording brings to mind his fondness for numerical conceits—for instance, *One Plus One, One American Movie, Numéro deux, 6 × 2,* "Ma démarche en quatre mouvements"—and his worries about knowing: *Le gai savoir,* the jokes about "what every woman should know" in *Une femme mariée,* Ferdinand's despair at knowing what Marianne is thinking in *Pierrot le fou.* The tentativeness of the title is consistent with the tone of his ensuing offscreen commentaries—for example, when he wonders whether Marina Vlady's hair is this color or that (1.5), whether to photograph Juliette or the leaves (12.33), or where he

0.3

$$\frac{1.0''}{0'05.0''}$$

0.4

$$\frac{1.0''}{0'06.0''}$$

0.5

$$\frac{1.0''}{0'07.0''}$$

has arrived politically (18.4). At the same time the playful alternation of numerals and phrases in shots 0.2–0.12, like the blinking neon signs in *Pierrot le fou* that flash VIE, RIVIERA, CINEMA, celebrate the power of film in a way that is also characteristically his. They give the title sequence the air of a trailer, an advertisement boasting

0.6

1.0″
0′08.0″

0.7

1.0″
0′09.1″

0.8

CHOSES
QUEJESAIS
D'ELLE

3.0″
0′12.1″

that as filmmaker he can and does know a thing or two (as we would say) about his subject.

In live-action cinema, titles are the only images that the film's author can compose in the same sense and to the same extent that he can the text. For this reason they can function in relation to the live-action images as a standard for sorting out what there belongs to him rather than to the world that he is photographing, what he declares responsibility for and responsibility for making sense of. Godard, in his parallel definitions of "elle" as region and woman, makes use of this possibility, proposing an equivalence between his voice and the title images. The graphic style of the titles, identified thereby as the counterpart of his voice, serves to locate that voice within the vocabulary of the film image, and in doing so tells us which elements of that vocabulary he takes to be unequivocally his—namely, color, flatness, and framing.

More specifically, the titles establish the special emphasis that the film is to give to the colors of the French and American flags: here blue, white, and red letters against a black ground. These colors announce a determination to link the politics of the Paris region to wider issues and to see Juliette Janson in political terms—as, for instance, in shot 3.1, where her blue cardigan is set against a red blanket and a white sheet. This color scheme informs so many shots that, for example, even when Juliette changes into a pink dress (as Anna Karina does in *Pierrot le fou*, where the color participates in an ongoing red/blue dichotomy), we continue to see the weakened hue in relation to the total scheme. The political sense of the tricolor relates in turn to an allegorical strain in the narrative: Juliette's friend is named Marianne, the figure on French coins (Anna Karina in *Pierrot* is called Marianne Renoir) and a national symbol; in Sequence 14 she performs an unnamed offscreen sexual act with the American John Faubus, who has the tricolor on his T-shirt in the form of the stars and stripes (Marianne draws out the sexual-political equivalence by remarking that his T-shirt is "America über alles"), while Juliette, whom we know from Commentary 2 to be "of Russian extraction," refuses to participate: "Non, pas ça."

Shot 0.13 puts the tricolor to work in a complex way. The graphics imply, but do not quite state, an equivalence of ELLE to LA RÉGION PARISIENNE (the vertical line connotes distinction as well as identity). Since the words of the latter phrase occur in blue, white, and red respectively, we trace connections like those of an electrical circuit between them and the letters of the word ELLE (E in blue, LL in white, E in red), as if the pronoun, unpacked, yielded the phrase. While the main function of this text is simply to gloss the word "elle" in 0.8 and 0.12, the analytical coloring has the sense of *correcting* (rather than explaining) the earlier shots, where the word appears in pale green—that is, without the political connotations of the tricolor. Because the playful color scheme has the effect of linking ELLE to LA RÉGION PARISIENNE, ELLE appears not merely broken into colors but *encoded,* suggesting that if this signifier is (or, remembering its opposition to 0.8 and 0.12, *should be*) presented as coded, then not only must its signified be understood as also coded but, more specifically, one of the codes of that signified might be color. Decoding, or knowing a few things about, the Paris region thus will involve tracing links of color—in particular those with political connotations, such as blue, white, and red.

The opposition here established between green and the tricolor (0.8 and 0.12 versus the other eleven shots of the sequence) extends to later sequences as well. In general, the imagery of the film avoids green, even yellow (although in some early scenes Juliette wears a yellow skirt and blue sweater). Whenever green occurs—for in-

0.9

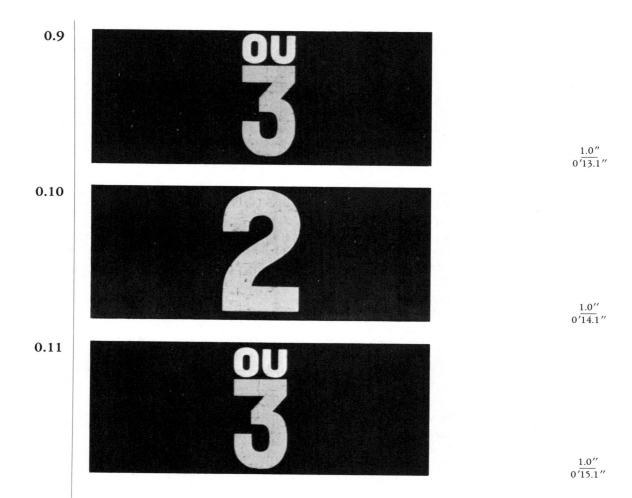

$\dfrac{1.0''}{0'\overline{13.1}''}$

0.10

$\dfrac{1.0''}{0'\overline{14.1}''}$

0.11

$\dfrac{1.0''}{0'\overline{15.1}''}$

stance, in the postcards on the grass (2.12 and 13.7), the leaves behind the service station (12.33), or the consumer products on the lawn (18.4)—the effect is exceptional and striking; more often than not, these shots mark the end of a sequence. As the film progresses, the opposition of green to the tricolor expands into that of the tricolor to the additive primaries (red, blue, green), a dichotomy connoting the political (or social) versus the natural (the colors yielded by the analysis of light). Similar connotations attend the opposition implied elsewhere of the tricolor to the subtractive primaries, those of the painter: red, blue (more accurately, magenta, cyan), and yellow.

Yet it is not enough to say that the main titles set out a palette with a particular (and coded) organization; one must add that they associate this organization with the image plane rather than with the illusory three-dimensional space that the image can evoke. They can do so because they are, as completely as it is possible to be, nothing *other* than an organization of the image plane. They differ in this respect even from the later closeups of book jackets (for example, 2.1), which are, after all, understood as planar segments of three-dimensional objects. Insofar as their color schemes are paradigms of those that follow, they suggest that the significance that colors may have in the film is an attribute not of the colored objects being photographed but of the image itself.

In 12.31 Godard makes the same point more explicitly by juxtaposing a definition of himself as "painter" to an extreme closeup of the surface of Juliette's red car. This definition is, of course, metaphorical, for in fact he has neither painted the car nor made the image of it by painting; all he has "painted" in the film are the title *cartons* (what we would call the "artwork"), and these only by proxy. The responsibility that his words claim is for the *significance* of the color, which does not result from any cultural code (for instance, Parisian call girls, Laurence Wylie tells me, like to drive small, red cars), but belongs, as Christian Metz would say, to the *système* of the film.[1] Consequently, the color organization of the image does not (or does not *only*) render information of the sort that the two African anthropologists in Jean Rouch's *Petit à petit* are after when they ask a Parisian what his yellow necktie means; rather, it is more like an argument which originates with the director and for which he takes responsibility.

As a sequence of shots, the titles proceed by filling the frame first in both dimensions (0.1), then vertically (0.2 and 0.3), and in the end horizontally

0.12

4.0″
0′19.1″

0.13

[The construction noise fades down just
before the cut.]

4.0″
0′23.0″

(0.13). This progression calls attention to the curious shape, particularly the width, of the Techniscope aperture, implying that its limits have something important to do with knowing about the Paris region. With respect to these limits, the titles differ from the ensuing live-action images: for the signification of the latter depends at least partly on the relation between what is included and what is excluded by the frame, whereas the meaning of the titles does not. Of them, as Stanley Cavell says of paintings, it makes no sense to ask what lies adjacent.[2] This difference obtains even in the case of the most planar of the live-action images, the book-jacket closeups, whose wit (for example, *Introduction to Ethnology* cut into a scene of prostitution) depends on our recognition that they are taken out of context—that is, that the frame is withholding information. By sustaining this feeling of excision throughout, Godard keeps before us the problem (recognized explicitly in the relation of Commentary 6 to shots 2.12 and 2.13) of the unphotographed, and ultimately unphotographable, "context" of the images. At times this context is the Paris region, which as a whole is inaccessible to vision, and at times the unphotographed process of producing the film. In either case what is included and what is excluded by the frame are frequently drawn into a relation that can only be described as dialectical.

The *decoupage* of the sequence has another effect as well. Instead of giving us the title of the film in the customary single shot, Godard breaks it into three parts and presents it in its entirety twice, with some repetitions and inversions. The intricacies of this arrangement (for instance, the palindrome formed by shots 0.5–0.11) are probably less important in themselves than for the difficulties they put in the way of reading. Our effort to read is, as a result, made to resemble Godard's own efforts later in the film to decipher the words around him—the car-wash sign (12.19) and the lettering that he associates with rediscovering "the b, a, ba of existence" (16.8). For us as for him, reading, insofar as it is a means, even a metaphor, for knowing two or three things, entails an act of assemblage, of putting pieces together.

The noise of the jackhammers accompanying shots 0.2–0.13 expands on this point in two ways. First, it associates reading with construction, specifically with that of the new apartment complexes on the outskirts of the city. This association, like the graphic style of the lettering, defines the sense in which Godard's film may be said to be constructivist, recalling (with some irony) Sergei Eisenstein's notion of putting together the elements of film according to the principles of the engineer and the architect. Second, the jackhammer noise aggravates the difficulty of reading. While we may wish to attribute this difficulty wholly to Godard, since it is he who authorizes the combination of image and sound, Godard clearly means to attribute it to the society that authorizes construction of the new apartment complexes. He signifies thereby that his film is not exempt from the problems of the society it portrays. "The society that produces these apartment complexes," he writes, "also distributes, in the form of paperback books, a bargain-rate culture that is assimilated in a piecemeal and rather ridiculous fashion by the population. All this takes place in a very loud din of jackhammers, motors, percolators, things crashing together, which, to a certain degree, impede communication."[3]

Sequence 1

1.1 [Silence.]

COMMENTARY 1

On August 19th a decree relating to the organization

Le 19 août, un décret relatif à l'organisation

of state services in the Paris region was published by the *Official Journal*.

des services de l'état dans la Région parisienne était publié par le *Journal officiel*.

$$\frac{10.4''}{0'33.4''}$$

With shot 1.1, a picture of construction, the construction noise on the sound track cuts to silence. The sudden absence of sound at this juncture, although puzzling in isolation, can, I think, be understood as a signifying element within the dichotomy noise/silence, that is, within a relationship of a structuralist kind between the sound/image combination of 1.1 and that of the title sequence. The picture of construction and its accompanying noise have been taken apart according to the same principle and on the same authority that the picture and sound of the title sequence are put together.

As for *what* we see being constructed in 1.1, it belongs, as we know from the preceding title, to the Paris region and as such is the manifestation of a particular policy. To examine and criticize this policy, even to speak of it, as Godard now begins to do, one must first turn off the noise that "impedes communication." That one *can* do this in a film, that one can separate the picture from the sound that belongs to it in reality, affirms that the construction we are shown, together with the policy it embodies, can be imagined otherwise. Yet it cannot be *pictured* otherwise, for there is no other Paris region, no other policy, to photograph. (It would not do to build sets representing Paris, as Jean Renoir does in *French Cancan,* since that Paris could not be under the authority of the Gaullist government.) The parallel implied between the construction we see in 1.1 and the director's work of construction (here the combination of 1.1 with silence) is therefore subject to some limitation—a point amplified in the monologues that Juliette and Robert deliver in 14.10–14.19 and 17.6 on the difference between reality and thought.

The relation of the images 0.13 and 1.1 implies much the same argument. In the essay "A Dialectic Approach to Film Form" Eisenstein suggests that shots, like frames, are not only successive but superimposed, and thus are perceived *on top of* one another.[1] Seen in this way, shot 1.1 repeats the design of 0.13, the curving roadway preserving the division of 0.13 by the white vertical line. The consequence of this repetition is to promote the reading of 1.1 in the terms of 0.13, that is, as colors and shapes divided and organized in a single plane. The fit of the elements of 1.1 into the oddly shaped Techniscope rectangle (the curve of the overpass vanishing in the upper left corner, the balance of man and wheelbarrow at the head of the shot) enforces this reading. To the extent that these elements are organized in the terms of 0.13, they are thereby identified as Godard's construction as opposed to the construction work associated with the reading of the image as a representation of space (two planes, one behind the other—in other words, a construction site), the organization of which is the responsibility of the prefect of the Paris region.

1.2 [Loud construction noise.]

[The construction noise fades down just before the cut.]

10.9″
0′$\overline{44.3}$″

Over 1.1, Godard's voice begins the inventory of things he knows about "elle."[2] His commentary adopts the style of a television newscast: dateline (August 19th, but no year), citation of source (the *Journal officiel*), impersonal tone, and passive voice. The accompanying picture is an exterior showing nothing out of the ordinary, plausible in this regard as an illustration for a television report on "state services in the Paris region." Yet it is in Techniscope, with a wide view, an enormous scale, and a wealth of finely resolved detail. Given these characteristics, the function conferred on it by the accompanying commentary as a replacement for a television image declares Godard's determination to bring what in Commentary 9 he calls the intensity of the biologist to the examination of material normally relegated to the evening news.

Just as Techniscope is in this context at odds with television, so Godard's delivery is in several respects at odds with the journalistic style of his text. First, he whispers it, as he does throughout, thereby intensifying—indeed necessitating—the absence of construction noise on the sound track. He thus establishes an opposition, at once formal and political, between the oppressive sound of the Paris region (and of the policy which that sound represents) and his own faint but clear voice. Second, the whispering itself connotes conspiracy, the guarded discourse of the political opposition (the censorship of the first sentence of Commentary 3 shows that there is something real to fear).[3] It signifies a trusting intimacy with the spectator, an assumption that we belong to his party (would he otherwise risk insulting the Lazards and the Rothschilds while we are listening?). Third, it draws out something latent in all voice-over image/sound relationships: namely, that the speaker is located outside the world shown in the image and that his words, as the term "voice-over" insists, are laid *over* it, added afterward. Although the commentator's voice emanates literally from the screen, his whispered delivery puts him, rhetorically at least, in the position of the spectator: facing the image, watching it, listening to the sound, whispering in our ear. Like us, he is so placed as to be able to observe, to reflect, to comment. His example encourages us to resist projecting ourselves into the world pictured, to acknowledge our position outside of it, and to make use of this fact in developing a critical relationship with what we hear and see. Finally, his whispering, in contradiction to the expository confidence of the text itself, reinforces the note of uncertainty in the film's title.

With the cut to 1.2 there is a straight cut on the sound track to very loud ambient noise. Because of the absence of actual sound in 1.1 the image there has a dreamy, underwater look (although it is not photographed in slow motion), as if the objects had no mass; it is work without the effort of work, a process open to looking and reflecting. But the cut to 1.2 does not have the sense we might expect of restoring a "realistic" sound/image relationship. It is too loud for that. Rather, it forms a dichotomy with the sound/image relation of 1.1, implying that the "reality" of what is represented cannot be simply declared but must be located with reference to two exaggerations standing in dialectical relation.

Two details of the sound mix confirm this conclusion. At the end of shots 0.13 and 1.2, just before the straight cut to silence, the mixer has faded the sound down slightly. This gesture toward a "normal" sound level reminds us that the sound/image relation is the director's doing as much as it is a fact of the world represented. More importantly, it sets off the unattenuated straight cut to the noise at the head of 1.2, confirming that this extreme and abrupt change in level was *chosen,* that it could have been otherwise. The extreme dynamic range marked out by the noise and whispering makes a similar point: because the playback level must be set so that the whispering is

1.3   [Silence.]

(A truck crosses left to right. Pause.)

COMMENTARY 2

Two days later the Council of Ministers names Paul Delouvrier prefect of the Paris region,	Deux jours après le Conseil des ministres nomme Paul Delouvrier préfet de la Région parisienne,

11.8″
0′56.2″

1.4   which, according to the communiqué of the Ministry of Information,   qui, selon le communiqué du Sécretariat à l'Information,

is thus endowed with definite and novel structures.	se trouve ainsi dotée de structures précises et originales.

11.5″
1′07.6″

1.5   [Actual sound fades up, starting on the cut.]

This is Marina Vlady. She is an actress. She is wearing a midnight-blue sweater with two yellow stripes. She is of Russian extraction. Her hair is dark chestnut or light brown. I don't know which exactly.	Elle, c'est Marina Vlady. Elle est actrice. Elle porte un chandail bleu nuit avec deux raies jaunes. Elle est d'origine russe. Ses cheveux sont châtain foncé ou brun clair. Je ne sais pas exactement.

intelligible, the noise will inevitably be very loud (one reason the film is so trying to watch). In these ways the sound mix establishes that in 1.1 and 1.2 the noise is not to be taken as alternately "turned off and turned on" but that the two are elements of a signifying dichotomy, neither pole of which "redeems" (or is capable of redeeming) the relationship that exists in reality.[4]

The relation of the two images 1.1 and 1.2 implies a parallel argument. Shot 1.1 does not "establish" any spatial continuum into which 1.2 can be subsumed. Though 1.2 might be a view from under the roadway seen from above in 1.1, the image track withholds information that would confirm or deny this. Such reticence characterizes the sequence as a whole, which consists mainly of long shots without cues to their places in a spatial whole. So assembled, they are a string of fragments in coordinate relation. Unlike the sounds, they are not organized into dichotomies, yet the lack of subordination or hierarchy among them makes something like the same point; for, like the sounds, they do not constitute an unproblematical description of "reality."

The status of the images as fragments and their failure to imply a spatial whole are reflected at the level of the shot by framing that emphatically dissociates the space shown from its surroundings. Shot 1.3 furnishes a good example: a truck, moving laterally, enters from offscreen left, crosses left to right at frame bottom, and leaves the frame; where it comes from and goes to are not shown. The feeling of excision thus established sets into opposition what is included and excluded by the frame, and does so even in cases where moving objects or frame entrances and exits are not in evidence. This dichotomy has nothing of the value it has, say, in Noël Burch's account of Renoir's *Nana*[5]—which, like most fiction films, exploits the notion essential to continuity cutting that what is offscreen is nonetheless somehow "present." Godard's point is just the reverse: that a condition of the image is exclusion, exclusion in the first instance of the immediate spatial surroundings and in the last of the cinema apparatus and director.

Commentary 2 does not begin until toward the end of 1.3, allowing us to feel the weight of the sound cut at 1.2/1.3 from noise back to silence and to conclude that it is not a technical mistake.[6] The image (which cuts to 1.4 on the word "qui") ironically measures the abstract legal connotations of the word "structures" in the text against the apartment complexes. The combination of image and text asks: aren't the objects shown in 1.3 and 1.4 "definite and novel structures"? The question has a Marxist edge, stemming partly from the connection of both the legal and the physical structures to the work process shown in 1.1 and partly from the intimation that structure, infrastructure, and superstructure have been confused. The irony of the question, which arises from the juxtaposition of the view "according to the communiqué of the Ministry of Information" with that of the camera, sets the sides of a topical political argument that occupies the film at least through Commentary 6.

With the cut to 1.5, Godard redefines "elle" as the woman shown in the accompanying shot and resumes the inventory of things he knows about "her." First, he knows that her name is Marina Vlady and that she is an actress. Although others, particularly film audiences, might know these facts, their recital here points to his identity as director. Second, he knows that she is wearing "a midnight-blue sweater with two yellow stripes," something that the image also reports and that the spectator can in principle see for himself. Third, "she is of Russian extraction," a fact that he might know in the same way he knows her to be an actress or that a spectator might infer from her name or face. Finally, a problematical item: "Her hair is dark chestnut or

MARINA
Yes, speak as if quoting truths. Old Brecht
said that. That actors should quote.

Oui, parler comme des citations de vérité.
C'est le père Brecht qui disait ça. Que les
acteurs doivent citer.

COMMENTARY 2 (CONTINUED)
**Now she turns her head to the right,
but that isn't important.**

Maintenant, elle tourne la tête à droite,
mais ça n'a pas d'importance.

$$\frac{44.8''}{1'52.4''}$$

light brown. I don't know which exactly." Since some of the things listed previously are knowledge of the real woman and some of the image of her, we cannot be immediately certain in which category this last observation belongs. If it refers to the image, it might be an acknowledgment that the colors of the image are not precisely those of the world, or, more importantly, that their signification has a different basis. (It is also undoubtedly a particular reference to shot 1.5, where the backlighting causes flare that makes the hair color hard to determine, and possibly a joke about the fact, which we learn in 11.1, that the hair is dyed.) If it refers to the woman, it points to something that is also true of the image, for what Godard does not know concerns not the phenomenology of color but categories as defined by words: "dark chestnut" versus "light brown."

Two things might be said about this uncertainty. First, it qualifies the earlier statement of equivalence between speaking and writing in which the latter is a paradigm for certain elements of the image (notably, color, flatness, and organization within a rectangle). The incommensurability thus stated of images and words is, as we know, a preoccupation of Godard's, addressed at some length in Sequence 12 of this film. Second, it is no accident that Godard's example of this incommensurability concerns color. The uncertainty he admits raises an issue that can be put in semiotic terms: for if the color cannot be categorized, then how can it enter into signifying dichotomies? That is, how can it pass from a fact of *langage* to a fact of *langue*—or at least of *système?* Might color be, in other words, "analogous" rather than "digital"? These questions record a reservation about a film's ability to make sense not only *of* color but *through* color, one that is surprising in light of the demonstration in the title sequence of how much Godard has invested in the expressive powers of color categories organized dichotomously. If the uncertainty exemplified by "dark chestnut" versus "light brown" (and underlined by the certainty with which the colors of the sweater are named just previously) does not threaten the film's ability to make sense of and through color, then it at least allows that color *outruns* this sense-making. If this is so, the film will (and can) have nothing to say about things like the color of Marina Vlady's hair, which the image, by its nature, reports unremittingly and exactly (though perhaps not faithfully).

In 1.5 we have the first recognizable sound mix: at the cut 1.4/1.5 synchronous sound, consisting first of children's voices in the distance, then Marina Vlady's speech, joins the voice-over track, heard alone in 1.1, 1.3, and 1.4. This coming together of elements gives a climactic feeling to shots 1.5 and 1.6, which themselves introduce a more complex principle of combination: a background composed of apartment blocks and cityscape such as we have glimpsed in 1.1–1.4, with the foreground figure of the actress. The formal density thus constituted confers a surprising weight on Marina Vlady's seemingly offhand first lines: "Yes, speak as if quoting truths. Old Brecht said that. That actors should quote." Besides recalling Godard's own quotation of "le *Journal officiel*," the lines exemplify the principle they cite: Berthold Brecht said that actors should speak as if quoting, and Marina Vlady, introduced as "an actress," quotes Brecht. What she is alluding to is probably Brecht's "Short Description of a New Technique of Acting which Produces an Alienation Effect," where he writes: "Once the idea of total transformation is abandoned the actor speaks the part not as if he were improvising it himself but like a quotation." Brecht annotates this prescription as follows:

Standing in a free and direct relationship to it, the actor allows his character to speak and move; he presents a report. He does not have to make us forget that the text isn't spontaneous, but has been memorized, is a fixed quantity; the fact doesn't matter, as we anyway assume that the report is not about himself but about others. His attitude would be the same if he were simply speaking from his own memory.[7]

But who is it that the actor quotes? In one sense it is the character; in another, it is the author whose text the actor has memorized. In the present case, as Marina Vlady reports, the process is short-circuited:

I have, in effect, no text to learn, since Jean-Luc speaks the text to me at the moment the scene is shot . . . Jean-Luc gives me banal sentences to say, like "pass me the salt," and then, at the same time, during the scene, he asks me questions, to which I must reply point blank, by means of a microphone which he speaks into and an earphone behind my ear.[8]

Of course, we have no way of inferring from the film all of what Marina Vlady reports about Godard's method. What we do notice is that often her speeches do not appear to be recited from memory and that her delivery is characterized by flatness, immediacy, and hesitation. At certain moments—for example, at the conclusion of her speech in 16.9—she appears to have difficulty hearing the lines Godard is feeding her, although the film alone does not allow us to understand the difficulty in just this way. On the other hand, we do understand that her lines are sometimes answers to questions that we do not hear: in 1.5 and 1.6, for example, three of her sentences begin with "yes" or "no," several are separated by pauses for the unheard question, and all have the tone of reply. The status of the lines as answers evokes Godard's agency and method and thereby invites a critical attitude toward what the lines declare: as answers, they cannot be construed as self-sufficient, unmediated expressions of the character. The actress, instead of becoming the character, answers questions about it. Although we do not know for certain when she is literally "quoting" Godard, we do know when she is answering and understand that in this context answering, like quoting, is Brechtian.

There is an equally important way in which quoting and answering are *not* alike. Quotation in Brecht's sense evokes either the absent author or the imaginary character, whereas answering implies the questioner's presence. In this connection the inaudibility of Godard's questions is especially puzzling. We may wish to explain it as a means of applying to sound the principle of opposition between what is included and excluded by the image: Godard is never onscreen and therefore, contrary to convention, his questions may not be heard. The physical basis of this analogy, however, is false; for although we do not expect to see what lies outside the frame (except by means of montage), we do expect to hear sounds whose source we do not see, especially when the figure onscreen hears them. But if, as Joel Haycock proposes, we understand the opposition onscreen/offscreen as "the space of the spectacle" versus "the space of the production," then it becomes clear that Godard's voice, taken as a sign of his presence, belongs only to the latter. Although it may, as an acoustical phenomenon, penetrate the space where the spectacle unfolds, this fact in no way addresses the central problem of how the director may represent himself there.

The exclusion of Godard's questions acknowledges that his absence is indeed a problem; it insists that we as spectators are in a position to be witnesses to the sign, but not to the act, of direction. Furthermore, because the questions that are inaudible

This is Juliette Janson. She lives here. She is wearing a midnight-blue sweater with two yellow stripes. Her hair is dark chestnut or else light brown. I don't know which exactly. She is of Russian extraction.

JULIETTE

It was two years ago in Martinique. Just as in a Simenon novel. No, I don't know which. Uh, yes, *Banana Tourist,* that's it. I have to manage. Robert, I believe, makes $225 a month.

Elle, c'est Juliette Janson. Elle habite ici. Elle porte un chandail bleu nuit avec deux raies jaunes. Ses cheveux sont châtain foncé ou alors brun clair. Je ne sais pas exactement. Elle est d'origine russe.

Il y a deux ans, à la Martinique. Exactement comme dans un roman de Simenon. Non, je ne sais pas lequel. Euh, oui, *Touriste de bananes,* c'est ça. Il faut que je me débrouille. Robert, je crois, a cent dix mille francs par mois.

COMMENTARY 2 (CONTINUED)

Now she has turned her head to the left, but that isn't important.

Maintenant, elle a tourné la tête à gauche, mais ça n'a pas d'importance.

49.3″
2′41.8″

to us are audible to Marina Vlady, we perceive that her position differs from ours. Godard is her director, not ours, and we have no means of responding to his questions or direction. Our appreciation of this difference is a further barrier to our identification with her. On the other hand, Godard's voice-over commentary, which he also speaks as director (perhaps more accurately as *metteur-en-cadre* than as *metteur-en-scène*), is audible to us but not to her. As I argued earlier, his delivery situates him, like us, before the image, whence his speech is, by convention, inaudible to the actors. Taken together, the inaudible questions and the voice-over commentary suggest the force of the opposition that the film requires between the image and the world that the image shows. They also specify that as spectators we belong neither to the space of the spectacle nor to that of the production. Indeed, our place outside both is another element of Godard's scheme that can be called Brechtian.[9]

Taken together, shots 1.5 and 1.6 confront us with a puzzle: although they are practically identical views of the same woman, Godard introduces her in the one case as Marina Vlady, an actress, and in the other as Juliette Janson, who "lives here." Excepting these, the four remaining sentences of his commentary are the same in both cases. Three of them refer to information in the image (the color of her hair and sweater and the like). The fourth, "she is of Russian extraction," occurs (unexpectedly) in a different place when the text is repeated: last, as if singled out. The English subtitles, perhaps in response to this emphasis, incorrectly translate the sentence in the negative ("she is not of Russian origin") when it recurs—a logical slip: obviously, Vlady is a Slavic name and Janson isn't, and we can't deduce her name from the image. But she does, after all, *look* Slavic, especially once we are told that she is. She jokes about this toward the end of the film (16.9), speaking of herself in the third person: "She looks like Chekov's Natasha, or else she's the sister of Flaherty's Nanook." The image must, of course, render this resemblance even when the narrative attributes a non-Russian name to her. By drawing attention to this fact through the twice-made reference to her "Russian extraction," Godard returns to an issue dealt with elsewhere in his work, notably in *Contempt*, where Fritz Lang is called by his actual name but Brigitte Bardot, equally recognizable, is not called by hers.[10] (Bardot's cameo appearance in *Masculine Feminine* is introduced by Elizabeth's line, "She looks exactly like Brigitte Bardot, doesn't she?") There, as here, the discrepancy contributes to a definition of the narrative and of the differing, even conflicting, possible relations of image and sound to it: for while it is not possible literally to photograph Juliette Janson, one may call a picture of Marina Vlady by that name. In this respect the narrative and the image are at odds—something that Godard chooses to recognize and accept.

The parallel texts introducing Marina Vlady and Juliette Janson both conclude by noting that "she" turns her head—in the first case to the right, in the second to the left—and that this "isn't important." If the gesture is truly without importance, why is it included? If it was done on the actress's initiative, could the director not have asked her to omit it?[11] Could he not have cut the shot earlier, eliminating it? In other words, is the authority to make the comment not the same as that which would render the comment unnecessary? The paradox of this relates to the "answering" format of what Marina and Juliette say. In Juliette's lines—in particular, the apparently pointless probing about the name of the Simenon novel ("No, I don't know which. Uh, yes, *Banana Tourist,* that's it"), it emerges that the director knows more about her than she does. This encourages us to continue to think of the woman that we see (despite Godard's statement to the contrary) as Marina Vlady and to entertain the possibility, developed

later, that she is in some sense a projection of him. His control of her text excludes the possibility that he means his remark, "that isn't important," as a renunciation of responsibility for her actions. Rather, it points with irony to a convention of film narrative according to which the action is portrayed as a spontaneous event (Christian Metz calls this "the referential illusion"[12]).

These turns of the head belong to the category of things one may know on the basis of the image. As such they exemplify the often remarked abundance, even superfluity, of information resulting from the photographic process—which, as Metz describes it, "obliges one to choose each element in all the detail of its perceptible appearance."[13] Taking the phrase "pas d'importance" to mean something like "without significance," we may usefully contrast this attribute of the image with Roland Barthes's definition of narrative as a system within which everything is significant.[14] Hence the sentence serves to indicate another respect in which narrative and the image are at odds. Yet if it restates the issue raised by Godard's doubt in naming the color of "her" hair, at the same time it gives that doubt a more consequential form: for there what was cited as resisting the signification mechanisms of the film was an attribute of the photographed world, the physical reality that Godard has not made (or painted, to use his metaphor) rather than a fact of what we must suppose to be the directed— hence *directable*—world of the fiction. If it is with respect to the narrative that the gesture is without importance, then the authority of the image has the effect of raising a question (one in which the film takes a special interest) about the adequacy of narrative as a theory, a set of terms capable of subsuming and explaining what we see.

A detail of Godard's phrasing complicates this account somewhat. Although his description in both instances comes after the gesture, in 1.5 it occurs in the present tense ("Now she turns her head to the right") and in 1.6 in the past ("Now she has turned her head to the left"). In the first case, his line resembles a stage direction, although it is of course not addressed to Marina Vlady, being part of a voice-over commentary that she does not hear. Rather, it dramatizes the act of direction to *us*. In the second case, his description is *narration*. He speaks of the gesture as an event in the story of Juliette Janson. The meaning of this distinction is illuminated by another passage from Brecht's discussion of quoting:

There are three aids which may help to alienate the actions and remarks of the characters being portrayed:
   1. Transposition into the third person.
   2. Transposition into the past.
   3. Speaking the stage directions out loud.
Using the third person and the past tense allows the actor to adopt the right attitude of detachment . . . Speaking the stage directions out loud in the third person results in a clash between two tones of voice, alienating the second of them, the text proper. This style of acting is further alienating by taking place on the stage after having already been outlined and announced in words. Transposing it into the past gives the speaker a standpoint from which he can look back at his sentence. The sentence too is thereby alienated without the speaker adopting an unreal point of view; unlike the spectator, he has read the play right through and is better placed to judge the sentence in accordance with the ending, with its consequences, than the former, who knows less and is more of a stranger to the sentence.[15]

Although what Brecht is proposing is a rehearsal exercise, not a performance technique,

1.7 [Loud noise of crane motor.]

(The upper crane is turning, moving downward in the frame.)

$$\frac{14.6''}{2'56.4''}$$

and although in Godard's case it is the director, not the actor, who speaks, and what he speaks of is a gesture, not a sentence, nonetheless the effect is much the same as Brecht describes.

In conventional narrative styles, a character's glance offscreen right or left can have the functional "importance" of cuing a cut to what the character sees out of frame in that direction (thus literally "putting us in the character's place"). That it does not function in this way here (or ordinarily elsewhere in the film, apart from circumstances where this function is a topic of discussion, as in 12.28/12.29 or certain shots in Sequence 8) is a measure of the extent to which the woman that we see is not such a "character." By declining the opportunity to see things from her viewpoint, Godard obstructs the comparison of our subjectivity to hers. He emphasizes this point by the very odd cut 1.5/1.6 and corroborates it in the references "right" and "left," which, as Joel Haycock points out,[16] do not describe *her* right and left (these would be just the reverse) but *ours*—that is, the screen's. In contradicting the coordinates of her space, these references not only acknowledge our actual location as spectators but, in doing so, affirm its authority as a position from which to understand what we see. Furthermore, they confirm what the whispering has already implied about the position of the narrator: that he, like us, is facing the screen. I say "facing the screen" rather than "behind the camera" (a distinction that *is* important) because the directive role associated with the latter phrase is signified in this code—or, more exactly, *système*—by silences (for instance, that which replaces his vividly evoked prompting, "*Banana Tourist*") in contrast to the audible, descriptive—but not literally directive—observations of the commentary.

If Juliette's turning her head has no importance within a *découpage* that invites the spectator to enter the character's space and subjectivity, it does affirm the contrary principle, which I associated earlier with Eisenstein's phrase "on top of." The essence of this principle is the relation of successive images as flat rectangles rather than as windows opening on segments of an integrable space. Thus the spaces depicted in 1.6 and 1.7 have no intelligible relationship (Juliette's glance downward at the tail of 1.6 in combination with the upward camera angle of 1.7 destroys even the possibility of one), while the turning of the crane in the latter shot clearly reads as "on top of"—and hence as a reenactment of—the movement of Juliette's head in the former (a similar link informs two cuts in Sequence 14: 14.7/14.8 and 14.8/14.9, which are also associated with offscreen "stage directions," Faubus's commands to stop and turn). Seen this way, the cut 1.6/1.7 declares the equivalence asserted in Godard's texts between "the Paris region," the new city under construction, and the Juliette/Marina figure. It wittily plays on this equivalence—and more particularly the Juliette/Marina equivocation—as one of the two cranes in 1.7 moves toward a position, barely achieved by the time the shot ends, of coincidence with the other, occluding it. The specific association of this coincidence with the image plane sustains and thus reaffirms the principle of the preceding cut. This cut also serves to evoke the woman/region equivocation in a pun of which Godard can scarcely be presumed innocent: *grue,* the word for crane, is also slang for "prostitute."

The two images of Marina/Juliette (1.5 and 1.6) themselves have some puzzling aspects. The exact parallelism of the accompanying texts ("Elle, c'est Marina Vlady" and "Elle, c'est Juliette Janson") leads us to expect either a repeated shot or at least a repeated camera setup, whereas the two shots that actually occur differ in several seemingly minor and troublesome details. In 1.5 Vlady is in shadow; when she turns to the

1.8 [Silence.]

COMMENTARY 3

I already have it figured that Paul Delouvrier, despite his pretty name, has done his class-work in the Lazard and Rothschild banking groups.*

Je relève déjà que Paul Delouvrier, malgré son beau nom, a fait des classes dans les groupes bancaires Lazard et Rothschild.*

I deduce from this that the Gaullist regime puts on the mask of re-

J'en déduis que le pouvoir gaulliste prend le masque d'un ré-

5.3″
3′01.7″

1.9 former and modernizer while wishing only to record and regularize the natural tendencies of big capitalism.

formateur et d'un modernisateur alors qu'il ne veut qu'enregistrer et régulariser les tendances naturelles du grand capitalisme.

* This sentence was deleted by the censor and is not heard in the finished film.

right, sunlight strikes her face. Shot 1.6 is backlit, with more flare around her hair. With respect to composition, the shots are mirror images: in 1.5 there is a building out of focus screen-left with distant cityscape and sky screen-right; in 1.6 there is an apartment building screen-right and distant cityscape screen-left. Yet the symmetry is not exact. Nor does its inexactitude correspond to distinctions drawn in the text (for example, "she lives here" versus "she is an actress"). Although the fundamental point—that the fiction is the mirror image of the fact—is clear enough, the elements of 1.5 and 1.6 that remain unexplained by it demonstrate that the category of visible details that aren't important is larger than Godard's single citation and hence requires of the viewer a sustained effort at discrimination and reflection.

Fragments of spatial relations unite shots 1.7–1.10. There is a crane like those of 1.7 in the background of 1.8; 1.9 appears to look out through a window on a space resembling that shown in 1.4. The overpass seen through another window in 1.10 might be that of 1.1. The AZUR sign in the background of 1.8 appears in mirror-image reflection in 1.10. More importantly, the three of these shots that accompany Commentary 3 (that is, 1.8–1.10) use these cityscapes as background to displays of consumer goods: gasoline, furniture, and radios respectively—all things that, like the roads and apartment buildings, figure in the sequences that follow. André Bazin's well-known argument would lead us to expect the deep focus of these shots to characterize the foreground objects as integrated with their possible place in the life of the streets and buildings behind them. Yet the effect is just the reverse, for we understand the deep focus in relation to the critical tone of the accompanying text, which associates the foreground elements (for instance, the furniture in the store window) with abstractions such as "the natural tendencies of big capitalism" and "the distortions of the national economy" and the background activity with "the everyday morality underlying it" (the last three words of this phrase in the French—"qui la fonde"—seem, in context, a literal reference to the background).

Given the critical posture of this text, it is hardly surprising that its opening sentence was censored. While this is the only instance of overt state censorship in the film, it is not the only such instance in Godard's career. In the case of his first feature, *Breathless,* the censors excised a shot of De Gaulle following Eisenhower in a parade along the Champs Elysées, where the Frenchman Michel is simultaneously pursuing Patricia, an American. They banned his second feature, *Le petit soldat,* altogether until the end of the Algerian war. In order to secure release of his eighth, he required the intervention of the minister of culture, André Malraux, and had to agree both to change its title from *La femme mariée* to *Une femme mariée* and to delete a sequence on the monokini and part of a speech by the maid, Madame Céline. He refers to this incident in an open "Letter to the Minister of 'Kultur,'" denouncing the suppression of Rivette's *La religieuse*[17] and has Anne Wiazemsky repeat this denunciation in *La chinoise.* In order to help the producer Georges de Beauregard out of financial difficulties caused by the suppression of *La religieuse,* Godard agreed to make a second film, *Made in U.S.A.,* virtually at the same time as *2 ou 3 choses.*[18]

This history may do something to explain the special irony of 0.1, the obligatory citation of the film's release permit. From one perspective the shot appears not to belong to the title sequence; silence rather than construction noise accompanies it. At the same time, its graphics do not differ from those of the shots following, and because of this its message is put on a par with theirs. Its red, blue, and white coloration has the effect of reminding us that the state exercises power not only over the Paris region but

I also deduce from this that, by system-atizing planning and centrali-

J'en déduis aussi que, en systématisant le dirigisme et la centrali-

11.1″
3′12.8″

1.10

zation, this same regime accents the dis-tortions of the national economy

sation, ce même pouvoir accentue les dis-torsions de l'économie nationale,

and still more those of the everyday mo-rality underlying it.

et plus encore celles de la morale quoti-dienne qui la fonde.

10.5″
3′23.3″

over films as well. In the case of the film whose "visa de contrôle cinématographique" number is 32167, the consequences of this power are complex. We do not know from internal evidence, but only from the Seuil/Avant-Scène script, either that there is certainly a lacuna at the beginning of Commentary 3 or that the cause of this lacuna is state censorship. What we do know is that logically the text begins with a non sequitur ("J'en deduis"); syntactically, the pronoun "en," which occurs twice, has no antecedent; and formally, the commentary is preceded by silence. As spectators, we have no means of distinguishing this silence from that which precedes Commentary 2 or even from that which replaces Godard's questions to the actors, where we also infer that there is a connecting link in the text that we do not hear. We have, therefore, some reason to characterize Godard's speech as "censored" in instances where he is the only possible censoring agent. This suggests if not a complicity, then at least a surprising and disturbing parallel between the functions of director and state.

This parallel reappears in the film's single overt reference to state censorship: in Sequence 9, Juliette instructs her client not to watch her undress and he, in his turn, observes that one never sees the two million Parisians in the Metro, where he works, "because the police do not allow photos to be taken." Godard, for his part, does not "take photos" of Juliette undressing. His reticence is consistent with his practice elsewhere: for example, when he excepts Nana from the prostitutes he shows nude in *Vivre sa vie*, or when he obscures with colored filters the shots of the bare-breasted women in *Pierrot le fou* and of Brigitte Bardot nude on the bed in *Contempt*. These traces of self-censorship contradict the motto "One must put everything into a film,"[19] which Godard uses as the title for an article on *2 ou 3 choses*. In another article on the film, he explains as follows:

Mark you, I myself will not tolerate indecency. Two people kissing, for instance. I have shown this once, with Belmondo and Seberg in *A Bout de Souffle* [*Breathless*], but never since. The characters in my films embrace and caress each other, but never kiss. The kiss is something intimate and private, purely personal and therefore unshowable. On a huge screen it is revolting to watch. When people kiss in the street I never look at them. I respect their intimacy. But sex is a different matter. One could study it and film it, just as love is studied and filmed.[20]

Can the attitudes Godard expresses in this passage be unconnected to his motives in publishing, at about the same time, the following diary excerpt?

Leaving the Blue Note, Albertine and I were kissing in my car while listening to Vivaldi. Suddenly someone knocked at the window, and the car doors opened. It was the police. They made us move on.[21]

Given these texts, what are we to conclude about the parallel between the censoring functions of the state and the director? Clearly, what is "censored" in the omission of Godard's spoken directions, promptings, and questions to the actors is not the content of his utterances, insofar as we can infer them, for they seem in no sense sexually or politically objectionable. To the extent that we may describe these omissions as censored at all, the object of the censorship is the voice itself taken as a sign of bodily presence, comparable to the sign of presence which in the case of Juliette and Marianne is excluded by the framing at certain moments of sexual transaction in Sequences 9 and 14. This line of argument, based as it is on the tenuous parallels of director/state and

sexual/political, leads to a hypothesis relevant chiefly in Sequence 8: namely, that the silence that replaces Godard's voice is a sign not simply of bodily absence but of bodily absence as a sign of sexual being.[22]

As for the distortion of meaning caused by the state censor, I should say that even if the omitted sentence in Commentary 3 were restored, the political position expressed would remain unclear. The vague terms of approval that the text offers—"reformer," "modernizer," "everyday morality," and the "pretty name" Delouvrier (that is, *de l'ouvrier,* "of the worker")—take no intelligible attitude toward what seems the center of the critique, "big capitalism." This vagueness surely contributes to the surprise we feel in Commentary 6 when Godard takes the Paris government to task for its "class politics" and speaks against it in the name of the region's "eight million inhabitants."

It is worth noting how little of Sequence 1 is related to the narrative. Neither Juliette nor any narrative element appears in any shot except 1.5 and 1.6. The remaining shots do, of course, describe the "setting," but the logic of their construction and presentation outruns that of the narrative and of "establishing the scene." In this way the sequence raises a question developed throughout the film about the adequacy of narrative to explain what is important about Juliette Janson and the Paris region, a question that is the counterpart of Godard's ambition to talk in political terms.

Sequence 2

2.1 [Actual sound, children off.]

JULIETTE
What am I looking at? The floor; that's all. I feel the fabric of the tablecloth against my hand.

Qu'est-ce que je regarde? Le plancher; c'est tout. Je sens le tissu de la nappe contre ma main.

$$\frac{9.3''}{3'32.6''}$$

2.2 ROBERT
It's amazing.

C'est fantastique.

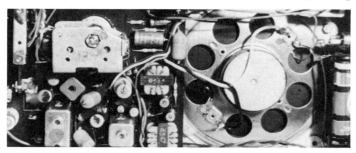

ROGER
Do you hear something?

Tu entends quelque chose?

ROBERT
Yes.

Ouais.

ROGER
What is it?

Qu'est-ce que c'est?

Commentary 3, which concludes Sequence 1, is indebted for its vocabulary, though not for its political position, to Raymond Aron's book *Dix-huit leçons sur la société industrielle* (Paris: Gallimard, 1962), the cover of which appears in 2.1. In the *Nouvel observateur* article entitled "La vie moderne" Godard declares that his film "endeavors to present one or two lessons on industrial society" and claims to "quote frequently" from Aron's book.[1] This book, like those shown in 4.1, 6.5, 9.2, 13.4, and 16.1, belongs to a series of Gallimard paperbacks called "idées," which Godard cites on four occasions in the film (2.11, 13.8, 16.14, 18.3) and describes, though not by name, in the text from which I quoted earlier. Indeed, the title of that text, "Grands ensembles et Vietnam ("Apartment complexes and Vietnam")," aptly names the "lesson" he gives in Sequence 2.

During shot 2.1 we hear Juliette's voice in the first of a series of brief interior monologues that extends through the film: "What am I looking at? The floor; that's all. I feel the fabric of the tablecloth against my hand." Often, as here, these monologues echo the concerns of Godard's commentaries, naming objects that Juliette perceives or remembers. Yet with the single (and important) exception of 8.27–8.29, they never command the image and are always represented as *off* rather than *over* (in 2.1, this is accomplished not only by means of voice recording that matches the room tone of the ensuing synchronized sound but through reference to objects that we can either see or infer as present in 2.3).

Godard once described *2 ou 3 choses* as "a continuation of the movement begun by [Alain] Resnais's *Muriel*."[2] As if in token of this, he places a poster advertising that film on the wall of the Jansons' living room and in the center of shots 2.3 and 2.5. As directors, Godard and Resnais do not much resemble each other. Resnais works from elaborate, and often very literary, scripts. He is attracted to experimentation, especially in the matter of chronology, and has collaborated with writers associated with the New Novel (notably Marguerite Duras and Alain Robbe-Grillet); yet he shows no inclination, at least in his feature films, to challenge the controlling place of narrative. Stylistically, he creates textures of great smoothness and highly worked rhythmic subtlety. His work has the seriousness and consistency of tone that one associates with French high art. Godard, by contrast, never collaborates with writers and never writes a script in the usual sense at all. He dislikes Robbe-Grillet, is impatient with narrative, and derives his scenarios from murder mysteries, newspaper stories, and other movies. His characteristic textures are rough ones, marked by angular, improvisatory rhythms and abrupt changes of tone.

What then can it mean for Godard to acknowledge *Muriel* as the predecessor of

ROBERT
Between Saigon and Washington.

Entre Saïgon et Washington.

5.9″
3′38.5″

2.3   JULIETTE
(She is seated to the right of Robert and
Roger. On the table is a shortwave radio.)
Hey, Christophe, what are you doing?
(As she says this, she gets up and crosses
left out of the frame.)

Dis donc, Christophe, qu'est-ce que tu fais?

ROGER
Who is talking?

Qui est-ce qui parle?

ROBERT
Johnson.

Johnson.

ROGER
Johnson? What's he saying?
(Roger picks up a soldering iron and sol-
ders.)

Johnson? Qu'est-ce qu'il dit?

ROBERT
"In 1965, in order to force Hanoi to negotiate, with heavy heart I ordered my pilots to
bomb North Vietnam."

"En '65, pour obliger Hanoï à négocier, j'ai
ordonné, la mort dans l'âme, à mes aviateurs de bombarder le Nord-Vietnam."

ROGER
And then?

Et alors?

ROBERT
"It was impressive. But it did not bring
Hanoi to the negotiating table. In 1966,
again with heavy heart, I ordered my pilots
to bomb Haiphong and Hanoi."

"C'était formidable. Mais Hanoï n'est pas
venu négocier. En '66, encore la mort dans
l'âme, j'ai ordonné à mes aviateurs de bombarder Haïphong et Hanoï."

ROGER
Hold on; let me listen for a bit.
(Robert passes him the headphones.)

Attends; laisse-moi écouter un coup.

"It was impressive, but it did not bring
Hanoi to the negotiating table. In July of
1967, still with heavy heart, I asked my
pilots to destroy China's nuclear installa-

"Ça a été formidable, mais Hanoï n'est pas
venu négocier. En juillet '67, j'ai demandé,
toujours la mort dans l'âme, à mes aviateurs, de raser les installations atomiques

2 ou 3 choses? First of all, Resnais's film is concerned with its setting, Boulogne, in somewhat the same way that Godard's is with Paris. It depicts Boulogne as a city of new structures standing in the place of those destroyed by World War II bombardment. One of its two plots concerns a soldier recently returned from Algeria and the memory he brings with him of Muriel, an Algerian girl who died after torture by his unit. The political questions evoked by the memory of the Algerian War in juxtaposition to the new city parallel those grouped under Godard's rubric "Apartment complexes and Vietnam." Like *2 ou 3 choses, Muriel* makes an issue of censorship. (Apart from the banned *Petit soldat*, it was, as Marie-Claire Ropars-Wuilleumier points out, the first French fiction film to speak openly about Algeria.)[3] The inclusion in *2 ou 3 choses* of the poster showing the partly torn-away image of a woman suggests that knowing something about "elle" is like remembering Muriel—that is, it is a task that involves assembling pieces and that has a political meaning. Resnais's discharged soldier, like Godard, works at this task by making a film; he shoots scenes of the city, presumably to supply pieces missing from the story of Muriel (whom we never see) and narrates this story over his 8mm footage of Algerian army life. His counterpart in *2 ou 3 choses* is John Faubus, the reporter fresh from Vietnam who "got fed up with the atrocities and the bloodshed" and who makes such a show of taking photographs. Indeed, the combination of the Algerian footage with the story of Muriel closely parallels that of the magazine photograph of the unidentified Vietnamese in 14.14 (which, in turn, recalls the photograph on the *Muriel* poster) with Juliette's meditation: "I can think of someone who isn't here, imagine him, or else evoke him suddenly with a remark—even if he is dead."

Godard follows Resnais not only in these details but in the general interest in comic strips that they both share with other French directors. *Last Year at Marienbad,* for instance, makes allusion to Mandrake the Magician, and after *Je t'aime, je t'aime,* Resnais tried (though without success) to produce a film on a scenario by Stan Lee. Chris Marker's *La jetée,* on which Resnais collaborated, is a filmed version of a *photo roman* and Roger Vadim's *Barbarella* of a comic strip. In *Alphaville* Lemmy Caution asks, as if of a colleague: "And Dick Tracy? Is he dead?" In *2 ou 3 choses* a comic-strip panel appears in shot 3.4, and in Commentary 16 Godard declares: "to live in society today is almost to live in a giant comic strip." This summary remark is a literal (if retrospective) description of Sequence 2, where the transmission Robert and Roger monitor on their shortwave radio is, in fact, a paraphrase of a Jules Feiffer cartoon that appeared in *Nouvel observateur* on August 24, 1966. What they hear and repeat aloud purports to be a speech by Lyndon Johnson narrating events of the Vietnam War. Surprisingly, these events extend through 1967, although, as Juliette's text in 14.11 reminds us, *2 ou 3 choses* was shot in the late summer of 1966. While we do not know from internal evidence that the source of this knowledge of the future is a cartoon, we recognize the message as emanating from what Juliette later calls "the beyond" (*l'au-delà*) and conveying a mixture of fact and grim joke: "In 1967, in order to force Hanoi to negotiate, again with heavy heart, I ordered my pilots to bomb Peking."

tions."

ROBERT
And then?

ROGER
"It was impressive, but it did not bring Hanoi to the negotiating table."

(He passes the headphones to Robert. Juliette enters left, crosses right, sits, picks up a copy of the magazine *l'Express,* and reads.)

ROBERT
"In 1967, in order to force Hanoi to negotiate, again with heavy heart, I ordered my pilots to bomb Peking."

ROGER
And then?

ROBERT
"It was impressive, but it did not bring Hanoi to the negotiating table. Now my missiles are aimed at Moscow."

ROGER
And then?

ROBERT
President Johnson says: "Let Hanoi understand this clearly: his [*sic*] patience has limits."

chinoises."

Et alors?

"Ça a été formidable, mais Hanoï n'est pas venu négocier."

"En '67, pour obliger Hanoï à négocier, encore la mort dans l'âme, j'ai ordonné à mes aviateurs de bombarder Pékin."

Et alors?

"C'était formidable, mais Hanoï n'est pas venu négocier. Maintenant, mes fusées sont pointées sur Moscou."

Et alors?

Le Président Johnson dit: "Qu' Hanoï le sache bien: sa [*sic*] patience a des limites."

1'57.9"
5'36.4"

2.4

Oh damn! I don't hear anything more.

JULIETTE
Say, don't you want me

Ah, merde! j'entends plus rien.

Dis donc, tu veux pas que je

4.7"
5'41.0"

2.5

"to sheathe my legs in anklets and stockings printed in trompe-l'oeil on tights designed by . . . uh . . . Louis Ferraud?

"gaîne mes jambes sous des socquettes et des chaussettes imprimées en trompe-l'oeil sur des collants dessinés par . . . euh . . . Louis Ferraud?

What in fact has Vietnam to do with Paris or with its new apartment complexes? In the text used as a preface to the Seuil/Avant-Scène script (p. 16), Godard answers the question this way:

While the Americans pursue an immoral and unjust war in Vietnam, the French government, whose connections with big capital are common knowledge, sees to the construction in and around Paris of apartment complexes whose inhabitants, either through boredom or through an anguish which this architecture cultivates or through economic necessity, are led to prostitute themselves, notably (incidentally) to Americans returned from Vietnam.

Sequence 14, in which Juliette and Marianne prostitute themselves to the American John Faubus, dramatizes this answer in the literal fashion of a *Lehrstück*. Sequence 2, on the other hand, proposes that the link between Vietnam and the apartment complex is precisely what we see in shots 2.2, 2.4, 2.6, and 2.8: the workings, tubes, capacitors, and wires of what we must suppose to be Robert's shortwave radio. As the soldering that Roger is doing in 2.3 reminds us, these electronic parts are not only colorful but color coded, so as to facilitate the tracing and making of connections. By the very em-

They make indecent dresses decent. They make the calf funny and charming, provided it is perfectly slim or perfectly young."	Ils rendent décentes les robes indécentes. Ils font le mollet drôle et charmant, s'il est tout à fait mince ou tout à fait jeune."
ROBERT Oh, cut the crap!	Oh, arrête tes conneries!
JULIETTE It's Madame Express who says that.	C'est Madame Express qui dit ça.
ROBERT Don't know her.	Connais pas.
JULIETTE You're uneducated.	Tu n'as aucune culture.
(She gets up and crosses left out of the frame.)	
All right, children, come say goodnight. Go on, quickly; we're going to say goodnight. Go on; you, Solange, come.	*Bon, les enfants, venez dire bonsoir. Allez, vite; on va dire bonsoir. Allez; toi, Solange, viens.*
(Christophe enters frame left and crosses right, followed by Juliette carrying Solange. Christophe kisses Robert and Roger.)	
We're going to sleep. Say goodnight to papa. Go on.	*On va dormir. Dites bonsoir à papa. Allez.*
(Juliette, Solange, and Christophe cross right and exit.)	
ROBERT It's the American generals now.	Ce sont des généraux américains maintenant.
ROGER What are the generals saying?	Qu'est-ce qu'ils disent, les généraux?
ROBERT They say that they want to send the North Vietnamese back to the Stone Age. Say, Juliette, *pierre*—that means "stone," doesn't it?	Ils disent qu'ils veulent ramener les Nord-Vietnamiens à l'âge de pierre. Dis donc, Juliette, *stone,* ça veut bien dire "pierre," hein?
JULIETTE *Yes.*	*Oui.*
ROGER Tell me, how did you pay for your Austin?	Dis donc, comment tu l'as payée, ton Austin?

phasis he gives to these shots, Godard suggests that the regularity of color elsewhere might also comprise a code, or, more precisely, signify the fact of codedness (even where the code's vehicle is other than color)—that is, of intelligible connections to be found or, remembering Roger's soldering, made. Robert, like other Godard protagonists, participates in this task by translating texts ("stone" is *pierre*) and writing in a

ROBERT
Oh, it's Juliette who found it. She's amazing.

[With the next sentence aerial bombardment noise fades up, becoming quite loud by the end of the shot.]
She always finds bargains.
ROGER
That's great! That's what I need: a woman who manages.
(This last sentence, which appears in the Seuil/Avant-Scène script, is scarcely audible because of the loudness of the bombardment noise.)

Oh, c'est Juliette qui l'a trouvée. Elle est formidable.

Elle trouve toujours des occasions.

C'est bien! C'est ce qu'il me faudrait: une femme qui se débrouille.

1'08.0"
6'49.0"

2.6 | (Smoke blows into the frame from the right.)

5.3"
6'54.3"

2.7 | [Rapid fade-out of the aerial bombardment noise to silence with the first two words of the commentary.]
COMMENTARY 4
O dear George Washington,

O dear George Washington,

notebook (the handwriting, red felt pen, and cross-hatched paper that we see in 15.9 and 15.11 are the same as Pierrot's).

The paradigmatic value assigned to color is here confirmed in the climactic 2.8 where, amid the circuitry, pieces of blue, red, and yellow tape have been conspicuously placed on what looks like a small piece of masonite. The tape is in two senses a sign of the director's hand. First, it appears to be neither a part of nor a key to the circuitry, but rather a decoration added as if in reply to the red, white, and blue of the "Made in U.S.A." poster of the shot preceding (and to the allusion that shot makes to Godard's film of the same name). Second, its colors are the subtractive primaries, those of the painter, which, as I have already noted, is one of Godard's metaphors for himself as director. Both points suggest that the circuits of the shortwave radio, which serve to introduce Vietnam into the apartment complex, are a metaphor for the film itself, especially for its succession of images. This conclusion is supported by two rather obscure details: first, that the part of Roger is played by Jean Narboni, an editor of the collection *Godard on Godard* and, like Godard, of *Cahiers du cinéma;* second, that the French word for wiring electrical connections, as Roger is doing, is *montage.*

Montage is, moreover, a second means by which the Vietnam War enters the Janson apartment—*montage* not in the French sense of "editing" so much as the Russian definition of the dialectical relation of shots and elements within shots. Such a relation obtains between the smoke and bombardment noise on the one hand and the radio wiring on the other. Significantly, this combination lacks the narrative frame of the guerrilla theater scenes in *Pierrot* and *La chinoise:* because we do not see who is blowing the smoke, the bombardment noise cannot seem simply an extension of the acted skit, as it does in the corresponding scene of *Pierrot.* Like the colored tape on the masonite, the smoke and noise point to the presence, or at least the proxy, of the director, who intervenes at the height of the battle to ask: "O dear George Washington,

what madness has made you play the role of the cruel William Pitt?

quelle folie t'a pris de jouer le rôle du cruel William Pitt?

5.5″
6′59.8″

2.8 [Aerial bombardment noise, propeller planes.]
(Smoke blows into the frame from the right and left alternately.)

8.8″
7′08.5″

2.9 [Midway through the shot, a rapid fade-out of the aerial bombardment noise to silence as the commentary starts.]

COMMENTARY 5
Pax Americana, supereconomical brainwashing.

Pax Americana, lavage de cerveaux super-économique.

6.8″
7′15.3″

what madness has made you play the role of the cruel William Pitt?" The director's visible and audible agency constitutes a means of representing the Vietnam War that is quite opposite to the documentary realism of the newsreel Ferdinand watches in *Pierrot* or of the newscast he and Marianne hear in the car at night. Godard's point is that the Janson apartment is, precisely, "far from Vietnam" (the title of a 1967 film to which he contributed) and that the "presence" of Vietnam there is not something one can immediately hear or see. In order to perceive this presence, it is necessary to look beyond the simple (though coded) surfaces of things into the *au-delà* of fantasy—something that to be seen must be acted out, but can be acted out only in the terms in which it is inscribed in reality—that is, in the radio, cartoon, and dishwashing soap that, like the poster of 2.7 advertising Prisunic stores, signify "Made in U.S.A." At the same time, the homemade crudeness of the bombardment and smoke (which we recognize, I think, as blown from offscreen cigarettes) argues that *how* Vietnam's presence is to be imagined must have the force of a question, of which Juliette's meditation over 14.10 and 14.11 is a paraphrase: "It's a strange thing that one person who is in Europe on August 17, 1966, can think of another who is in Asia."

The *pax* (2.9) following the bombardment is not simply "peace" but the logo of a dishwashing soap, linking Vietnam to Juliette via a specifically American style of packaging: "Pax Americana, supereconomical brainwashing." In context, the aggressive red and white logo connotes blood and bandages, subverting the sense of the word "pax" and providing a witty gloss of the narrator's phrase "Pax Americana." (For me the wisecrack has a hermetic, Parisian ring to it, especially the easy play on *Pax Romana,* the imperial Roman peace of conquest and bloodshed: among the things Godard forgets to forget in his closing commentary are Algeria and Dienbienphu.) The line

2.10 [Actual sound.]

JULIETTE

(To the camera:)

In the "proof of the beyond" genre:

(She turns away, sprinkles Pax into the sink, and puts the box down. She begins to wash the dishes. When delivering a number of the lines in this shot, she turns her head to look at the camera.)

I was in the middle of doing the dishes. I began to cry. I heard a voice saying to me: "You are indestructible." I, me, myself, everybody.

Dans le genre "preuve de l'au-delà:"

J'étais en train de faire la vaiselle. Je me suis mise à pleurer. J'ai entendu une voix qui me disait: "Tu es indestructible." Je, me, moi, tout le monde.

It's preferable . . .

ROBERT

Juliette!

(This word renders the conclusion of Juliette's sentence inaudible.)

JULIETTE

It is very confused. Time? I don't know very well. No, a definition doesn't assert itself unavoidably.

ROBERT

Juliette, Roger is leaving!

JULIETTE

Yes, I'm coming! Yes, but one very often tries to search out, to analyze the meaning

C'est préférable . . .

Juliette!

C'est très confus. Le temps? Je ne sais pas très bien. Non, une définition ne s'impose pas forcément.

Juliette, Roger s'en va!

Oui, j'arrive! Oui, mais on essaie très souvent de chercher, d'analyser le sens des

parodies the language of television commercials, and the mise-en-scène, framing, and text of the shot immediately following (2.10) continue the parody. Here, as it were, is the commercial that follows the newscast of Sequence 1: Juliette standing at her sink, holding the box of Pax that we see in supercloseup in 2.9, delivering a testimonial (*preuve*) to the camera. Surprisingly, the object of the testimonial is not the soap but "the beyond." Even though Juliette appears quite serious when she reports hearing a voice tell her "you are indestructible," the evocation of the mise-en-scène of a commercial reduces the authority of her testimony to that of an advertisement. Indeed, the image maintains that what is being advertised is, contrary to what she says, soap—the Pax Americana. Moreover, the bombardment noise, which rages most violently over the logo "pax" at the head of 2.9, argues that the voice from the real "beyond" is Lyndon Johnson's and that its message is that Juliette, like *tout le monde* (meaning both "everybody" and "the whole world"), is anything *but* indestructible: "Now my missiles are aimed at Moscow." The conclusion implied is that the hopeful messages of the dishwashing soap and the *au-delà*—namely, peace and indestructibility—are ideological masks for the real (and contrary) messages conveyed by the radio circuits—that is, the film.

In light of this conclusion and of the clear evidence in 2.10 that Juliette is answering questions which, as in Sequence 1, we do not hear, it is not implausible to think of her "proof of the beyond" as a joking description of Godard's technique of speaking to her via a concealed microphone during the filming: "I was in the middle of doing the dishes . . . I heard a voice saying to me: 'You are indestructible.' " In this interpretation the message "you are indestructible" is Godard's, a fact that unexpectedly implicates him in the ideology he is criticizing (this is the first of a number of such worries about complicity that extend throughout the film). At the same time Juliette's speech begins with the phrase "In the 'proof of the beyond' genre," which sets what follows in quotation marks, attributing it to the character rather than to the actress or director. And if Godard is responsible for what Juliette hears, he is also responsible for conveying the Feiffer text through the earphones that Robert and Roger, in their clumsy vaudeville routine, laboriously pass back and forth. What then is the *au-delà?* In Juliette's text it is simply "the beyond" or "the afterlife," the assurance that "you are indestructible"; as such, it names an issue that recurs in 8.26 and 17.3. As it applies to the offscreen microphone, the concealed earphone, the radio transmission, and the origin of the smoke and bombardment noise, it refers to what is "beyond" the view of the camera and the sensitivity of the recorder: namely, the director and the act of production. Through this ambiguity the sequence reinvokes the opposition between production and spectacle, associating that opposition with the ideological conflict of competing messages—the "idées" of 2.11.

After the line "Tu es indestructible," Juliette might say, "Je, tu, il, tout le monde": a movement outward, like the zoom in 2.12, progressing stepwise from herself to everybody. Instead she says, "Je, me, moi, tout le monde": a paradigm of the first-person-singular pronoun followed by a leap of generalization like the cut to the master shot 2.10 from the extreme closeup 2.9. Both phrases, the possible as well as the actual one, are grammatical paradigms and as such dramatize the movement from the self to everybody in linguistic terms. But the phrase we expect is logically as well as linguistically organized (this is why we expect it). The one that actually occurs, therefore, appears to offer grammar *in place of* logic, as if in anticipation of Juliette's line in 3.3: "Language is the house man lives in." The logic in question here is spatial, as I have

of words, but one wonders too much. One has to admit that nothing is simpler than to think that such or such a thing goes without saying.

mots, mais on s'étonne trop. Il faut admettre que rien n'est plus simple que penser que telle ou telle chose va de soi.

1′19.3″
8′34.5″

2.11 [Silence.]

COMMENTARY 6

It is certain that the development of the Paris region

Il est sûr que l'aménagement de la Région parisienne

4.2″
8′38.7″

indicated by comparing the phrases to shots. Denying this logic is part of the "proof of the beyond," for, as Stanley Cavell writes in *The World Viewed* (p. 18): "What is heard comes *from* someplace, whereas what you can see you can look *at* ... This is why our access to another world is normally through voices from it." In this instance denying the logic of space entails affirming the structure of language, on which partly depends the character and even the validity of the generalization from "I" to "everybody."

The possibility of a generalization such as Juliette's is of central importance not only to the philosophical problematic of the film as a whole but to the imminent Commentary 6, where Godard, the "je" of the title, wishes to make a large political statement in the name of everybody in the Paris region. Clearly, this statement depends in some measure on the precise meaning of Juliette's line, which portrays the act of generalization not as a widening circle, and not only as an invocation of the structure of language, but as a comparison or equation of terms, like that expressed in the two senses of *elle* (woman and region): the phrasing "je, me, moi, tout le monde" carries the connotation "I, like everybody" or "I, who am everybody." The line thus poses a question that, as Godard writes, he means constantly to put before the spectator: "Does Marina Vlady embody a heroine representative of the inhabitants of the apartment complexes?"[4]

Accompanying Juliette's line is the first music heard in the film, the opening phrase of Beethoven's String Quartet Number 16, Opus 135 (all of the film's musical fragments except the very last—which is from Quartet Number 12, Opus 127—are drawn from this work). It has a complex effect. First, it makes Vlady's delivery of the line sound like the recital of a charm, adding to the otherwordly aura of the message from the beyond. At the same time, it plays a role in the parody, lending her line the bright, snappy conclusiveness of a commercial tag: "Indestructibility: I have it; everybody does." Finally, in an odd way, it authenticates the *preuve,* both by according it an

...will favor the government's policy of class-discrimination...

(At the cut the image is out of focus and is in the process of coming into focus.)

is going to permit the government to pursue its class politics more easily

va permettre au gouvernement de poursuivre plus facilement sa politique de classe

(The image is now sharp.)

and the big monopolies to organize and direct the economy without tak-

(Zoom-out begins.)

ing account of the needs and the aspiration for a better life of its eight million inhabitants.

et au grand monopole d'en organiser et d'en orienter l'économie, sans te-

nir compte des besoins et de l'aspiration à une vie meilleure de ses huit millions d'habitants.

$\dfrac{13.9''}{8'52.6''}$

unexpected gravity and by exemplifying it: a musical phrase as well known as this one evidences the immortality of its composer and thus itself qualifies as a voice from the beyond.

The cut from 2.9, the extreme closeup of the Pax box, to 2.10, in which the box is inserted in a spatial context, implies a connection (probably unrecognized by most viewers because of the extreme change of scale) which shot 2.12, a long zoom, locates in the traversal of the intervening space. It is significant that the object shown at the head of 2.12 is itself an image, a postcard. The camera begins by bringing it into focus, as if to emphasize its status as a picture, which by definition locates it in a single plane. The focusing is an act of searching for that plane in space, and, as it is found, the satisfying coincidence between it and the plane of the film image dramatizes the planarity of both. It is also significant that the camera then zooms, rather than tracks, out, since a zoom reads as a widening of the frame, an extension of the limits of view of a plane, whereas a track is a movement *through* planes, through space. In this way Godard stresses the equivalence between the postcard and the film image (he comically underlines this by placing the postcard sideways, so that it better fits the proportions of the Techniscope frame). As the zoom (the first in the film) widens to include the natural green of the surrounding grass (also the first in the film), the bouquet of flowers that the postcard shows is made to look even more artificial than at first. But insofar as the postcard—which belongs to a category of printed materials that includes the Pax box, the pornographic picture (13.9), and the book jackets—is a proxy of the film image, the opposition natural/artificial is weakened. A qualification is thus attached to the promise held out by the zoom to insert the object in a context that somehow explains it; for context and object, both images, resemble each other. The exciting cut to

2.13 [Loud ambient noise: children playing, dogs barking, traffic, whistles.]

(Pan right.)

(Hold, then pan left.)

(Hold.)
JULIETTE
My eyes   *Mes yeux,*

26.4″
9′19.0″

2.13, which commutes the zooming movement into that of a pan on a grander scale, dismisses this qualification. The spatial disjunction, felt as a problem in 2.9/2.10, is overborne in 2.12/2.13 by the continuity of zoom and pan, which affirms that a satisfactory explanatory context might indeed be the spatial and might therefore be accessible to view. The termination of the pan simultaneously fulfills and deflates this promise: we are given the first long, clear view of the apartment complex, accompanied by the recognition that the sweep must, after all, stop at *something*. This is, so to speak, all the "beyond" that there is.

Shot 2.13 is the first (and perhaps only) occasion in the film on which Techniscope functions as a conventional means of rendering monumentality. The enormous scale of the image, together with the pan right, gives whatever support there is to the accusation made in the accompanying commentary that what governs the region is a "class politics" that ignores "the needs and the aspiration for a better life of its eight million inhabitants." At the same time the commentary stands as a measure of the image, which, even with Techniscope, has no means of showing eight million people, still less of representing their needs and aspirations. The image/sound combination here is not, I think, entirely under Godard's control. Clearly, it is meant to parallel and correct Juliette's "je, me, moi, tout le monde." But whatever the precise meaning of her text, the film presents it with some irony, whereas no textual qualification attends Godard's claim to be able to speak for the Parisian millions. What qualification there is stems exclusively from the movement of the camera, which, having finished the pan right, retraces its path in a pan left back to its starting point—producing, as Michael Fried puts it, a sense of erasure. However one interprets this gesture, it seems quite opposite in feeling to the zoom, as if the camera is unable to find what it is looking for. Thus the symmetrical pans acknowledge the hollowness of the explanatory promise of the context that is to be found beyond the frame, of a satisfying visible totality.[5] What is in question here is not, of course, optics, but rather the significance that can be borne by, or assigned to, the image. In speaking of the needs and the aspirations of eight million people, the commentary makes clear precisely what is (unavoidably) lacking in the image, though unfortunately it does so by arrogating this to itself.

Sequence 3

3.1 [Outdoor ambient noise continues over the cut and is then mixed with actual sound. During the shot the level of the outdoor noise lowers very subtly.]

are the body and the noise is . . .

(Sound of a door opening. Juliette in bed opens her eyes, lifts her head, and looks off-screen left.)

CHRISTOPHE
Tell me, mama, do you dream sometimes?

JULIETTE
Hurry up, you're going to be late for school.

CHRISTOPHE
I'd like to know.

JULIETTE
Before, when I dreamed, I had the impression of being sucked into a big hole,

c'est le corps et le bruit, c'est . . .

Dis, maman, est-ce que tu rêves parfois?

Dépêche-toi, tu vas être en retard à l'école.

Je voudrais savoir.

Avant, quand je rêvais, j'avais l'impression d'être aspirée dans un grand trou,

of disappearing into a big hole. Now when I dream, I have the impression of shattering into a thousand pieces. And before, when I woke up, even if it took a long time, I woke up in one piece. Now when I wake up, I'm afraid there are pieces missing.

de disparaître dans un grand trou. Maintenant, quand je rêve, j'ai l'impression de m'éparpiller en mille morceaux. Et avant, quand je me réveillais, même si c'était long, je me réveillais d'un seul coup. Maintenant, quand je me réveille, j'ai peur qu'il manque des morceaux.

The musical phrase in 2.10 invites a comparison between *2 ou 3 choses* and *Une femme mariée,* whose sound track also includes passages from Beethoven string quartets. The two films have much in common. Both follow a married Parisian woman through a day that includes sexual infidelities. In both cases the woman's son is played by Christophe Bourseiller, who in *Femme mariée* delivers a memorized speech like that in 3.2. The counterpart of the allusion to *Muriel* in Sequence 2 is a segment of *Night and Fog* that the heroine of *Femme mariée* watches at the Orly movie theater. In both *2 ou 3 choses* and *Femme mariée* book jackets, cityscapes, and interior monologues figure prominently. Both films narrate a 24-hour period of ordinary activities, which claim our attention less by being conventionally dramatic than by seeking to be representative in the manner of a sociological document.

However, *2 ou 3 choses* is not so much a restatement as it is a revision of the earlier film. It differs in depending for its organization less on narrative and more on a central metaphor (namely, prostitution). Its narrative line is sketchy and constantly interrupted. Clues important to the plot are thrown away, fragmented, overborne, and submerged in other material, chiefly philosophical and political speculation. The time scheme, which includes such ostentatiously precise references as "3:37 P.M.," also contains gross contradictions: in 14.11 Juliette gives the date as August 17, 1966, whereas in Commentary 24 (in Sequence 12) Godard says that it is the end of an "October afternoon."[1] And, of course, in Sequence 2 the year appears to be 1967 rather than 1966, as it is on the wall calendar we see in 17.3. Nonetheless, *2 ou 3 choses* does have a discernible narrative line, beginning in the evening as Juliette puts the children to bed and washes the dishes (Sequence 2) and continuing the next morning as she and her son wake up and recount their dreams (Sequence 3). During the day that ensues, she leaves the children at a sort of daycare center (Sequence 5), shops for a dress (6), has a coke in a café (8), meets her first client (9), has her hair washed (11), takes her car to the garage where her husband works (12), goes with her friend Marianne to meet her second client (14), returns to the apartment complex (16), puts the children to bed (17), and goes to bed herself (18).

Clearly, this narrative scheme, like that of *Femme mariée,* is indebted to the chronological presentation of an ordinary day of city life in Joyce's *Ulysses.* In *Pierrot le fou,* Ferdinand suggests a further aspect of this debt:

I've found an idea for a novel. No longer to write about people's lives . . . but only about life, life itself. What goes on between people, in space . . . like sound and colours. That would be something worth while. Joyce tried, but one must be able, ought

CHRISTOPHE
*Say, mama, you know, last night I dreamed . . .
something!*

JULIETTE
What did you dream?

*Dis, maman, tu sais, cette nuit, j'ai rêvé . . .
quelque chose!*

Tu as rêvé de quoi?

47.8″
10′06.8″

3.2   [Outdoor noise continues to be mixed with
the actual sound, though at a lower level.]

CHRISTOPHE
OK, here goes: I dreamed that I was walking all alone on a road at the edge of a
precipice; there was room for only one person.

Hein, voilà: j'ai rêvé que je marchais tout
seul au bord d'un précipice sur un chemin;
il n'y avait place* que pour une seule personne.

Then, all of a sudden, I see two twins appear, two twins walking in front of me. So
I wonder how they are going to manage to
get through! And then, all of a sudden, a
. . . one of the twins makes his way toward
the other; they . . . reunite; they . . . they . . .
they . . . they form one single person. And,
at that moment, I discover that these . . .
that these two persons are North Vietnam
and South Vietnam

Puis, soudain, je vois apparaître deux jumeaux, deux jumeaux qui marchaient devant moi. Alors je me demande comment
ils vont faire pour passer! Et puis, soudain,
un . . . l'un des jumeaux se . . . se dirige
vers l'autre; ils se réunissent; ils s'es . . . ils
se . . . ils s'i . . . ils se forment une seule
personne. Et, à ce moment-là, je découvre
que ces . . . que ces deux personnes . . . c'est
le Vietnam du Nord et le Vietnam du Sud

38.8″
10′45.6″

3.3   *reuniting.*

qui se réunissent.

* This word appears in the Seuil script but is unintelligible in the film.

to be able, to do better.[2]

This is, I think, less accurate as a description of *Ulysses* than of *Pierrot,*[3] which expends little energy on its confused, opaque plot and a great deal on sound, color, space, and allusion to painting. It is also a passable description of *2 ou 3 choses,* where, however, sound, color, and space have less poetic and more political connotations. And *2 ou 3 choses* owes further debts to *Ulysses* in its representative protagonist and its parody of styles and forms: the newscast, the commercial, the interior monlogue, the philosophical meditation, the literary conversation, the interview, the question-and-answer catechism, and the aleatory composition.

In 3.1 and 3.2 Christophe and Juliette recount dreams that sound more like messages from the beyond than convincing emanations of the characters' psyches. We find it hard to believe that a child such as Christophe actually dreams in political allegory. Rather, we understand what he says as a text, a "citation," identified as such by his introductory "Voilà." (The phrase "Dans le genre 'preuve de l'au-delà' " in 2.10 serves a similar purpose.) His is a clearer case than Juliette's, which sounds more like a real dream. But the mise-en-scène and composition of 3.1 establish that hers too is in some sense a text. Her jersey does not look like something one would normally wear to bed; the room is brilliant, neither darkened as a bedroom would be nor warmly lit by morning light as is the cityscape in 2.13; the frame is a studied arrangement of blue jersey, red blanket, and white sheet—all of which portrays her at her least individual and most iconic, that is, as the embodiment of her industrial society. We therefore understand her current dream of being split into a thousand pieces in relation to the film's preoccupation with "ensemble," its critique of the city as "un ensemble" and of the apartment complexes as "grands ensembles." It thus stands as a comment on her function as representative of the "thousands of people" that, as she says in 6.3, comprise "a city." The dream that she had "formerly" (*avant*), the dream of being sucked down a hole, is, as Michael Fried points out, an allusion to Baudelaire's "La gouffre": "J'ai peur du sommeil comme on a peur d'un grand trou,/Tout plein de vague horreur, menant on ne sait où" ("I am afraid of sleep as of a great hole filled with nameless horror, leading one knows not where"). This citation secures the present definition of her as the speaker of a text rather than the reporter of an authentic dream. In doing so, it distinguishes "her" past from that of the psychologically unique individual Juliette Janson and identifies it with that of her culture. As a consciousness representative of Baudelaire's Paris ("avant"), she fears disappearing down a hole but is eventually reassured on waking; as a consciousness representative of her own ("maintenant"), she is split into a thousand pieces and on waking fears that some are missing.

Whether or not we understand Juliette's text in precisely this way, we cannot miss the contrast between its subjective vocabulary, literary allusion, and evocations of the unconscious (the sexual and mortal fears of being sucked into a hole and split into pieces) and the terms of Christophe's dream: the exterior landscape, concrete geography, narrated incident, familial relationships, and transparency of meaning. Clearly, the relation of mother and son is schematized, the son's unconscious belonging to the younger, preindustrial struggle in Asia and hers to the industrial society of Europe. Godard must also mean us to compare the symbolic, fearful vagueness of her dream with the explicit, concrete hopefulness of his, just as we compare her images of the hole and the thousand pieces to his of the precipice and unification. Taken together, the two texts imply that the hope for a unity, an "ensemble" (a hope expressed as the fulfill-

(Pause.)

Mama, what is language?

Juliette
Language is the house man lives in.

(She looks at the camera and pushes back a strand of hair.)

[The outdoor sound ceases with the entrance of the music.]

(She puts her head on the pillow and closes her eyes for an instant, then looks offscreen at Christophe.)

Maman, qu'est-ce que c'est, le langage?

Le langage, c'est la maison dans laquelle l'homme habite.

$\dfrac{20.7''}{11'06.3''}$

3.4 [Silence.]

$\dfrac{6.3''}{11'12.7''}$

ment of a wish, that is, a dream), is placed outside the society that we see, Juliette's society, and given a concrete political context.

The political hope for ensemble is defined further by the contrast between Christophe's version of how the Vietnamese struggle will end and his father's version, in which the United States risks nuclear war rather than lose. Both are visions of the future: what the adult world listens to, translates, notes down, and credits is the report of technology (the radio and newspaper cartoon), which is that the *side* of technology, the side of imperial America, will prevail. Christophe answers this in visionary, familial terms: the two Vietnams are twins, with a blood relationship, and they get through the narrow place by merging, as figures often do in dreams.

The presentation of Christophe's speech as a "text" rather than a convincing account of a dream does something to soften the non sequitur with which he concludes: "Mama, what is language?" What underlies the placement of this question, I think, is Lacan's idea that the discourse of the unconscious has a structure like that of language. Juliette's answer, "Language is the house man lives in," quotes Heidegger while bringing to mind the house she literally lives in, namely, the *grand ensemble* (in Sequence 6, she makes this link explicit by specifying *ensemble* as a condition of speech). The musical fragment that follows her answer, the second phrase of the Beethoven quartet, gives it enormous, almost comic, weight. Because the fragment is only the second such in the film and because it is, in Beethoven, the immediate continuation of the phrase heard in 2.10, it functions in the fashion of a leitmotiv, connecting Juliette's answer to her phrase in the preceding scene: "je, me, moi, tout le monde." What was puzzling about that phrase (that it offers a linguistic paradigm where the context makes us expect a logical movement from part to whole) is explicated here: it is not logic that can secure the Cartesian path from the *je* to the world, but language, the manifestation of the *ensemble,* and, moreover, specifically by means of its structuredness ("je, me, moi").

Shot 3.4, the comic-strip panel, comprises a second answer, or an elaboration of the first, to Christophe's question. The context leads us to expect an illustration of "language"—something, for example, like the closeup of the Pax box in 2.9. Since we are instead given a picture, moreover, a picture of a sort that normally includes words, the cut to 3.4 has the effect of defining "language" so broadly as to include that of images. Godard draws this point out in the passage from Commentary 16 that I cited earlier: "More and more there is an intermingling of image and language. And at the extreme, one can say that to live in society today is almost to live in a giant comic strip." Shot 3.4 thus exemplifies the metaphoric "house" of "society today" that Juliette lives in. The differences between it and her literal house (as shown, say, in 2.13) define an opposition between the film and the culture that the film depicts: on the one hand, a melodramatic, dreamlike fantasy of wealth and romance represented by a woman with a vividly implied psychology, a Bentley, and snow-capped mountains; on the other, a sketchy narrative of the economic realities of Juliette, her red Austin, and the outskirts of Paris. But, as I have tried to show, Godard recognizes that his film is irretrievably part of the culture it criticizes. The parallels that exist between the dramatic situation shown in 3.4 and that of *2 ou 3 choses* allow that the cartoon is also in some respects a paradigm for Godard's imagery, specifically in its flatness and unmodeled areas of primary color.

Sequence 4

4.1 [Silence.]

$\dfrac{7.4''}{11'20.1''}$

4.2 [Actual sound.]

(A young woman is seated in a bathtub, washing herself. She puts on a headband,

then turns on the hand shower, rises, and rinses herself. Knocking is heard at the door.)

YOUNG WOMAN

(In Serbo-Croatian throughout:)

Who is it?   Ko je?

(More knocking.)

Who is it?   Ko je?

As Godard acknowledges (Mussman, p. 274, and Seuil/Avant-Scène, p. 17), the points of departure for *2 ou 3 choses* were two articles in the weekly magazine *Le nouvel observateur*. The first, by Catherine Vimenet, describes casual daytime prostitution by women living in the *grands ensembles*. The second is a two-part response to the first: a long anonymous letter from such a woman together with a symposium on the social and economic problems of those relocated in the new housing. Godard's debt to these articles is quite specific. Sequence 2, for example, derives from the opening paragraph of the first:

Eight o'clock in the evening. On the seventh floor of an H.L.M. (three rooms, kitchen, bath) the two children have taken their shower. All clean in their clean bathrobes, they come in to kiss mama, papa, and a guest, then go to bed. The adults dine, not at all badly. Mama clears the dishes, herself not badly off either in her new dress and permanent redone three days before. While she is in the kitchen, papa and his friend finish the bottle of wine. "My wife is amazing," says papa, who makes 95,000 francs [$200] a month, family supplements included. "With the little I give her, she does miracles: she feeds us, she outfits the kids, she dresses well—you've seen! I don't understand how she does it!"[1]

With the exception of the sentence about dinner, the paragraph precisely describes Godard's scene, even providing a bit of the dialogue between Robert and Roger: "Tell me, how did you pay for your Austin?" "Oh, it's Juliette who found it. She's amazing. She always finds bargains."

In Sequence 4, the scene of the woman in the bath and Commentary 7—despite the initial reference to *On Classes: Further Lessons on Industrial Societies,* another book by Raymond Aron (4.1)—also derive from Vimenet's article (p. 18):

The sole fact of suddenly enjoying a convenience that one has never known increases its use. Certain tenants who at last have hot water and gas use them without moderation: someone quotes me the case of a young woman who, mad with joy at having a shower at her disposal, used it five to ten times a day without thinking that at the end of the month she would have to pay the bill.

When Godard dramatizes this case in 4.2, he adds only one detail: he has the young woman speak Serbo-Croatian, identifying her as one of a series of immigrants he includes among the inhabitants of the *grands ensembles*: the *pied noir* Paulette Cadjaris (11.5), the Algerian boy (13.6–13.8), and the black couple (16.2).

The action of 4.2, in which the man from the electric company interrupts the

(A meter reader enters. The young woman covers her body with a towel.)

METER READER
(In French throughout:)
Madame: the electric company.

Madame: L'électricité de France.

YOUNG WOMAN
Wait!

Hej!

METER READER
Where is the meter?

Où est le compteur?

YOUNG WOMAN
What are you doing here?

Šta radite ovde?

METER READER
Ah . . .

Ah . . .

(He crosses leftward through the frame.)

YOUNG WOMAN
I beg your pardon, what right do you have to enter a foreigner's apartment?

Sa kojim pravom ulazite u tudj stan, molim vas?

METER READER
(Enters left and crosses right, stops, takes out a pencil and notebook.)
Oh, this is going to hurt! A hundred bucks!
(He makes a note of the reading in his book.)

Oh, ça va faire mal! Cinquante mille balles!

YOUNG WOMAN
(As he is writing:)
Sir, I beg your pardon, can you explain to me what this is all about?

Gospodine, molim vas, hoćete li mi objasniti o čemu se radi?

45.1″
12′05.2″

young woman's bath to read the meter, recalls the scene in *Les carabiniers* in which Ulysses falls through the movie screen trying to get a better view of the "Bain d'une femme du monde." Both scenes are in Godard's low-comedy manner. But here the actress seems self-conscious and embarrassed by her nudity. Godard does too. The camera movements are discreetly (though rather clumsily) orchestrated in concert with hers, so as not to show her genitals.[2] The action is similarly arranged in the "Femme du monde" excerpt, but to comic effect, since Godard is ostensibly not the author of that film. Here the joke is that the man who reads the meter is impressed by the electric bill that the young woman has run up, not by her body, but this seems too feeble to be worth the 45 seconds of screen time it takes. I suppose the scene is meant to suggest that the young woman will wind up paying for the electricity with her body, but its more immediate function is as a particular instance which sets up (unnecessarily, I

4.3 [Silence.]

Commentary 7

The sole fact of suddenly enjoying a convenience one has never known

Le seul fait de jouir soudain d'un confort qu'on n'a jamais connu

$$\frac{5.0''}{12'10.2''}$$

4.4 makes one use gas and hot water without thinking that at the end of the month one must pay for them.

pousse à dépenser du gaz et de l'eau chaud, sans penser qu'à la fin du mois il faut payer.

It's always the same story. No money to pay the rent, or else no television, or else a television but no car, or else a washing machine

C'est toujours la même histoire. Pas d'argent pour payer le loyer, ou alors pas de télévision, ou alors une télévision, mais pas d'auto, ou alors une machine à laver,

$$\frac{13.4''}{12'23.6''}$$

think) the general statement of Commentary 7.

Commentary 7 and the accompanying images (4.3–4.5) allude to two segments of a sequence from *Le joli mai*: in the first, over telephoto shots of crowds crossing the street, the narrator tells us: "Emptiness as always is filled with dreams, the dream of a car, of a TV set, hovering over Paris"; in the second, over the following closeup of a young woman reflected in a window, the narrator proposes,

"If we dissect this many-faced crowd, we find that it is made up of a sum of solitudes." Godard's shot 4.4, the reflection of a young woman's face, clearly alludes to this closeup while the commentary accompanying it (to be precise, the commentary extending from 4.3 to 4.5) pointedly answers Marker's poetic tone ("a sum of solitudes") by insisting on the concrete commercial and sociological circumstances behind what we see.

The first sentence of Godard's text conflates the two already quoted from Vimenet's article. The second and third paraphrase others from the same source (p. 19): "It's always the same haunting thought: 'no money to pay the rent.'" On the other

4.5   but no vacation.   mais pas de vacances.

In other words, any way you arrange it,   C'est-à-dire, de toute façon, pas une vie
no normal life.   normale.

                                                        6.3″
                                                     12′29.9″

hand, "normal life" is an idea that belongs more particularly to Godard and is one of the few flashes of a positive vision in the film. But what would normal life be? Hot water *and* a car? Shots 4.3 and 4.5 expand on the point a little: segments of sky, buildings, a crane, and letters from giant advertisements—legible in 4.5 as the word "AZUR," with its simultaneous evocation of Baudelaire, sky color, and gasoline—exhibit the commercial intrusion into the natural and the literary (Commentary 23 makes clear the moral force Godard attaches to the role of writer), and in doing so hint at what life might be in the absence of this intrusion.

Sequence 5

5.1 [Actual sound.]

(Hold on M. Gérard, then pan right with
him. He opens the bedroom door, enters,
disappears left, then reappears with a ham-
mer in his hand.)

M. GÉRARD
(As he leaves the bedroom, he says to the
couple inside:)

Only seven minutes more.   Plus que sept minutes.

(The doorbell rings as he closes the bedroom door. Pan right and track left with
him as he crosses to the front door and
opens it.)

Hello, Madame Janson.   Bonjour, Madame Janson.

(Juliette enters leading Solange, who cries

The action in shot 5.1 has a farcical air: doors opening and closing, doorbell ringing, Monsieur Gérard trudging back and forth (like Clov in the opening pantomime of *Endgame*), the commerce in processed food, the bizarre sexual tableau revealed through the door. As the shot unfolds, we gather that Monsieur Gérard is operating both a brothel and a daycare center out of an apartment in the *grand ensemble,* where the medium of exchange is not money but small consumer goods. This scene too derives from the Vimenet article, which reports that the site of prostitution is sometimes an apartment in the complex, rented from an old man, "pas riche," in return for a meal.

The most striking feature of this extremely elaborate *plan séquence* is the behavior of the camera, which in the course of the shot executes a nearly 360-degree clockwise

and whines until the end of the shot.)

JULIETTE
Hello, Monsieur Gérard. I'm bringing you
Solange.

Bonjour, Monsieur Gérard. Je vous amène
Solange.

(Pan right with Juliette, who says to Solange:)
Look at them; go play with the others.
(She puts Solange down with the other
children.)

Regarde-les; va jouer avec les autres.

(Pan left with Juliette; she crosses out of
the frame. M. Gérard appears through a
door to the right of the table.)

M. GÉRARD
Oh, Madame Janson, have you forgotten . . . ?

Eh, Madame Janson, est-ce que vous avez
oublié de . . . ?

turn composed of many smaller and more complex movements: tracks and pans first with Monsieur Gérard, then Juliette, then Monsieur Gérard—in sum, a kind of participation in the farcical nature of the action. Because the camera remains at adult height and in medium shot, Solange is often out, or nearly out, of the frame (an effect exaggerated in the 16mm print). And since Solange cries so inconsolably from her entrance until the end of the scene, Monsieur Gérard's reminder to Juliette that he wants to be paid—"have you forgotten . . . ?"—makes us, as Cavell points out, want to say—both to Juliette and to the camera—"Solange." The image and sound, however, never

(Pan left with him. Solange enters right and crosses left in front of him.)

JULIETTE
Ah, yes.

Ah! oui.

(The pan left with M. Gérard puts Juliette back into the frame. She gives him a chocolate bar; he puts it on the table, which is already loaded with carefully arranged boxes and bottles of food and drink.)

Since this is all I have, next week I'll give you something better.

Comme c'est tout ce que j'ai, la semaine prochaine je vous donnerai quelque chose de mieux.

M. GÉRARD
Oh, thank you!

Oh, thank you!

JULIETTE
(To Solange:)
Go on. Go.

Allez. Va.

(Pan left with Juliette and Solange as they cross to the apartment door.)

M. GÉRARD
(To Juliette:)
Goodbye, Madame Janson.

Au revoir, Madame Janson.

(Juliette leaves. To Solange:)
Look, go back there with the two little girls.

Tiens, va là-bas, avec les deux p'tites filles.

(Pan left and track right with him and Solange back to the bedroom door as he looks at his watch.)

Come, come back here.

Viens, viens là-bas.

(He opens the door.)

quite make this answer, and it is hard to know whether they are meant to call attention to this forgetting or to seem accomplices to it.

The only decorations in Monsieur Gérard's virtually empty apartment are some travel posters.[1] These pictures bear a relation to the film image that is indicated in two ways: about midway into the shot the camera reveals a poster showing Anna Karina in *Vivre sa vie,* Godard's earlier film about prostitution, whose heroine is, like Zola's,

Three minutes more.

(As he says this, the doorbell rings again. He closes the bedroom door. To Solange:)

Yes, very well. Come on, go back there with the others.

(Pan right and track left with him as he crosses to the apartment door and opens it. A young woman enters, followed by a young man.)

YOUNG WOMAN

Hello, Monsieur Gérard. May we come in?

M. GÉRARD

Yes, that way please.

(He points right. The young woman crosses out right as the young man gives M. Gérard a can.)

Encore trois minutes.

Ouais, très bien. Viens, va là-bas avec les autres.

Bonjour, Monsieur Gérard. On peut venir?

Oui, par là, s'il vous plaît.

YOUNG MAN

All I have is catfood.

(He follows the young woman out.)

M. GÉRARD

(To Solange:)

Look, go back there with the other little girls.

(M. Gérard crosses right. Pan right, as if with him, as he exits by the door through which the young man and woman just

Je n'ai que du ronron.

Tiens, va là-bas avec les autres petites filles.

called "Nana." (The sexual tableau we see when Monsieur Gérard opens the door to announce "seven minutes left" resembles those we glimpse through the hotel-room doors in Tableau 10 of *Vivre sa vie*.) More importantly, at the end of the shot, the cam-

went. Solange appears at the bottom of the frame crossing left toward the apartment door. M. Gérard reappears through the door to the right of the table.)

Come, come. We're going to play. Come, we're going to read a story. Come,
(Pan right with M. Gérard and tilt down as he sits.)
we're going to read a little story. Come, my little girl, come.
(He reaches for Solange.)

Viens, viens. On va jouer. Viens, on va te lire une histoire. Viens,

on va te lire une petite histoire. Viens, ma petite, viens.

(The pan continues without interruption rightward past him and the children, toward the window.)
Here, sit down there. Look, we're going to read a little story. You'll see. Come. "Pic and Pouc."

(The camera holds on the view out the window. Juliette and others stop to watch two young men, handcuffed to a policeman, led off right. They are followed by a group of children.)
"Pic and Pouc are walking along the bank of the river . . .

Regarde, assieds-toi là. Tiens, on va te lire une p'tite histoire. Tu vas voir. Viens. "Pic et Pouc."

"Au bord du fleuve, Pic et Pouc se promènent . . .

era abandons its principle of following the characters' movement and continues on its own (as it were) the pan set in motion by Monsieur Gérard, going past him and the

See . . . Concealing her eggs, Madame Pelican   *Voir . . . Couvant ses oeufs, Madame Pélican*
. . ."   *. . ."*

2'18.5"
14'48.4"

5.2 | [Silence.]

8.0"
14'56.4"

5.3 | [Loud construction noise.]

(A barge moves right.)

15.2"
15'11.5"

5.4 | [Silence.]

children to look out the window. This held view stands in series with the poster images (particularly as it is "framed" by the window), inviting comparison with them: exotic, romanticized pictures versus an ordinary street scene, which includes, as if by chance, a policeman leading off two handcuffed suspects, a curious crowd, and Juliette.

Formally, the exterior scene relates in two ways to the interior action: first, it represents a view, achieved after a nearly 360-degree turn, of what Monsieur Gérard was watching almost three minutes earlier when the shot began; and second, it constitutes an ironic comment on what he begins to read to the children offscreen: "Pic and Pouc are walking along the bank of the river . . . Concealing her eggs, Madame Pelican . . ."[2] The text/image combination here resembles that at the conclusion of Tableau 1 of *Vivre sa vie,* where Nana's estranged husband quotes a schoolchild's theme on "La Poule" (the context invokes both the slang and the literal meanings of the word), while the camera, beginning in two-shot of Nana and him at a pinball machine, executes an abrupt and short pan left, centering her in the frame: "The chicken is an animal composed of an outside and an inside; if you take away the outside, the inside is left; and when you take away the inside, then you see the soul."[3] Tableau 2 of the film concludes with a parallel structure: the camera tracks to, then holds on, a view out the window of the record shop where Nana works, as offscreen her friend reads a purple passage about suicide from a magazine story. In the present case the text/image relation is much less pointed (in the earlier film, the street has a more specific connotation, representing the desperate alternative to suicide, that is to say, prostitution), for the moment asserting only that there *is* a relation between the stylized narrative and the ostensibly unstaged public incident.

But in what, precisely, does this relationship consist? Shots 5.2–5.4, documentary views of the city, retrospectively confirm the terminal framing of 5.1 as another such.

(Pause.)

COMMENTARY 8

Always the same story:

Toujours la même histoire:

10.4″
15′22.0″

5.5   Apprentice seamstress, she gets her C.A.P.* and joins a small firm. She meets a boy who gets her pregnant and leaves her. A year later, a second guy, a second child, a second desertion.

Apprentie brodeuse, elle réussit son C.A.P.* et entre dans une petite entreprise. Elle rencontre un garçon qui lui fait un enfant et la quitte. Un an après, deuxième type, deuxième enfant, deuxième abandon.

(A young man with glasses enters left, crosses to her, says something that we do not hear.)

At the lying-in hospital, they moralize at her,

A la maternité, on lui fait la morale,

(She replies to him, but we do not hear her words.)

but it is also at the hospital that friends explain to her what to do

(He exits left.)

to earn money to feed her two children.

mais c'est à la maternité aussi que des copines lui expliquent comment faire

pour gagner de quoi nourrir ses deux

* Certificat d'aptitude professionelle (trade diploma).

Over the last of these, Godard begins to tell the archetypical story, presumably of the woman we see in 5.5. Although spectators are unlikely to know that this story is taken almost verbatim from *Le nouvel observateur,* they probably will recognize its similarities to that which Godard tells of Nana and that which Yvette tells of herself in *Vivre sa vie:* the child, the absent father, the bad jobs, the shortness of money, the nice guy who

When she leaves, she takes up her work again; but in the evenings she prostitutes herself.

enfants. En sortant, elle reprend son travail; mais, le soir, elle se prostitue.

One day by chance a nice guy falls in love with her and marries her.
(She looks at the camera.)
They move with the chil-

Un jour, une chance, un gentil type tombe amoureux et l'épouse.

On s'installe avec les en-

31.5″
15′53.5″

5.6   (Juliette crosses the street away from us.)

dren into an obviously too expensive modern apartment. Two years later, a third child. They can't manage any longer and it's the husband himself who asks his wife to go out on the street.
(Juliette turns and waits on the far side of the street, as if for a taxi.)

fants dans un appartement moderne évidemment trop cher. Deux ans après, troisième enfant. On n'y arrive plus et c'est le mari lui-même qui demande à sa femme de faire le trottoir.

20.2″
16′13.7″

proposes marriage.[4] Indeed, shot 5.5, which Commentary 8 accompanies, specifically reprises an image of Nana from Tableau 10 of *Vivre sa vie:*

But if *Vivre sa vie* attributes prostitution to a broken marriage and a slide into poverty, Commentaries 7 and 8 (linked by the repeated phrase "always the same story") blame it on the financial strains of family life in new buildings such as those in 5.2 and 5.4. The *Nouvel observateur* articles thus supply the film not only with much of its narrative material (the stories of Juliette, the young women of 5.5 and 8.2, the secretary of Sequence 10, and Colette and Isabelle of Sequence 8), but with a central metaphor as well. In "One must put everything into a film," Godard describes it as one of his most "rooted" ideas: "the idea that, in order to live in Parisian society today, at whatever level or on whatever plane, one is forced to prostitute oneself in one way or another, or else to live according to conditions resembling those of prostitution" (*Godard on Godard,* p. 239).

Sequence 6

6.1   [Actual sound mixed with loud outdoor ambience, traffic noise.]

    (Hold, then pan left with Juliette as she
comes up the stairs of a dress shop and
crosses left. She looks at the dresses on a
rack, takes off her raincoat, picks up a shirt
and holds it up in front of her.)

JULIETTE
(To Salesclerk 1:)
Is this cotton?   C'est du coton?

SALESCLERK 1
Yes, it's cotton.   Oui, c'est du coton.

(Juliette puts the shirt down. Track in, pan
left and track right with her. She inspects a
red dress.)

In this scene Juliette goes into a store in downtown Paris and selects a dress that she says she will pick up after stopping "at the bank." In Sequence 9, we learn that the bank is in reality a hotel room and a client. This anecdote derives from the Vimenet article (p. 19): "At Les Halles, empty shopping basket in hand, women wait for a client, find one, lead him to a hotel, and then go shopping, as they could not have done a moment earlier." The scene in the store dramatizes what Godard's preceding commentaries describe: the pressure to consume, to overspend, to shop without knowing precisely what one is shopping for. At the conclusion of the scene, Juliette puts this in

JULIETTE
(To Salesclerk 2:)
Do you have dresses like this?　　　　　　Vous avez des robes comme ça?
SALESCLERK 2
Yes, Madame, on the third floor.　　　　　*Oui, Madame, au second.*
JULIETTE
Thank you.　　　　　　　　　　　　　　Merci.
(Pan left with Salesclerk 2 as she crosses in
front of Juliette. She stops and addresses the
camera:)
SALESCLERK 2
I get off at seven o'clock. I have a date at　　Je sort à sept heures. J'ai rendez-vous à huit
eight with Jean-Claude.　　　　　　　　heures avec Jean-Claude.

We go to a restaurant, sometimes to a　　　On va au restaurant, certaines fois au
movie.　　　　　　　　　　　　　　　cinéma.
(She exits left. Pan left with Juliette, then
track backward as she approaches.)
JULIETTE
Yes, I know how to talk.　　　　　　　　Oui, je sais parler.
(She glances at the camera, takes a red skirt
off the rack.)

(Pan left with her to a mirror.)
All right, let's talk together.　　　　　　D'accord, parlons ensemble.

55.2″
17′08.9″

more philosophical language: "In certain cases you know the object of your desire. In other cases you do not."

However, the issues with which the sequence is preoccupied seem remote from these economic and social facts. It begins by returning to the discussion of language broached in the exchange between Juliette and Christophe in 3.3. Here Juliette is again under interrogation, this time by the unheard director. The question that elicits her initial reply, "Yes, I know how to talk," does not, of course, reflect a simple, literal doubt. Rather, it calls to mind the scene of *Vivre sa vie* to which the poster on Monsieur Gérard's wall specifically refers, the one in which the philosopher Brice Parain and Nana discuss the possible identity of thought and speech and the rebirth of speech through the death of not-speaking. There, however, the terms of the discussion are existential, even mystical, whereas in the present context we understand that knowing how to speak indicates social and political circumstances.

While Juliette's line, "All right, let's talk together," expresses confidence that she and the director *can* talk to each other, the sound track contradicts her confidence by reporting only one half of this dialogue. From our point of view—that is, from the

6.2 [Rapid fade-out to silence on the cut.]

6.7″
17′15.5″

6.3 [Actual sound throughout the shot; starting at the head, outdoor noise slowly fades up until by midshot it is quite loud.]

Ensemble, "together"—that's a word I like very much.

CHILDREN'S VOICES
She isn't here. She's left.

JULIETTE
An *ensemble*—there are thousands of people, a city perhaps. No one today can know what the city of tomorrow will be.

(She holds up a yellow skirt.)

Ensemble. C'est un mot que j'aime bien.

Elle est pas là. Elle est partie.

Un ensemble, ce sont des . . . des milliers de gens, une ville peut-être. Personne aujourd'hui ne peut savoir quelle sera la ville de demain.

A part of the semantic wealth that belonged to it in the past . . . It is going to lose this, certainly . . . Certainly.
(Pause.)
Perhaps.
(Pause.)
The creative and formative role of the city will be assured by other systems of communication. Perhaps. Television, radio.
(Pause.)
Vocabulary and syntax. Knowingly and de-

Une partie de la richesse sémantique qui fut sienne dans le passé . . . Elle va la perdre, certainement . . . Certainement.

Peut-être.

Le rôle créateur et formateur de la ville sera assuré par d'autres systèmes de communications. Peut-être. Télévision, radio.

Vocabulaire et syntaxe. Sciemment et

point of view that the film permits us—they do not "talk together" at all. Godard pursues this point by having her reflect: *"Ensemble,* 'together'—that's a word I like very much. An *ensemble*—there are thousands of people, a city perhaps." Her movement from the adverb, with its reference to her first-person-plural dialogue with the director ("parlons ensemble") to the noun that suggests "thousands of people, a city," not only recalls Commentary 6 and the widening of view from shot 2.12 to 2.13 but also parallels the progression "je, me, moi, tout le monde," adding to it the missing term "nous." The apartment complex is, of course, also "un ensemble," that is, the specific sort of *ensemble* (in the adverbial sense) resulting from the administrative policy of the Paris region. Godard puts us in mind of that policy here in two ways. First, he mixes the ambient sound of the shop and the traffic outside with the synchronous track of Juliette, in 6.3 and 6.8 raising the level of the noise—slowly, to assure us that its presence is not a technical mistake—until it all but overwhelms what she says. If her speech represents the already curtailed and doubtful possibility of "talking together," then the noise once again functions as Godard's sign for the policy governing the region. The sound mix thus establishes an opposition between the false *ensemble* brought into being by that policy and *un ensemble* in its structured aspect, a society capable of speaking and communicating, capable, in short, of discourse. Second, Godard inserts a brief shot (6.2) of a traffic jam beneath a freeway overpass, as if to illustrate what it is like to be "together" in these circumstances. The silence that accompanies the shot is an absence of speech—Juliette's speech—as well as of the traffic noise that belongs spatially to this scene rather than to the interior of the shop. Juliette's following sentence, "No one today can know what the city of tomorrow will be," ironically ignores the answer framed by 6.2—the overpass, the traffic jam, the absence of speech.

Juliette goes on to discuss communication, talking together, in the city of tomorrow first as the loss of semantic wealth (quite an understatement in a context where the problem is simply hearing what is said!), then as the emergence of "other systems of communication." These, curiously, include radio and television rather than film,[1] and "vocabulary and syntax," the components of knowing how to speak, rather

liberately . . .   délibérément . . .

1′08.4″
18′23.9″

6.4 [Actual sound mixed with loud outdoor ambience.]

SALESCLERK 3

(She glances repeatedly at the camera as she
speaks:)

Lunch is at three o'clock.   Déjeuner, il est trois heures.

(Toward frame right:)

Sea-blue shetlands?   Des shetland bleu marine?

JULIETTE

A new language will have to be constructed.   *Un nouveau langage devra être construit.*

SALESCLERK 3

I got up at eight o'clock. I have brownish-   Je me suis levée à huit heures. J'ai des yeux
green eyes.   marron vert.

15.1″
18′39.0″

6.5 [Fade-out to silence on the cut.]

4.8″
18′43.8″

6.6 [Actual sound, apparently mixed with outdoor ambience, fades up at the head of the
shot.]

than language. As if to illustrate her prediction, she concludes with two puzzling adverbs, "knowingly and deliberately," which might or might not belong to the sentence she speaks offscreen in the next shot: "A new language will have to be constructed." Between this sentence and the preceding adverbs a clerk onscreen delivers two sentences: "Lunch is at three o'clock. Sea-blue shetlands?" Are these examples of the new language or of the inadequacy of the old—that is, of the present state of knowing how to speak? If, in the dramatized scene as a whole, Juliette and the clerks can be said to "talk together," they do so only in a limited sense, only about their business, buying and selling. Indeed, there would be no reason to expect otherwise were it not for the more interesting talk that they address to the camera: in Juliette's case, speculation about desire and language, and in that of the clerks, accounts of daily routine and physical features.

The second large issue broached here is color. One might say that Juliette acts

(Hold, then slight pan right with Juliette as she enters and crosses right to a rack of fur coats.)

SALESCLERK 4

(Enters right and crosses left to Juliette.)

Good day, Madame, do you desire . . . ?

Bonjour, Madame, vous désirez?

JULIETTE

May I try this one?

Je peux essayer ça?

SALESCLERK 4

Yes, of course.

Oui, bien sûr.

(She exits right. Juliette takes a brown coat from the rack. Pan left with her to a mirror. She looks around the room.)

JULIETTE

In this room there is blue, red, green.

Dans cette pièce, il y a du bleu, du rouge, du vert.

(Pan right with her to the rack of coats. She hangs up the brown coat.)

Yes, I'm sure of it.

Oui, j'en suis sûre.

(She takes a white coat from its hanger.)

My sweater is blue.

Mon chandail est bleu.

(She turns toward the mirror and holds the coat up in front of her.)

SALESCLERK 4

The white will suit you very well.

Le blanc vous ira très bien.

(Salesclerk 4 enters right at the end of this sentence.)

JULIETTE

Mademoiselle, I'd like a . . . uh . . . cotton dress with sleeves.

Mademoiselle, je voudrais une . . . euh . . . robe en coton avec des manches.

(Juliette hands her the white coat and she puts it back on the hanger.)

SALESCLERK 4

Yes, I'll show you.

Oui, je vais vous montrer.

(Juliette turns. The camera pans left with

toward color much as Godard does, noting what colors are in the room and trying to decide which will suit her (the salesclerk tells her: "The white will suit you very well").[2] She begins by asking for a red dress and winds up settling for pink (a mixture of red and white?), something which we can easily miss amid the philosophical interrogation and which we might measure against Godard's own success in "choosing red" in the climactic views of the car, 12.30 and 12.31. By noting "my sweater is blue," she recalls Commentary 2, where he describes her sweater as midnight blue. Her appropriation of this line dramatizes her assumption of a role that was previously his. But, unlike him, she encounters no problem naming colors: "In this room there is blue, red, green. Yes, I'm sure of it." The salesclerk is equally sure when she tells us that her eyes are "brownish green." In ordinary social discourse one does, after all, know how to

her to a dress rack. She glances at the camera once quickly as she walks.)

JULIETTE
Because I see that it's blue.

Parce que je vois que c'est bleu.

SALESCLERK 4
It's this way, please.

C'est par là, s'il vous plaît.

(Pan right with Juliette as she crosses right and closer to the camera, then stops; short hold.)

JULIETTE
If one was mistaken at the outset and mixed up blue and green?

Si on s'était trompé au départ et qu'on ait melangé le bleu et le vert?

48.7″
19′32.5″

6.7 | That would be serious.

Ce serait grave.

(She crosses away from the camera; slight pan left to reframe. She picks out a pink dress.)

Good, that's it. This one will do very well. What bothers me is that . . . When do you close?

Bon, voilà. Celle-là va très bien. Ce qui m'ennuie, c'est que . . . Vous fermez à quelle heure?

SALESCLERK 4
At seven o'clock.

A sept heures.

JULIETTE
Well, put this aside for me. I'll stop by again because . . .

Alors, gardez-la-moi; je repasserai parce que . . .

SALESCLERK 4
I really can't put it aside for you.

Je ne peux absolument pas vous la garder.

JULIETTE
Why?

Pourquoi?

SALESCLERK 4
Well, talk to . . .

Eh bien, adressez-vous . . .

(Short pan right with Juliette.)

JULIETTE
(To manageress:)

speak and by what name to call the color of one's own features. Juliette knows her sweater is blue because, she says, she sees that it's blue. But "if one was mistaken at the outset and mixed up blue and green ... that would be serious." Why? Colors might have any name. Godard's point is that they do not. Salesclerks know what color their eyes are. If one mistook the names of things, there would be no communication, talking together would be threatened. This, then, is an instance of how the physical world guarantees the possibility of "ensemble." The meaning of blue, red, green, the colors that Juliette finds in the room, is not that they signify a particular thing but that one needs to have them, to get their names straight, in order to talk and to be understood.

This argument about color applies equally to the film image. Blue, red, green, the additive primaries, are in a sense the colors of *any* room, since it is by recording their quantities and distribution that the film is able to render color. Godard's definition of himself as a painter, even as it is here dramatized by Juliette's choices as a shopper, depends on this mechanism and on its guarantee that the colors she names are recognizably those that we see. If one called the blue-sensitive layer of the emulsion green, this would no longer be the case. As the author of Juliette's line, Godard, the "painter in letters" (as he aptly calls himself in Mussman, p. 275), is of course not referring to this photochemical mechanism so much as to the *système* based on it: we may think in this connection of the importance the film reserves for green and of the consequences of confusing it with blue. That is, to "talk together" via the image, insofar as it is a configuration of colors, presupposes an "ensemble" with a different basis, a *système* or code rather than a language (to use Metz's terms). Having said this, I should add that throughout the scene there is a distance between Juliette, who is confident about the possibility of talking together, of "ensemble" (red plus white is pink), and of naming,

Can you put this aside for me for an hour or two? I have to stop at the bank.

MANAGERESS
Of course, Madame. Not after six o'clock.

JULIETTE
I'll stop by before six.

MANAGERESS
All right.

(Pan right with Juliette as she puts on her raincoat and speaks:)

JULIETTE
It's because my impressions do not always refer to a specific object.

Vous pouvez me la garder une heure ou deux? Je dois passer à la banque.

Mais bien sûr, Madame. Pas après six heures.

Je passerai avant six heures.

D'accord.

C'est parce que mes impressions ne se réfèrent pas toujours à un objet précis.

46.7″
20′19.2″

6.8 [Actual sound throughout; as the shot progresses, outdoor ambience fades up subtly and slowly, until it is quite loud.]

Yes, for example, desire.

Oui, par exemple, le désir.

Yes, in certain cases you know the object of your desire. In other cases you do not. For example, I feel that I am lacking something, but I scarcely know what; or I'm afraid, and . . . or although nothing in particular could be making me afraid . . . What expression? . . . does not refer to a specific ob-

Oui, dans certains cas on connaît l'objet de votre désir. En d'autres on l'ignore. Par exemple, je sens que quelque chose me manque, mais je sais pas trop quoi; ou j'ai peur et . . . ou bien que rien de particulier ne puisse me faire peur . . . Quelle expression? . . . ne se réfère pas à un objet précis.

and Godard, who is on each of these counts more ironic, reserved, doubtful, or critical: the possible confusion of primaries is more consequential for him than for her.

Juliette's closing speech—"my impressions do not always refer to a specific object . . . for example, desire"—also has something to do with color. She defines desire as the feeling that something is lacking ("quelque chose me manque"), terms that she used in recounting her dream in 3.1 ("il manque des morceaux") and that here refer to the preceding action: wanting a dress, not knowing which, asking for red and settling for pink. This action, like the speech itself, follows from the clerk's question in 6.6: "Do you desire?" Here too we may think of Monsieur and Madame Expresso's cocktail party in *Pierrot,* where the monochromatic shots dramatize Ferdinand's complaint of feeling "plusiers" (like Juliette's "impression of splitting into a thousand pieces") and

ject. Oh, yes! Order. Logic. Yes, for example, uh . . . something can make me cry; but . . . but the cause of the tears is not to be found in . . . integrated with their traces on my cheeks; in other words, one can describe everything that is produced when I do something without indicating, for all that, what makes me do it.

(She turns to face offscreen left:)

I'll be back at six o'clock.

(She turns back.)

Ah, oui! Ordre. Logique. Oui, par exemple, euh . . . quelque chose peut me faire pleurer; mais . . . mais la cause des larmes ne se trouve pas dans . . . integrée à leur traces sur mes joues; c'est-à-dire qu'on peut décrire tout ce qui se produit quand je fais quelque chose sans indiquer pour autant ce qui fait que je le fais.

Je reviens à six heures.

1'27.2"
21'46.3"

the full-color image his wish to feel "unique."

Juliette's list of *expressions* that do not refer to a specific object includes "order" and "logic" and, curiously, "tears." Her meditation on the relation of her tears to what makes her cry comments on a passage in Maurice Merleau-Ponty's essay on "Film and the New Psychology" in *Sense and Non-Sense,* a work jokingly cited in Commentary 18. By "the new psychology" Merleau-Ponty means gestalt psychology or the *Psychologie de la forme,* the French title of the book by Wolfgang Köhler that appears in shot 6.5. The passage in question is the following:

We must reject that prejudice which makes "inner realities" out of love, hate, or anger, leaving them accessible to one single witness: the person who feels them. Anger, shame, hate, and love are not psychic facts hidden at the bottom of another's consciousness: they are types of behavior or styles of conduct which are visible from the outside. They exist *on* this face or *in* those gestures, not hidden behind them.[3]

Describing everything that is produced when Juliette does something is, of course, precisely what the film image does. But by "cause" Juliette surely means psychological cause, that which is, in Merleau-Ponty's terms, "accessible to one single witness." Yet we understand the word more broadly, since her speech stands as the conclusion to a dramatic action, buying a dress, and since the film aspires to give this action a broad though as yet not completely defined context (immediately sociological and economic, but ultimately political), we have reason not to be satisfied with her view. We do, after all, know something about the meanings of her expressions with no specific object, the cause of the tears, though we do not (perhaps cannot) know it on the basis of what the image reports about surfaces—things "which are visible from the outside." Furthermore, the scene leaves open the possibility that what is under discussion is not only desire for the dress but *sexual* desire, the means by which the dress will be paid for. This possibility is supported by the odd framing of 6.8 (more odd than it should be in the 16mm reduction). The width of the Techniscope frame and the consequent wastes of background area to either side of Juliette's face point to the separation of her head from her body (as if the view of her body had been censored) and at the same time set her phrase "everything that is produced when I do something" in relation to our close, sensual view of her skin and of the perspiration "produced" by the real heat of the August day.

Sequence 7

7.1 [Loud construction noise: this appears to be the same as the outdoor ambience of the preceding shots, but louder.]

(The steam shovel swings right, dumps soil, then swings left, digs up more soil, swings right, and again dumps.)

$$\frac{31.9''}{22'18.2''}$$

7.2 [Silence.]

(Early in the shot, the illumination changes from diffuse skylight to direct, full sunlight. Pause.)

The five shots of this sequence all include construction. Shot 7.1 shows the same site as 1.1, although here the camera looks to the right rather than to the left of the overpass and construction noise rather than silence accompanies the image. As in Sequence 1, the noise alternates with silence, the pattern being noise, silence, silence, noise, silence. But in place of the political terms of Commentaries 1–3, Godard now describes what we see as biological evolution; as filmmaker, he examines "the life of the city and its inhabitants and the links that unite them with as much intensity as the biologist examines the relations of the individual and the race in evolution." The word "evolution" applies to the construction that we see in the accompanying shot, 7.2. The phrase, "les rapports de l'individu et de la race," retrospectively describes the cut 6.8/7.1, which compares the turn of Juliette's head to that of the steam shovel. It also introduces shot

I examine the life of the city and its inhabitants and the links that unite them with as much intensity as the biologist examines the relations of the individual and the race in evolution.

Je scrute la vie de la cité et de ses habitants et les liens qui les unissent avec autant d'intensité que le biologiste scrute les rapports de l'individu et de la race en évolution.

$$\frac{22.9''}{22'41.1''}$$

7.3 (Juliette crosses the street toward us.)

It's only thus that I can attack the problems

C'est seulement ainsi que je pourrais m'attaquer aux problèmes

of social pathology, forming the hope of a truly new city.
(Juliette exits frame left.)

de pathologie sociale en formant l'espoir d'une vraie cité nouvelle.

$$\frac{9.5''}{22'50.5''}$$

7.4 [Loud construction noise.]

$$\frac{14.4''}{23'05.0''}$$

7.3, which shows her crossing the street toward us (presumably on her way from the dress shop to the café), so confirming her as an example of "l'individu." Here, perhaps more than in 7.2, the gaze of the camera represents the act of scientific study and the director the biologist.[1]

However, it does not seem to me that the metaphor is a very good one. Construction is not much like evolution; the city does not look organic here (as it does,

7.5 [Silence.]

$\dfrac{11.4''}{23'16.3''}$

say, in Hilary Harris's film *Organism*); and Godard's procedures do not really resemble those of a scientist. Godard tacitly acknowledges this, for, apart from Juliette's passing reference to Paris as "naturelle" (14.6), the metaphor does not recur.[2] In contrast to Godard's characterization of himself as a painter, it seems merely a decorative figure of speech, without power to explain—or even masking a confusion about—the central relation of the film: the two definitions of *elle*, the woman and the city. Moreover, by invoking the disinterested stance of the scientist, it denies the partisanship clearly evident in the film as a whole. As a result, the argument of the sequence appears schematic and contradictory and the hope Godard holds out for "a truly new city" seems an opaque version of that which he describes more convincingly in Commentary 23.[3]

Sequence 8

8.1 [Actual sound, including the noise of a pinball machine.]

(Short pan right with Juliette as she enters a café.)

BARTENDER
Hello, Madame.   Bonjour, Madame.

JULIETTE
Hello, Monsieur.   Bonjour, Monsieur.

(Short pan left as Juliette approaches the camera.)

To define myself? One single word? Indifferent.   Me définir? Un seul mot? Indifférente.

JULIETTE'S FRIEND
Say, hello!   *Tiens, bonjour!*

(Pan left with Juliette as she crosses to the

As I recounted earlier, one of the points of departure for *2 ou 3 choses* was a letter in *Le nouvel observateur* from a woman who read the Vimenet article and wished to corroborate it with her own first-hand testimony. This woman reports how, after years of hard work and debt, she was finally persuaded by a friend to go to a café where part-time prostitutes, "shooting stars," met potential clients:

At the end of ten minues, a man—a handsome man—looked at me fixedly. I gave him the shadow of a smile, hoping with all my might that he would leave without insisting. My hopes were disappointed, and when I lifted my eyes, I saw him, with an imperceptible sign of his head, invite me to leave. Numbed, I paid for my drink and went out. I was in a fog. I led him automatically to a nearby hotel.[1]

Is this passage a plausible description of the very ambiguous dramatic action of Sequence 8? Specifically, is Juliette trying to pick up a client? Is it her first? She implies affirmative answers to all these questions when in 8.4 she tells the pimp who tries to engage her: "I'm doing this temporarily. I hope it's not going to last." Moreover, the young man at the café table acts like the handsome man of the letter, casting repeated glances at her. On the other hand, the dialogue about the Austin in 2.5 indicates that she is already engaged in prostitution. In the café she shows none of the anxiety expressed by the author of the letter: as she enters, she says, "To define myself? One single word? Indifferent." When she leaves, it is not with the young man, and her lyrical account of this moment (over 8.27–8.29) is opposite in tone and content to "I was in a fog." Yet as we learn in Sequence 9, she, like the writer of the letter, is at this mo-

booth where her friend is sitting.)

8.2 | [Actual sound.]

JULIETTE
Hello!   Bonjour!
(Slight pan left as Juliette sits.)
How are you?   Comment ça va?
FRIEND
All right.   Ça va.

I came this morning. I'm staying a little   Je suis venue ce matin. Je reste un petit
while longer. I'm waiting for Jean-Paul.   peu. J'attends Jean-Paul.
JULIETTE
Oh! I'm going to stay until this evening.   Oh! Moi, je vais rester jusqu'à ce soir.
(To the bartender:)
Do you have any Winstons?   Vous avez des Winston?
BARTENDER
Yes, Madame.   *Oui, Madame.*
(Short pan right with Juliette as she gets
up and exits frame right. Her friend glances
in that direction and the camera quickly
pans right and tilts up, catching Juliette exiting frame left along the bar and a young
woman getting up onto a stool. Track in
on the young woman. Another woman, followed by the young man with glasses,
crosses left to right through the frame.)

ment on her way to a hotel and a rendezvous with a client.

In the opening shots of this sequence what is problematical is not the narrative but the blocking and camera movement. The camera follows Juliette until she sits down in 8.2, then moves with her after she gets up (but only when prompted by her friend's glance in her direction), catches a young woman getting up onto a bar stool, centers on her, then tracks in, prompting her to recognize the camera and speak. What

YOUNG WOMAN ON STOOL
(Looking offscreen right, presumably at the young man with glasses:)
Say, you have new shoes!
(The tracking stops. She looks left, then at the camera:)
I live in the big buildings near the Autoroute du Sud.
(She looks off left, smokes, then addresses the camera:)

Tiens, vous avez des nouvelles chaussures!

Je vis dans les grands bâtiments, près de l'autoroute du Sud.

I come to Paris twice a month. You know? The big blue-and-white buildings.
(She looks off left.)
JULIETTE
A pack of Winstons and some matches, please.

BARTENDER
Yes, Mademoi-

Je viens à Paris deux fois par mois. Vous savez? Les grands bâtiments bleus et blancs.

Un paquet de Winston et des allumettes, s'il vous plaît.

Oui, Mademoi-

$$\frac{1'02.6''}{24'31.0''}$$

8.3 *selle . . . Madame.*
JULIETTE
Thank you.
(The bartender hands her a pack of cigarettes. Pan left with her. She stops and lights a cigarette.)

selle . . . Madame.

Merci.

she says is that she lives in the big blue-and-white buildings near the Autoroute du Sud and comes to Paris twice a month (leaving us to guess why). To whom is she talking? Whom does she mean when she asks "Vous savez"? The director? The spectators? "Vous savez" implies that she is addressing someone who regularly drives on the Autoroute du Sud, but I also want to say "the camera" because of the intricacy of its preceding movements.[2] In any case the speech, like the pimp's mention of Isabelle and Colette, is testimony that there are others besides Juliette, like her, doing this for reasons like hers. The elaborate, conspicuously directed choreography of the camera and actors argues that these instances are linked in other ways as well (though not, of course, merely as movement). Godard does not specify what these links are. Instead, he restates

YOUNG MAN WITH GLASSES
Yes, they're American shoes!

Oui, c'est des souliers américains!

YOUNG WOMAN
It's with those that they walk on the feet of the Vietnamese . . .

C'est avec ça qu'ils marchent sur les pieds des Vietnamiens . . .

YOUNG MAN WITH GLASSES
. . . and the South Americans.

. . . et des Sud-Américains.

(Juliette walks toward the camera, blacking out the frame as a phone rings offscreen. She crosses right, out of the frame.)

$\underline{25.7''}$
$24'56.8''$

8.4   We've seen each other before, I believe.
(He pulls Juliette back into the frame.)
JULIETTE
Yeah!
(She exits again.)
YOUNG MAN WITH GLASSES
But
(He pulls her back again.)
don't talk that way! You still don't want me to take you on? Only ten percent?

On s'est déjà vus, je crois.

Ouais!

Mais,

ne parlez pas comme ça! Vous voulez toujours pas que je m'occupe de vous? Dix pour cent, seulement?

JULIETTE
Yes, I know that.
YOUNG MAN WITH GLASSES
Ask Colette what happened to Isabelle.

Oui, je connais ça.

Ben, demandez à Colette ce qui est arrivé à Isabelle.

the connection between the *grands ensembles* and Vietnam: the pimp's new shoes are American, the kind used for stepping on "the feet of the Vietnamese and the South Americans." The line means, I suppose, that the pimp makes his money just as, on an international scale, the imperialists do—but isolated as it is, the accusation is hermetic and facile; we have no access to the arguments that might or might not persuade us.

JULIETTE
I know. A razor slash in the face.

YOUNG MAN WITH GLASSES
And that doesn't scare you?

JULIETTE
In the first place, the war is over.

(She begins to cross right, out of the frame.)

and in the second, I'm doing this temporarily. *I hope it's not going to last.*

(To the bartender:)

A coke, please.

BARTENDER
Yes, Madame.

Je sais. Un coup de rasoir dans la figure.

Et ça ne vous fait pas peur?

D'abord, la guerre est finie,

et puis je fais ça provisoirement. *J'espère que ça ne vas pas durer.*

Un Coca, s'il vous plaît.

Oui, Madame.

$$\frac{24.6''}{25'21.4''}$$

8.5   (As the bartender pours her coke, Juliette takes a notebook out of her purse.)

(She makes a note in the book, then puts it away.)

$$\frac{21.2''}{25'42.5''}$$

With shot 8.5 begins one of the richest and most complex segments of the film. On the one hand, the fiction suddenly takes on a tremendously heightened vividness, not at all the sort of thing in which actors are quoting. Interchange ceases between Juliette and Godard and with it our sense of the woman as actress rather than character.

8.6

(After taking a sip of her coke, Juliette looks off right.)

[Actual sound lowers just before the cut.]

11.4″
25′53.9″

8.7 [Low actual sound under the commentary.]

(A hand turns the pages of the magazine.)
COMMENTARY 10

Here is how Juliette, at 3:37 P.M., saw turn the pages of that object which, in journalistic language, is called a magazine.	Voici comment Juliette, à 15 h 37, voyait remuer les pages de cet objet que, dans le langage journalistique, on nomme une revue.

10.1″
26′04.0″

In his commentary Godard switches to speaking of the dramatic action as if it were an unfabricated, independent reality (Metz's "referential illusion" again) which it is his role to reveal, to represent, and to wonder how to represent accurately. He fixes the action (like that of *Cleo from 5 to 7,* in which he, Anna Karina, and Eddie Constantine played cameo parts) at a precise moment, 3:37 P.M., and pretends that it retains its integrity and continuity when seen from another perspective, that of the young woman of the couple. He observes an object on the table and classifies it almost scientifically, according to "journalistic language" (in fact, it is the August 1966 issue of *Lui*).

In the midst of characterizing the mise-en-scène and action in this way, Godard

8.8	And there is how, about one hundred and fifty frames further along,	Et voilà comment, environ cent cinquante images plus loin,

	another young woman, her likeness, her sister,	une autre jeune femme, sa semblable, sa soeur,

$$\frac{6.4''}{26'10.5''}$$

8.9	[Silence.] saw the same object.	voyait le même objet.

	Where then is the truth? In full face or in	Où est donc la vérité? De face ou de

$$\frac{4.2''}{26'14.7''}$$

8.10	profile? And anyway, what is an object?	profil? Et d'abord, un objet, qu'est-ce que c'est?

(Pause.)

$$\frac{7.7''}{26'22.3''}$$

surprises us by measuring the elapsed time in frames: shot 8.9, he says, represents the woman's view "about one hundred and fifty frames," or roughly six seconds, "further along." Thus he calls into question the very convention he invokes, according to which the action exists independently of his representation: 8.9 is, he insists, not precisely "how . . . another young woman . . . saw the same object," but rather—or perhaps also—a point-of-view *shot*. Consequently, the questions he asks in reference to 8.7, 8.9, and 8.10—"Where then is the truth? In full face or in profile?"—not only pose a metaphysical problem but state the practical dilemma of which angle he as director should pick. (We may recall here that in 1.5 Marina Vlady speaks of "citations de vérité," then turns her head from full face to profile.) In this respect they raise an issue of some complexity. Movies have the power, celebrated by the cubists and constructivists, to pick both—that is, to alternate. Yet while most styles of *découpage* exploit that power, this movie so far does not, inclining instead toward either *plan séquence* or shorter shots (like those of Sequence 1) that resist spatial integration. If the present sequence deviates from this norm and frankly alternates viewpoints, Godard's questions imply dissatisfaction with the practice, seeing it as a sort of epistemological confusion whose counterpart is expressed in Commentary 12: "I cannot tear myself from the objectivity that crushes me nor from the subjectivity that exiles me."

In context, the terms "full face" and "profile" refer not only to the viewpoints on Juliette and the young woman but also to the graphic conventions of the magazine pictures, 8.9 in particular. These drawings, in their outline style and word balloons, resemble comic strips, earlier a term of comparison for the film image. They are a further reminder that what we as spectators are watching are images, that one hundred and fifty *images* (the French word for "frames") have passed before 8.7 yields to 8.9. This kinship between the magazine and the film[3] suggests that in the narrator's description of the woman as "sa semblable, sa soeur" "sa" refers as much to the women in the drawings as to Juliette. Godard's line is, of course, a paraphrase of Baudelaire's poem "Au lecteur," at the conclusion of which the "hypocrite reader" is unexpectedly addressed. The bored young woman thumbing the magazine is something like a modern equivalent of that reader and the message on the page from her "semblable." In this context a fair translation of "semblable" might be "likeness," with the connotation of

8.11

$$\frac{3.2''}{26'25.5''}$$

8.12

$$\frac{2.9''}{26'28.5''}$$

8.13

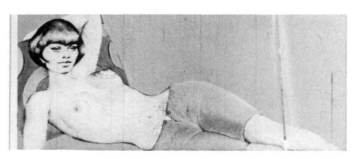

$$\frac{3.6''}{26'32.0''}$$

8.14 [Loud room sounds, pinball machine.]

looking alike. The young woman does indeed look like Juliette, and lest we miss her even more striking likeness to the magazine figures, Godard has her wear big, purple earrings so as to underline the resemblance and give her their air of commercial sexuality. If she is already an "image" by virtue of this resemblance, then the filming process makes her, as well as Juliette, *literally* into images—a train or band of images outrunning the unity that Godard attributes to "the truth."

In so admitting the kinship of the filming process to the mildly pornographic magazine, Godard gives a more complex sense to the film's central metaphor. It is not simply that, as he writes in a text quoted in the preface to the Seuil/Avant-Scène script (p. 17), the director must be included among those whom modern life forces into prostitution; it is that the camera itself at best evinces untruths and at worst is a party to voyeurism: as he says in Commentary 11, "I do not cease to find myself guilty although I feel innocent." Consequently, the word "object" in his concluding question, "And anyway, what is an object?", has the connotation associated with slogans attacking the notion of women as objects. In the strictest sense of his text, the object is what is perceived. For him—at least within the rhetorical premises of this commentary, which portray him as a witness to the action rather than to the image—the magazine and Juliette are objects. *In* the image—that is, for us—they are properly not objects, only representations, a "full face" or "profile." But in addition, images themselves are objects: the magazine is an object with a particular name "in journalistic language." Making images turns things into objects of this sort, and if there is any comparison between the women in *Lui* and those in this scene—and Godard uses all the resources of montage and commentary to draw one—then the women too have been made into objects—a point emphasized by holding on the young woman (8.10) rather than on the magazine during the question "And anyway, what is an object?"

Shots 8.10–8.13, because they are accompanied by the silence that is in fact a prolongation of the acoustic background of the commentary, appear to constitute an answer to the question: we see the magazine, then the woman, in virtually identical framings, then the magazine again, as if to stress equivalence—image for image, object for object. The two succeeding shots (8.14 and 8.15) restore the room sounds, and in

(She looks up, left.)

2.9″
26′34.9″

8.15

[Room sounds lower when music enters midway through the shot.]

14.9″
26′49.8″

doing so transform the woman from a term of equivalence to the magazine pictures back into an inhabitant of her own space, whence she looks at Juliette and smiles. The addition of a shot of Juliette (8.15) to the alternation woman/magazine in 8.8–8.14 suggests that all that applies to the woman—image, object—also applies to her "semblable" and "soeur," the heroine of the film. Music intervenes here, measures 10 through 14 of the Beethoven quartet, giving a mysterious feeling that something has been revealed and recalling, in the fashion of a leitmotiv, the earlier moments in which

8.16 | [Low actual sound, including clinking of spoon, but no room ambience or noise of pinball machine.]

(The coffee is stirred and the spoon is put down on the saucer.)

COMMENTARY 11

Maybe an object is what permits us to relink . . .

Peut-être qu'un objet est ce qui permet de relier . . .

3.2″
26′53.0″

8.17 | [Silence.]

to pass from one subject to the other, therefore to live in society,

(The young man looks at Juliette. She returns his gaze.)

to be together. But then,

(He looks down again.)

since social relationships are always ambiguous,

de passer d'un sujet à l'autre, donc de vivre en société,

d'être ensemble. Mais alors,

puisque la relation sociale est toujours ambiguë,

since my thought divides as much as it unites, since my speech brings nearer through that which it expresses and isolates through that about which it is silent,

(He looks at her again, then back down. She returns his gaze, then looks away.)

puisque ma pensée divise autant qu'elle unit, puisque ma parole rapproche par ce qu'elle exprime et isole par ce qu'elle tait,

the questions of Juliette's representativeness and language were raised.

Commentary 11 gives a second answer to the question of what an object is: "Maybe an object is what permits us to relink . . . to pass from one subject to the other, therefore to live in society, to be together." Despite its association with 8.16 and 8.17, Godard's sentence by no means equates the *possibility* of living in society, which the film can represent only by means of metaphor or montage, with the actual society represented (as it were) by the three people at the café table. *Ensemble* in this instance is a more vexed and hedged possibility than in Juliette's casual "Oui, parlons ensemble." Indeed, these people do not "talk together." They are together in a sense that is on the one hand restricted to the space of the mise-en-scène and on the other denied by the images, which fragment the group by means of mirrors, *découpage,* shallow focus, one-shots, and two-shots.

In order to understand what the narrator means by associating the possibility of being together with the mediation of objects, we must recall that in this context "objet," though here exemplified by a coffee cup (8.16) and earlier by the magazine, is not synonymous with "chose," a thing; rather, it stands in a complementary relation with "sujet." The sequence dramatizes the two terms of this relation with images of, respectively, what is seen (the magazines, the cup) and the person doing the seeing. It does not, however, propose this dramatization as an equivalence. What it does propose, given the implication of Commentary 10 that the film image turns all subjects into objects, is that the people we see *represent* subjects and that the point-of-view shots *represent* their subjectivity.

The power of the shots to effect this representation derives from a conventional figure of film rhetoric. This crucial qualification is reflected in the "peut-être" that begins Commentary 11. Restoring the link between, or passing from, one subject to another, from Juliette in 8.15 to the young man in 8.17, is an act that can be performed only with respect to the image track and only at the level of its syntax. Godard's very portrayal of this act as possible indeed depends on the perfect suitability of his verbs *relier* and *passer* as descriptions of the physical task of editing, where, in order to pass from one shot to the next, one first cuts apart strips of film and then restores a link between them, that is, splices them together. Apart from film (and the arts that resemble it), passing from one subject to another is a contradiction in terms, for, as Commentary 12 acknowledges, subjectivity is inescapable. Natural language too maintains an absolute distinction—exemplified both in the title of the film and in Juliette's "je, me, moi"—between subject and object. Therefore, being together, as defined in Commentary 11, is a possibility that belongs specifically and exclusively to the rhetoric of the film image.[4]

On the word "passer" in the phrase "passer d'un sujet à l'autre," Godard cuts to 8.17, the profile of the young man with Juliette out of focus frame-left. The right-hand portion of the frame, counterbalancing Juliette, is strikingly empty, creating an uneasy and problematical composition, especially since the young man looks toward the empty space as Juliette looks at him. The attention thus directed frame-right makes that space seem not simply vacant but *vacated,* as if it were the sign of someone not present. Whose coffee cup is it, after all? A silly question? The image never answers outright, although we know from 8.4 and 8.5 that Juliette is drinking coke and the young woman beer; we also know that the young man is smoking and in the closeups of the coffee faint traces of smoke are visible. These things, along with the cut 8.16/8.17, imply that the cup may be his and, as if to confirm this implication, 8.18 (the high-angle closeup

since an immense gulf separates the subjective certitude that I have of myself

puisqu'un immense fossé sépare la certitude subjective que j'ai de moi-même

21.0″
27′14.0″

8.18   [Actual sound: clinking of spoon.]

from the objective truth that I am for
others, since I do not cease to find myself guilty although I feel innocent, since
each event transforms my daily life, since
I ceaselessly fail to communicate—

(The spoon enters the frame and stirs the
coffee.)
**I mean, to understand, to love, to be
loved—**
(The spoon leaves the frame.)
**and each failure makes me experience my
solitu-**

et la vérité objective que je suis pour les
autres, puisque je n'arrête pas de me
trouver coupable alors que je me sens
innocent, puisque chaque événement
transforme ma vie quotidienne, puisque
j'échoue sans cesse à communiquer—

je veux dire à comprendre, à aimer, à
me faire aimer—

et que chaque échec me fait éprouver ma
solitu-

20.2″
27′34.1″

8.19   [Silence.]

de, since . . .

de, puisque . . .

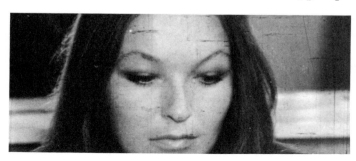

(Juliette looks up, off left.)

of the cup and saucer) appropriates his spatial viewpoint.

With Sequence 8, the commentary changes in character. Until this point it has separated dramatized scenes, accompanied "documentary" material, or indicated, as in 1.5, a documentary aspect of the narrative. The whispering places the speaker near us, facing the image, and outside of it. He neither intrudes into the space nor interrupts the continuity of the world pictured. Although in Commentaries 3 and 9 he uses the first person, he does not speak in a personal vein. But in the present scene, and most decisively with the closeups of the coffee cup (8.16 and 8.18), these patterns are broken. The scale of the image, the whispering, and the tone of what is said for the first time match, signifying that the narrator has entered the space shown (this is not the case, say, in the closeups of the radio in Sequence 2, where we have reason to imagine the narrator close to the spectator but not to what is pictured): we can, and do, I think, imagine that the director is speculating over a cup of coffee—if not that it is his coffee cup, then at least that he is a person like those in the image, with habits like theirs, a person who might frequent a café and think about epistemology and politics. His, we might say, is the space left vacant in 8.17. In 8.17/8.18, as in 8.23/8.24 and 8.25/8.26, he preempts, displaces the young man, and although it is clear that he does not mean us to see the young man as his surrogate (he has excluded this possibility by making him an anonymous figure who does not appear elsewhere in the film), it is also clear that the young man is invested with the properties of a subject, that he is lent them, more ostentatiously than is necessary simply to illustrate the phrase "to pass from one subject to the other."

Once the *ensemble* is dissociated from the figures of montage that create it and invest objects with the power of catalyzing it, then it is left in doubt. Indeed, reasons for this doubt, nine in all (each introduced by the word *puisque*), occupy the remainder of Commentary 11 and the whole of Commentary 12. The first, that "social relationships are always ambiguous," applies not only to the human condition but also to the images that the phrase immediately accompanies. Is the young woman a prostitute? Is the young man her client? Her prospective client? Her pimp? Are they a couple? Is Juliette soliciting him? The peculiar suggestiveness of 8.17 makes the phrase, among other things, an acknowledgment of these Resnais-like narrative ambiguities. In a similar way the phrase that almost immediately follows, "My speech brings nearer through that which it expresses," concerns the commentary itself. *What* does Godard's speech, his act of commentary, bring nearer? Is it the *ensemble*, which is here in doubt? Does speech promote—or equal—*ensemble* itself, as in Juliette's phrase "parlons ensemble"? Here, as we know, *ensemble* describes the group at the table; and they, of course, do not speak. Godard speaks, but not to them, not so that they can respond. Yet the vision of society, of *ensemble*, that his speech holds out locates in them the possibility of, if not *ensemble*, then at least *rapprochement*, just as Commentary 9 locates in an image of construction the hope of "a truly new city." In this instance, however, a doubt accompanies the hope, for Godard's speech also "isolates through that about which it is silent." This silence is both his inaudibility to the figures in the image, isolating him from them, and that which elsewhere replaces his questions to Juliette, dramatizing, as in 6.1, a radical qualification on the possibility of talking together.

The following phrase, "an immense gulf separates the subjective certitude that I have of myself from the objective truth that I am for others," extends these concerns to the realm of the image, which on the words "vérité objective" cuts from the young man (8.17) to the high-angle view of the coffee cup (8.18). Godard, the film's director,

$$\frac{4.5''}{27'38.6''}$$

8.20   [Actual sound, including the noise of the
pinball machine.]
    (The bartender looks off right,

then at what he is doing, then off right
again, then again at what he is doing. He
exits left.)

$$\frac{6.2''}{27'44.8''}$$

8.21

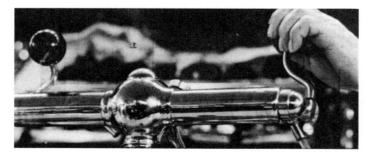

(A hand pulls the faucet, lets it go, pulls it
again, lets it go again.)

is not an objective truth in the sense that the young man or the coffee cup is. We do not see him in the film, as we do, say, at the beginning and end of *Numéro deux*. Instead we confront a paradox: at the moment the film most insistently affirms the objective truth of the image (the French word for a lens being *objectif,* "vérité objective" proposes the equation of objective truth with the truth of the lens), it invokes his "presence" by other means: the empty space in 8.17 and the implication of the editing that the young man is his stand-in.

Here, as the film moves closest to first person, not just in the grammatical sense but with respect to the increasingly personal, even hermetic, tone and content of the commentary (particularly the passage that starts "each event transforms my daily life"), it fulfills most rigorously the promise of the title phrase that the knowledge it purveys will be that of a subject. If "les autres" includes, as it must, the trio at the café table, then the director is, as we see, anything but an "objective truth." He would be so only either in the space of the production, to which no reference is made here, or if he were to be released from his role as director. If the image track shifts from one subject to another, it may do so only in the case of subjects who belong to the mise-en-scène, not in that of the subject who constitutes the *je* of the film, that is, of the commentaries (this conclusion will require qualification in light of 8.27–8.29). In this respect the director's position differs from the characters', for example, that of Juliette, who crosses the Cartesian gulf between subjective certitude and objective truth with the incantation "je, me, moi, tout le monde." For us this incantation has validity both because it is marked as such by its association with a musical phrase and also because we see Juliette but do not see the director. We as spectators—that is, those who look via the mediation of the lens—are specifically excluded from the hypothetical *ensemble* of *autres* who have access to "la vérité objective que je suis," just as we are excluded from the space of the production by the silence that replaces the director's questions. His existential isolation is thus dramatized, or perhaps constituted, by his function as director, which bars him from the two *ensembles* in question: that of the audience and that of the mise-en-scène.[5]

The cut 8.19/8.20 is, I think, a brilliant gesture. The meditation breaks off in midsentence ("puisque . . ."), the noises of the café return, and we have a plain and not obviously necessary picture of a bartender filling a shot glass. What makes this moment so astonishing is not simply the reminder that we are in a café; it is, rather, that the reminder interrupts the meditation at its most metaphysical, personal juncture and takes the form of the most ordinary, literal image in the sequence: the rough, alien, and not very handsome bartender, who displaces, even disallows, speculation and metaphor.

What can this gesture mean? Are we returned to the scene or to the mise-en-scène? To the narrative or only to the space in which the narrative is set? Insofar as the preceding shot, 8.19, reads as the narrator's *regard,* it illustrates the feeling of solitude that he describes. Juliette exacerbates this feeling by not returning "his" look (8.5–8.29, unlike some other scenes, observe the conventional prohibition against actors' looking at the camera), but instead, at the tail of the shot, looking screen-left. At the cut 8.19/8.20, there is an interlocking of glances, implying that she is looking at the bartender and he at her. Do these looks have a sexual meaning? We learn shortly that Juliette does not leave with the young man and that therefore, to the extent that he is the narrator's surrogate, the fictional action dramatizes the narrator's avowed failure "to love and be loved."

In this reading, a great deal depends on whether in 8.17 the young man's two

[With the word "puisque," rapid fade-out of actual sound to silence.]

COMMENTARY 12

since . . .   puisque . . .

12.1″
27′56.9″

8.22   since I cannot tear myself from the ob-   puisque je ne peux pas m'arracher à
         jectivity that crushes me   l'objectivité qui m'écrase

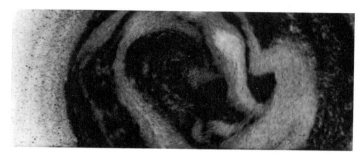

nor from the subjectivity that exiles me,   ni à la subjectivité qui m'exile, puisqu'il
since I am permitted neither to lift my-   ne m'est pas permis ni de m'élever
self to being nor to fall into nothingness,   jusqu'à l'être, ni de tomber dans le
I must listen, I must look around me   néant, il faut que j'écoute, il faut que je
more than ever at the world, my like-   regarde autour de moi plus que jamais
ness, my brother.   le monde, mon semblable, mon frère.
(Pause.)

27.9″
28′24.8″

8.23   [Room sounds slowly fade up.]

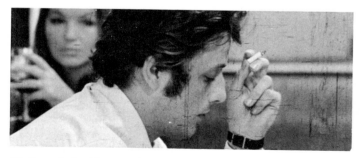

(Juliette is looking at the young man. He
turns to look at her, then they both look
away. Pause. Just before the commentary
starts, Juliette again looks at him.)

glances at her and his concluding glance downward, presumably at his coffee, constitute a signifying dichotomy. Do these glances, in other words, set in opposition the act of meditation, interwoven as it is with that of directing, and the possibility of sexual *ensemble?* If so, then shot 8.18 and the increasingly closer shots of the coffee (8.22, 8.24, 8.26) signify that the tension is resolved in favor of the former—that is, that both the young man and the narrator, insofar as he appears to us as the director of the shots, choose speculation rather than Juliette. And if this in turn is so, does Juliette's glance then constitute a response, a turning away from the ambivalent sexual initiative of the composite figure young man/narrator toward the bartender? In other words, is the bartender an image of sexuality? We see both that he is an opposite physical type to the young man (as he is to Robert) and that he resembles Eddie Constantine, who in *Alphaville is* just such a figure of atavistic sexuality, the foe of logic and prostitution and the champion of poetry and love. At the same time, if the glance is here a sexual sign, the bartender's dark glasses mark him as someone who sees but is not seen: he is, as it were, out of the arena. As the example of *Alphaville* suggests, however, the exchange of glances among him, Juliette, and the young man, if they have to do with sexuality, then it is with sex as a commodity in prostitution, which the sequence does not on any account equate with "aimer" or "faire aimer."

The beginning of Commentary 12, which continues the sentence started in Commentary 11, comes as an intrusion at the tail of 8.21, the luminous and beautiful shot of the beer taps. The cut to 8.22 falls on the repetition "puisque . . . puisque," as if the narrator, earlier interrupted by the cut to 8.20, must now prompt the image to change—that is, must demonstrate the difficulty of dispelling the "objective" world of the café—before he can continue his meditation.

The allusion in Commentary 12 to Sartre's *Being and Nothingness* brings to mind the existential terms of the discussion between Nana and Brice Parain in *Vivre sa vie*. There, as here, the text touches on whether thought and speech are identical, the relationship of speaking to silence, the body, and love. Here there is an additional, and more concrete, meaning: Godard, the director, is "crushed" by the objectivity of the world he films, which, once filmed, *has* no mode but that of objectivity. The "exile" it imposes on him is dramatized by his whispering, his tentativeness, and the various means he has used to show the difficulties that attend representing himself within it. Still, he has not found it possible to lapse into nothingness, which here includes among its meanings the conventional absence of the director in his filmed world, still less to elevate himself unambiguously into being, rather *a* being, a surrogate, as the young man is in some respects.

This reading is not to diminish the philosophical meanings of the sentences, rather to remind ourselves that they occur in a narrative film, indeed in the first scene of it in which the mediating director has intruded into the space of the narrative. Seen in this perspective, the long deferred conclusion—"I must listen, I must look around me more than ever"—though vague as a philosophical resolution, is precise as a response spoken by the persona of director in reference to the situation of the film—for the film, unlike the world, *has* a director, a figure for whom this answer is appropriate, perhaps even adequate. Godard does not feel it necessary to specify that in this context looking is really filming and listening is really recording, for the earlier reference to a frame-count establishes firmly enough the concern of the scene with film and direction.

Look at what? Shot 8.23 shows the young man again, part of the trio that includes the two women and himself, filled out by the unseen fourth member whose

[Room sounds rapidly fade out to silence as the commentary starts.]

COMMENTARY 13

The world by itself   Le monde seul

18.3″
28′43.1″

8.24   today, when revolutions are impossible,   aujourd'hui, où les révolutions sont impossibles,

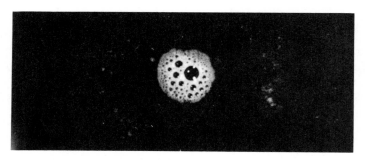

when bloody wars threaten it, when capitalism is no longer very sure of its rights and the working class is in retreat, when the advance . . . the lightning advances of science give to future centuries a haunting presence, when the future is more present than the present, when distant galaxies are at my door: my

où des guerres sanglantes le menacent, le capitalisme n'est plus très sûr de ses droits et la classe ouvrière en recul, où le progrès . . . où les progrès foudroyants de la science donnent aux siècles futures une présence obsédante, où l'avenir est plus présent que le présent, où les lointaines galaxies sont à ma porte: mon

23.1″
29′06.1″

"semblable" and "frère" the young man is. There is an important syntactical ambiguity in "le monde, mon semblable, mon frère," which occurs near the end of 8.22. The phrase can be heard either as an appositive—"the world, which is my likeness, my brother"—or as a list of things in coordinate relation: "the world *and* my likeness *and* my brother." The first reading expands on the implication in Commentary 11 that things have a unity which the narrator's thought divides. Access to that unity is not the visible and audible in themselves but as conjoined with quotation, that is, with another's thought. The assertion of this link has a complex effect. It plants a hint, developed in Sequence 15, of an *ensemble* different from the one we hear and see, in which the speaker claims membership. Moreover, just as the source of the quotation brings to mind Juliette's dream in Sequence 3, so its substance recalls Christophe's allegory of unification and brotherhood. In Godard's paraphrase of this source, "le monde" replaces Baudelaire's "hypocrite lecteur," as if stating an equivalence: the world is, or at least includes, the "hypocrite reader."

Who is this hypocrite reader? In one sense it is the spectator, since it is only to the spectator that the director is speaking; we alone can hear him. In another sense it is the young man, who, as we saw in 8.5, is reading a newspaper, just as Juliette's "semblable" and "soeur" reads a magazine. Insofar as the phrase, like the later formulation "the landscape is like a face" (8.29), means that the world *is* "mon semblable, mon frère," then it implies that this newspaper reader is *our* brother as well, an interpretation reinforced by the narrator's never entirely relinquished position as *our* likeness, our fellow-spectator. The progression "le monde, mon semblable, mon frère" is, moreover, nearly the mirror-image of Juliette's "je, me, moi, tout le monde" (a relationship obscured by the custom of translating *monde* as "world" rather than "people" and *tout le monde* as "everybody" rather than "the whole world"); it summarizes Godard's effort not only to understand himself as included within the world but to represent this effort as an elaboration and correction of that expressed in Juliette's phrase. If that phrase asks us to consider whether Juliette is not representative of her world, then Godard asks whether this world, constituted as it is by his likenesses, must not include him. The literary allusion argues that the achievement of this inclusion, the perception of the unity of things and the dissolution of the gulf between the subjective and objective—or, more precisely, the representation of these things in a film—is not possible directly but only via another "système," of which the quoted poem, or perhaps quotation itself, is an instance.

Commentary 13 develops a paradox, first listing attributes of today's world that make it hostile and alien, then reaffirming that it is nonetheless "mon semblable, mon frère." While this paradox in itself may be persuasive, I think that the description of the modern world which it entails is not. Can we believe, for example, that "the lightning advances of science give to future centuries a haunting presence" or that "the future is more present than the present"? To my ear this sounds like "journalistic language." It may do as a description of the premise of *Alphaville* or of the short *Anticipation*, where images of the present stand, with some irony, for the future. But it does not precisely describe, nor is it really supported by, anything in *2 ou 3 choses*—neither Juliette's speculation about "the city of tomorrow" nor the narrator's hope of "a truly new city" nor the construction which threatens that hope.

There is, I suppose, a certain wit in characterizing the world as a place where "distant galaxies are at my door" (the car Lemmy Caution drives across intersiderial space to Alphaville is a Ford Galaxie) while showing coffee bubbles that resemble swirl-

8.25 [Room sounds slowly fade up.]

likeness, my brother. **semblable, mon frère.**

(The young man smokes, looks down.)

(He looks at Juliette, then looks away.)

13.2″
29′19.3″

ing nebulae. But this, after all, is not the doing of scientific progress so much as of metaphor making, filming, which until this point Godard has not hesitated to claim responsibility for. There is some playfulness in his not admitting that it is he who makes the coffee look like galaxies, but, I'm afraid, not enough indication that the authority for this resemblance does not wholly derive from the recited "facts" about the modern world. After all, one wants to say, galaxies aren't at his door, and scientific progress is not in evidence here.

Nor is he more persuasive when he complains that "the working class is in retreat," "revolutions are impossible," and "capitalism is no longer very sure of its rights" (it seems sure enough to me). In these three instances, however, the problem arises because his phrases are adapted from a text by Merleau-Ponty:

The class struggle is masked. We are at an ambiguous moment in history. Neither capitalism nor revolution fights openly any more: because capitalism is unsure of its own future and cannot project itself in terms of a positive theory, and because Marxism—even if it retains a palpable influence on the mode of production and the economic structure of those countries in which it has triumphed—has ceased to animate a proletarian politics.[6]

Unlike the passage from Baudelaire, this is not sufficiently known for Godard's paraphrase to be understood as such. How, therefore, can we help but ask what basis he has, as narrator of this film, for such conclusions as "revolutions are impossible"?

Commentary 14 is on surer ground and closer to the important concerns of the scene (though I admit I find the introductory paraphrase of Genesis awkward and weak):

. . . to say that the limits of language are those of the world, that the limits of my language are those of my world. And that in speaking, I limit the world, I end it. And that one logical and mysterious day death will come to abolish that limit and there will be neither question nor answer; everything will be fuzzy.

These sentences, in part a paraphrase of Wittgenstein, expand on Juliette's formulation, "Language is the house man lives in." They link the existential conditions of life both to natural language and to the "language" of the image, its sharpness and delimitation of view. They are at once mystical and concrete: death will abolish not only the limits imposed by language, a condition of life generally, but question and answer, a procedure associated specifically with this film and its directorial method, along with sharpness, to which its imagery is manifestly committed.

In outline, the argument resembles that which Brice Parain sets out in *Vivre sa vie:* living and talking cannot be separated; to speak well it is necessary to have passed through a death, which is the nonspeaking life. This may help explain Godard's concern with speaking well (the young woman in 15.3 defines speaking as "dire des bêtises ou des choses très bien") and the curiously affirmative role given to death as the release from the limits of language.

But if by chance things again become sharp, this can be only with the appearance of consciousness and conscience. After that, everything will connect and proceed.

Does "after that" (*ensuite*) mean "after death"? If so, then "the appearance of consciousness" is the afterlife, an unironic equivalent to the assurance "you are inde-

8.26 | [Silence.]

(A sugar cube plunges into the coffee. Pause.)

COMMENTARY 14

Where does it begin? But where does what begin? God created the heavens and the earth, of course. But that is a bit cowardly and easy.

(The image is out of focus and is becoming more so.)

One should be able to say something better, to say that the limits of language are those of the world, that the limits of my language are those of my world. And that in speaking, I limit the world, I end it. And that one logical and mysterious day death will come to abolish that limit and there will be neither question nor answer; everything will be fuzzy.

(The image starts to come into focus, becoming sharp after the word "nettes.")

But if by chance things again become sharp,

Où commence? Mais où commence quoi? Dieu créa les cieux et la terre, bien sûr. Mais c'est un peu lâche et facile.

On doit pouvoir dire mieux, dire que les limites du langage sont celles du monde, que les limites de mon langage sont celles de mon monde. Et qu'en parlant, je limite le monde, je le termine. Et que la mort, un jour logique et mystérieux, viendra abolir cette limite et qu'il n'y aura ni question, ni réponse; tout sera flou.

Mais si par hasard les choses redeviennent nettes,

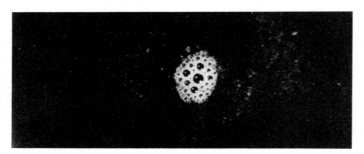

this can be only with the appearance of consciousness and conscience. After that, everything will connect and proceed.

ce ne peut être qu'avec l'apparition de la conscience. Ensuite, tout s'enchaîne.

$$\frac{53.5''}{30'12.8''}$$

structible." On the other hand, it is plausible that the narrator's adversative means that he takes "the appearance of consciousness" and "death" to be opposites; that sharpness is not on the other side, the *au-delà*, of death, but an alternative event. The context gives some support to this reading, since the present sentences introduce Juliette's testimony in 8.27–8.29 on the theme "everything will connect and proceed," a feeling that she associates not with death but with "the smell of the trees." In what sense can this "appearance" happen "by chance"? If "apparition de la conscience" and "la mort" are opposites, then so are "par hasard" and "logique": death is the logic of time, represented in this sequence both by the fictional hour, 3:37 P.M., and the count of frames in the image track,[7] while the appearance of consciousness, if it comes about, will do so neither through logic nor through intention. However, "par hasard" takes on another sense when heard, as it must be, in relation to the image, in which at this moment things literally "again become sharp." Because this happens in no sense "by chance," it argues that the appearance of consciousness will be achieved not in the face of logic but through the ordinary, unmysterious work of filming as it has been presented to us so far: taking shots, linking them together, and taking care to focus the camera.

What then are we to understand by the phrase "apparition de la conscience"? It is worth recalling that in French *conscience* has the sense both of "consciousness" and "conscience" (that is, moral consciousness). The apocalyptic tone of the preceding sentences, especially the longing expressed in the phrase "one logical and mysterious day," makes it clear that both "l'apparition de la conscience" and "la mort" are mystical ideas. But by associating them respectively with (literally "avec") fuzziness and sharpness, properties manifested in the accompanying shot (8.26), Godard not only illustrates them, acts them out (in a disconcertingly literal and rather embarrassing way) but also *equates* them with the simple act of focusing the camera. Hence the "apparition de la conscience" is, in one sense, an aesthetic presciption, or at least begins from one: seeing things sharply or, more precisely, taking sharp pictures—a condition of the director's taking action on the injunction to look around himself more than ever.

Commentaries 13 and 14 accompany a very simple but significant shot structure: two extreme closeups taken of the surface of the coffee from the same camera setup (8.24 and 8.26), intercut with two shots of the young man (8.23 and 8.25). The shots of the coffee are without ambient sound, which returns (in *place* of the commentary) during those of the young man. This structure is introduced, and hence informed, by the prescription "I must listen, I must look around me more than ever," that is, hear the sounds of the room, of the world, and look at *it*, not (to put it crudely) just at one's coffee. The shots of the coffee are not only self-absorbed and meditative; they *represent* self-absorption and meditation, especially the moral deficiency of those things.

It is in this connection that the moral connotation of *conscience* comes into play. *Conscience* consists in the act of looking up and around, in listening and, by implication, distrusting the representations of subjectivity, the equivalences one might find in one's cup. The prediction "After that, everything will connect and proceed" applies as much to what follows from this act as to a mystical vision of death and rebirth. As if to correct the identification of the swirling coffee at the tail of 8.24 with the galaxies, atoms, and "revolutions" (a lame pun) that constitute the narrator's "world," at the head of 8.26 a flash barely recognizable as a sugar cube pierces the dark surface of the liquid, vividly reminding us that what we are looking at is, after all, a cup of something that someone is going to drink, not just use as a background for meditation.

8.27 (Pan right with Juliette.)

JULIETTE
I don't know where or when. I
remember only that it happened.

Je ne sais pas où, ni quand. Je me souviens seulement que c'est arrivé.

$$\frac{8.3''}{30'21.0''}$$

8.28 (Tilt down and pan right with her.)

It's a feeling that I searched
for the whole day. There
was the smell of the trees.

C'est un sentiment que j'ai recherché
toute la journée. Il y avait l'odeur des
arbres.

$$\frac{13.3''}{30'34.3''}$$

In light of this, it is not enough to say of the tail of 8.26 that the camera is focusing; we must add that it is focusing *on the coffee* and so wittily linking the "apparition de la conscience" to the fact that drinking coffee, especially black coffee, wakes you up. Moreover, in the context of shots 8.22–8.26, to focus on the coffee is also not to focus on Juliette, who in 8.23 and 8.25 is and remains out of focus. This helps dramatize the choice, which I earlier described as having sexual overtones, by the young man and narrator of meditation over Juliette. Is it too much to say, therefore, as William Rothman does, that the sequence represents this act of meditation as evidence of sexual impotence?

With the phrase "Mais si par hasard . . ." begins the slow movement of the Beethoven quartet, which provides the sort of affective gratification ordinarily excluded by the austerity and abruptness of Godard's style. As the string instruments enter one by one, they construct the concord of a D-flat major triad, exemplifying for us the clarity and connectedness that the accompanying words describe. The crescendo that begins when the fourth instrument, the cello, enters immediately follows the phrase "tout s'enchaîne," underlining its summary, climactic place and conferring on it the visionary, transcendental aura associated with the late Beethoven quartets. The phrase itself contradicts, and so appears to displace, the terms Godard uses earlier to describe his condition: "isole," "exile," "fossé," "divise," "solitude." The word "enchaîne," moreover, also designates the specifically filmic kind of connection known as the lap-dissolve (*fondu enchaîné*), which, although not used here or elsewhere in the film, may be thought of as a "surface structure" of the overlapped action at the cuts 8.27/8.28 and 8.28/8.29 (the cut 15.5/15.6 and all those in Tableau 1 of *Vivre sa vie* also follow this pattern).

I think it is fair to say that what chiefly occupies the segment 8.5–8.26 is the narrator's struggle to insert himself in the world, a struggle dramatized in the language of philosophy but always with reference to his situation as film director. It may not be going too far, therefore, to hear the staggered entrances of the four string instruments at the tail of 8.26 as affirming not simply that everything will connect and proceed but that the trio at the table has now, in some visionary sense, definitively become a quartet—in other words, that the narrator's struggle has been successfully resolved. After this moment the music, having switched its emphasis from harmony to melody—that is, from a vertical linkage of voices to a horizontal, temporal linkage like that connoted by *enchaîne* and manifested in the image track—continues under shots 8.27–8.29, which reenact the drama of insertion into the world, this time through the persona of the heroine.

In other words, in 8.27–8.29 Juliette becomes the narrator's surrogate. She assumes his role as voice-over commentator (this is the first time in the film that any voice but his is used over, as opposed to off[8]); the music prompted by his text continues under hers; and what she says addresses and resolves his concerns in the commentaries preceding. Her testimony "I was the world, the world was me" recasts his paraphrase of Baudelaire, giving it the authority of a "feeling" as immediate as "the smell of the trees" (does Godard know Eliot's passage about an idea being as immediate as the smell of a rose?) rather than that of a quotation. It also recalls the source and vocabulary of her own "je, me, moi, tout le monde." But as I argued earlier, the irony that surrounds that line measures Godard's distance from it. And inasmuch as 8.27–8.29 directly continue the scene 8.5–8.26 and are linked to it by music, it would seem that two premises of the earlier segment also apply here: namely, the director's

8.29 (Pan right with her.)

That I was the world. And that the world was me.

Que j'étais le monde. Et que le monde était moi.

(Hold.)

surrogation by the young man rather than by Juliette, and the sexual intrigue that sustains absolute distinctions of gender. In this respect Juliette cannot stand for Godard, or cannot stand for him simply. Consequently, this moment can neither be taken without qualification to represent his "apparition de la conscience" nor resolve either the issues of the film so far or even those of the preceding segment. Rather, it relays these issues to Juliette, to whom nothing of consequence has happened until this point, and thereby to the narrative, which begins in earnest only with the end of this sequence.

The camera movement in 8.27–8.29 is complex and lyrical. All three shots pan with Juliette, seemingly from the same vantage point, as she walks down the street. They repeat in an overlapping fashion portions of the action: the second (8.28) begins earlier in Juliette's walk than the first (8.27), starting with a tilt down, then a pan; the third (8.29) picks up the action also earlier than the first but later than the second and follows her to a point beyond the tail of either, then halts as she exits from the frame. The abruptness of the jump cuts to 8.28 and 8.29 is softened in both cases by not showing her at the head of the shot: she emerges from behind a woman in 8.28 and from behind a man in 8.29 (in 8.27 from behind a tree).

What are we to make of all this? First, the pans, with their elaborately interwoven stopping and starting points, even on first viewing convey the feeling of intricate design, like that of the accompanying music; they designate the importance of the moment and of Juliette's text, as if responding to it, acting out its central idea "I was the world and . . . the world was me." More specifically, the Marienbad-like repetitions of the action seem equivalents of the act and effort of remembering: "I remember only that it happened. It's a feeling that I searched for the whole day." In this reading, therefore, the scene entails not only an insertion of the heroine, the subject, into the world—that is, a simple enactment of the concerns of the preceding meditations—but also the identification of the image with her subjectivity—at least to the extent that image syntax and voice-over make this possible.

Several considerations must qualify this reading. First, Juliette appears in what is represented to us as her own memory. She begins her speech by saying that she does not remember where or when this happened, but the image does—and indeed must. Second, as we learn in the next shot but one (9.1), she is on her way to a rendezvous with a customer, a fact that retrospectively discredits the lyricism of the moment. Third, careful listening reveals that her speech is recorded not in a neutral acoustical space like that of the commentaries but in a noisy city environment like, or perhaps in fact, that which we see when this text is reprised (16.9). Indeed, one sentence—"Il y avait l'odeur des arbres"—appears to have been recorded in a *different* environment from the others. In the sound mix each of her phrases is adroitly faded in and out, thus preventing their connective ambience from prevailing and thereby associating itself, rather than the music, with the space pictured. These acoustical details qualify the conclusion that her voice-over is precisely analogous to Godard's. They testify, rather, that it is he who authorized the recording of the phrases, assembled them (from at least two sources), separated them with pauses, and *placed* them over the image—in short, that he has a controlling relationship to her text which is inscribed in its delivery, recording, and mix. Finally, as we sense even on first viewing, the shots are different takes of the same action. They resemble in this respect the near repetitions in the famous escape sequence from *Pierrot le fou* (which are, incidentally, also linked to a controlling voice-over text: "Partez en vitesse, partez en vitesse," and so forth). Here, more than in *Pierrot,* we have explicit contextual support for mentioning the filming process

[Straight cut from music to outdoor ambience on the next word:]

The landscape is like a face.

Le paysage, c'est comme un visage.

16.9″
30′51.2″

8.30 [Loud construction noise.]

11.6″
31′02.8″

in our interpretation: the narrator's identity as director, his resolve to listen and look around him, his measurement of the elapsed time in frames, and his question about which perspective, full face or profile, is the truth.

Thus, in the present context, we might ask an equivalent question—namely, which *take* is the truth—and the answer given by the triad 8.27–8.29 is all and none, since memory is not strictly equivalent to any filmed or filmable image. The triplication, besides acknowledging this fact, rehearses the earlier implication that the director's situation is not Juliette's, that is differs precisely with respect to the work of directing, which by definition includes the making of images. It is through this work and not through her act of remembering that we see her. Her final line, "The landscape is like a face," admits the relevance of this point. The abrupt end to the music and the switch of tone that set this line off from the preceding lines force us to recognize that it does not belong to her character in the way that they do. Rather, it enunciates a structural principle that the director has followed and that hence belongs to *him:* namely, the alternation of narrative scenes, faces, with interludes of Parisian "landscape": it is *his* premise, *his* argument, that the two are alike. When Juliette repeats the tag much later (16.9), it is in a speech where his presence is strongly felt as the unheard, offscreen prompter. The cut to 8.30, the picture of the barge, illustrating a "landscape" presumably like Juliette's "face" in some way that we are still struggling to understand, is "his" (in the same sense that the cuts 8.27/8.28 and 8.28/8.29 are "hers"), and had his voice spoken the line that prompts it, no problem would ensue and no issue of surrogation would arise. But even if the cut 8.29/8.30 does not immediately seem "his," we nonetheless recognize it as one of a whole *class* of cuts to interlude material, the imagery of the Paris region, which has examples throughout the film and which, as the film's title insists, are his indisputably.

Sequence 9

9.1 [Actual sound.]

(Juliette hangs up her raincoat as a young man closes the hotel room door. She exits left; he takes off his coat as she reenters. He pays her.)

JULIETTE
Thank you.   Merci.

YOUNG MAN
Is this a hotel reserved for Jews?   C'est un hôtel réservé aux juifs?

JULIETTE
Why?   Pourquoi?

(She locks the door. Pan right with her.)

YOUNG MAN
It has only one star.   Il n'y a qu'une seule étoile.

(Juliette takes the blanket off the bed. Pan left with her as she throws it on a high shelf above her coat. Pan left with her to

In this, the first of the two scenes of Juliette with clients, the main issues are voyeurism and censorship. Her client wants to watch her undress; she objects, even

the mirror over the sink. Hold. She washes
her hands.)

(Pan left with her to the window. Hold.)

JULIETTE
Don't watch me undress.

YOUNG MAN
Why?

JULIETTE
Because I don't want you to.

YOUNG MAN
In two minutes you'll be completely naked.

JULIETTE
That's not the same thing.
(He appears in the mirror over the sink, re-
moving a second mirror opposite.)

YOUNG MAN
I'm

Ne me regarde pas me déshabiller.

Pourquoi?

Parce que je veux pas.

Dans deux minutes, vous serez toute nue.

Ce n'est pas la même chose.

Je suis

$\dfrac{43.8''}{31'46.6''}$

though, as he says, "in two minutes you'll be completely naked." "That's not the same thing," she replies. He explains that he works in the Metro and that there are two million Parisians there, "but no one sees them because the police do not allow photos to be taken." Then, with her consent, he positions a mirror so that he can watch the sexual act. Later, she herself proposes sex "Italian style," him standing and her kneeling: "that way you can watch me."

Shot 9.2, a closeup of the jacket of a book called *Introduction to Ethnology,* jokes about the scene's concern with observation as well as about the sociological perspective it shares with the film as a whole.[1] But the joke is ambiguous. In one interpretation, the director is the ethnologist and Juliette and her client the objects of his scrutiny. In another, the client himself is the ethnographer. His speech about the Metro, in combination with the shot of the book jacket, suggests that the introduction to ethnology consists in his desire to see. His assumption that you don't see what you can't photograph, though puzzling both in itself and as a reply to Juliette, is explicable as a statement of the scientist's need for data. Therefore when in the shot following he sets up his mirror, we understand that what we are witnessing is a comic version of ethnographic research.

In certain respects Juliette's client and Godard resemble each other. As a young man Godard studied ethnology at the Sorbonne. His previous film, *Masculine Feminine,* includes a major scene shot in the Metro. The obvious care he has taken in 9.1 in placing the camera so as to multiply Juliette's reflections in the two facing mirrors is

9.2   *a Parisian.*   *Parisien.*

I work in the Metro. There are two million Parisians who are there too, but one never sees them

Je travaille dans le métro. Il y a deux millions de parisiens qui sont là aussi, mais on ne les voit

$$\frac{11.9''}{31'58.5''}$$

9.3   (Juliette crosses left through the frame as he positions the mirror on the floor so that it will stand up.)
because the police do not allow photos to be taken.
(Juliette crosses right through the frame.)

jamais parce que la police a défendu qu'on prenne des photos.

(Pan left and tilt down with the young man as he sits on the bed and looks in the mirror.)
Will it bother you if I put the

Ça ne vous dérange pas si je met la

$$\frac{23.0''}{32'21.5''}$$

echoed by the client's positioning of the mirror in 9.3. On the other hand, the client is a worker, not a student. He may wish to take photographs, but does not actually do so (in contrast to Juliette's other client, John Faubus, who not only photographs her but uses a camera that produces pictures proportioned like Godard's Techniscope). And while *Masculine Feminine* includes a scene in the Metro, this film, which attempts to speak for the Parisian millions, does not.

The joke about ethnology is played out in the series of exotic poster images with which the hotel room (like Monsieur Gérard's brothel) is decorated. As Juliette enters, she passes a poster advertising Seville, which shows two women seen, as she herself momentarily is, from the back, and another for Mizoguchi's *Ugetsu Monogatari*. Later in shot 9.1, her receding mirror reflections are juxtaposed to a San Francisco travel poster, which repeats the blue and yellow of her skirt and blouse. As William Rothman notes, this also serves Godard as an allusion to *Vertigo*, which, like *Ugetsu*, comments on the relationship between looking and making images, in particular those of women. Shot 9.3 adds to this repertoire an advertisement for the Near East with a stylized drawing of an Arab woman holding food and another showing a Japanese

(She looks in the mirror over the sink and straightens her hair.)

JULIETTE

No. It isn't my fault if I have a passive side.

Non. C'est pas de ma faute si j'ai un côté passif.

(Slow pan left with her past the window.)

To have sexual relations . . . I don't see why I should be ashamed of being a woman!

Avoir des relations sexuelles . . . Je vois pas pourquoi je serais honteuse d'être une femme!

(She stops in front of a poster.)

Or then . . . Yes, often it's being happy or indifferent. Yes, that's what I'm sometimes ashamed of. Oh well, yes . . . he is going to put his sex between my legs.

Ou alors . . . Oui, souvent c'est d'être heureuse ou indifférente. Oui, c'est de ça que je suis honteuse quelquefois. Eh bien, oui . . . il va mettre son sexe entre mes jambes.

(With the previous sentence, pan right with her.)

I feel the weight of my arm when I move it.

Je sens le poids de mon bras quand je le bouge.

(She stops at the mirror, uncaps her lipstick. Hold.)

Maybe I should leave Robert.

Peut-être il faudrait que je plaque Robert.

(She puts on lipstick.)

woman in a red kimono. After the cut to 9.4, we see the second of these in the mirror as Juliette meditates on her passivity. She crosses left and stands in front of it, speaking about her femininity and the things she is ashamed of, then delivers the line: "He is going to put his sex between my legs." When she crosses back to the mirror to put on heavy red lipstick, then wonders whether she should leave Robert, it continues

He doesn't want to get ahead in society. He is always satisfied with what he has. In Martinique it was already that way.

YOUNG MAN
Why do you use lipstick?

JULIETTE
(Turns to him:)
That's none of your business!

Il veut pas s'élever dans la société. Il est toujours content avec ce qu'il a. A la Martinique, c'était déjà comme ça.

Pourquoi vous mettez du rouge à lèvres?

Ça te regarde pas!

56.9″
33′18.3″

9.5

(She crosses leftward close to the camera. He follows her with his gaze as she leaves the frame. We infer that she sits to his right on the bed. Her hand touches his forehead.)
What do you like?

YOUNG MAN
I don't know.

JULIETTE
Do you want it Italian style?

YOUNG MAN
What's that?

JULIETTE
You stand and I kneel; that way you can watch me.

Qu'est-ce que tu aimes?

Je sais pas.

Tu veux à l'italienne?

Qu'est-ce que c'est?

Tu restes debout et moi, je me mets à genoux; comme ça, tu peux me regarder.

31.9″
33′50.3″

to form the background, though now in a metaphoric sense, to her thought and action.

As Juliette stands at the mirror, the young man asks: "Pourquoi vous mettez du rouge à lèvres?"—literally, "Why are you putting red on your lips?" The lipstick is indeed unlike the makeup she ordinarily wears. For us, it signals both the imminent sexual act and her transformation from wife to prostitute. Insofar as it recalls the magazine mannequins (8.9 and 8.11), whose lips are painted in the patterns of the British and American flags, it repeats the film's contention that this transformation has a political cause. Red is the painter's color of 12.31, the color of politics. Here it fills out the painter's primary triad, whose other components, the yellow and blue of Juliette's skirt and blouse, complete both the comparison of her to the red, yellow, and blue of the San Francisco poster visible screen-left and the concomitant allusion to Alfred Hitchcock and *Vertigo*. More importantly, it acknowledges her appropriation of the image of the Japanese woman, particularly of its connotations of submissiveness, and, at one remove, that of *Ugetsu*. By these means Godard expands on her contention, "It isn't my fault if I have a passive side." She is a creature, if a willing one, of images, which he as ethnologist has assembled as terms of comparison and explanation. His argument may appear simply to repeat the point made by her citation of Madame Express's advice on dress in 2.5 or of the underwear advertisements in *Une femme mariée;* in actuality it is more complex, since in this instance blame attaches not to commercial exploitation but to serious cultural expressions, one of which, *Ugetsu,* he (with reason) admires greatly.[2]

This treatment of Juliette's submissiveness issues in her proposition in 9.5 of sex Italian style. Just before the young man's assent, Godard cuts to 9.6, a mirror image of the word "beauty," evidently part of a sign painted on a window, in deep red. The cut,

9.6

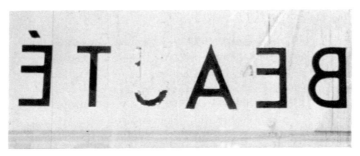

YOUNG MAN
OK.

Ouais.

JULIETTE
To be independent of a man sexually, that tempts me.

Etre indépendente d'un homme sexuellement, ça me tente.

9.6″
33′59.9″

9.7   (She looks at the camera:)

But in fact it horrifies me.
(She looks down.)

Mais, en fait, ça me fait horreur.

No, humility isn't really good. Yes, because

Non, l'humilité n'est pas vraiment bonne.

we might say, represents an act of censorship, denying us a view of something forbidden. But what? The inversion of the letters suggests that the answer is sex Italian style, while the dark red puts us in mind of the lipstick and the act of prostitution. As the shot is held, Juliette meditates, "To be independent of a man sexually, that tempts me," then, following the cut to 9.7, adds, "But in fact it horrifies me." As she says this, she looks at the camera and we hear, for the second time in the film, the opening phrase of the Beethoven quartet. The leitmotiv links what she says here with "je, me, moi, tout le monde," suggesting that what horrifies her in the prospect of sexual independence isn't the specific possibility, left to our imaginations, of lesbianism, masturbation, or abstinence, but the loss of a link to other people, of *ensemble*.

Shot 9.6, in addition to displacing a view of a sexual act, offers a comment on it: sex Italian style and the various possibilities of sexual independence turn beauty the color of prostitution, of shame, and get it backward. More precisely, they put it in mirror image. But, we might ask, in whose mirror is the word "beauty" so seen? The obvious answer is "the young man's." If this is the case, shot 9.6 is, as it were, a picture of Juliette, who has turned her beauty around and reddened it. The cut to 9.7, a low-key closeup prominently displaying her red lips, corroborates this.

However, 9.6, although a "mirror image," is not something literally seen in a mirror, for mirrors, besides reversing things left to right, also return a view of the perceiving self. At least, they do so when regarded frontally, as are the letters in 9.6. If that self is the young man, then shot 9.6 can be said to withhold a view of him. His absence here, pointed up by the numerous mirror reflections of him in the shots preceding, brings to mind that of the narrator in the previous sequence. What this instance adds to that is a connotation of sexuality: the image of the body has been not simply omitted but effaced, censored. It is forbidden to take photos.

The ambiguity about whether, in the scene's metaphor of ethnology, the client is the student or the studied has a counterpart in the dichotomy that his lines suggest between camera and mirror. The cut to 9.3, showing him setting up his mirror, occurs at the beginning of his phrase about the police not allowing photos. In combination, the text and image remind us that someone here *is* taking photos, namely Godard. His instrument of observation is the camera, just as the young man's is the mirror. We infer that 9.6 is not a picture taken in a mirror because we do not see the camera. By virtue of the dichotomy camera/mirror, we understand not only that 9.6 is a camera image but that it aspires to say something about what such an image is. What it says is, precisely, that a shot is not a mirror. A shot implies, but does not show, the perceiving self. If that self is to be shown, it must be by proxy. The shot is not directed back to the perceiving self but outward, to us, to *tout le monde*.

Several details of the dialogue bear on this point. When the young man asks why Juliette is putting red on her lips, she snaps: "Ça te regard pas!" Insofar as we understand her annoyance, we sense that it is provoked as much by his intrusion on her thoughts about leaving Robert as by the content of his question. But to whom has she in fact been speaking in the moments preceding? Clearly, at the beginning of 9.4 she is answering him: her admission that she is not ashamed of her passive side in sexual relations seems to explain why she doesn't mind his mirror. But after she crosses to the Japanese poster, it is no longer clear whether she is answering the director's unheard questions (several of her lines begin with "oui") or continuing to answer the young man's. While she does not look directly at the camera (as she does, say, at the head of 9.7), she either looks toward it or seems to be glancing down a bit, as she

it's sad. Yes, I'd say the same thing about shame.

(She puts a cigarette in her mouth.)

That can stop people from arguing,

(The young man's hand enters right, holding a match to Juliette's cigarette. Juliette looks at the camera.)

since it rules everyone's actions

(She looks away.)

according to approval and blame, other people's blame. Yes, it's also sad, then . . . and then, it's bad.

(She looks at the camera, then away.)

Yes, like contempt for oneself

(She looks at the camera, then away.)

and all feelings of that kind.

YOUNG MAN
Do you want it like this?

(She looks offscreen right, glances down, then up.)

JULIETTE
No, out of the question!

Oui, parce que c'est de la tristesse. Ouais, je dirais la même chose de la honte.

Ça peut éviter aux gens de se disputer,

puisqu'elle règle les actions de chacun

d'après l'approbation et le blâme, le blâme des autres. Oui, c'est aussi de la tristesse, alors . . . et alors, c'est mauvais.

Oui, comme le mépris de soi-même

et tous les sentiments de ce genre.

Est-ce que vous voulez comme ça?

Non, pas question!

60.0″
34′59.8″

would be if she were talking to the young man seated on the bed. As for the literal content of her reply to the question about the lipstick, its verb, *regarder,* touches on the scene's thematic concern with looking, echoing her earlier reprimand "Ne me regarde pas me déshabiller" and anticipating her invitation "Comme ça, tu me peux regarder." But if the act of putting on lipstick does not look toward the young man (so to speak), then toward whom does it look? One plausible answer is toward us, since we understand it in some of the ways I have already outlined. An effect of Juliette's lines, therefore, is to call our attention to what is denied to *our* view. We do not see Juliette undressing. We do not see her completely naked. We do not see sex Italian style. Finally, we do not see what the young man is proposing when he asks offscreen, "Do you want it like this?" As if to confirm the centrality of these omissions, the scene ends abruptly on Juliette's reply, "No, out of the question!"

Juliette's meditation preceding this moment, ostensibly about herself, serves to acknowledge and comment on the censorship whose consequences we are experiencing. "Shame," she says, "rules everyone's actions according to approval and blame, other people's blame." Who are these "other people"? As we know, state censorship exists in France, and the film makes an issue of this at the outset. But the censor has evidently allowed the nudity of 4.2. And the single example cited in the present sequence is questionable: *have* the police forbidden taking photos in the Metro? *Masculine Feminine* belies this. Or is Godard himself the censor? In "One or Two Things" (Mussman, p. 281) he writes:

There are other taboos in France, and one of them—no matter what they think abroad—is sex. It is extremely difficult, if not impossible, to make a frank film about sexual problems. Let's be honest: in order to make a frank film, one must oneself be affranchised, and this, I find in my own case, takes some effort. I still retain ingrained traces of my Protestant upbringing, and I have struggled to get rid of them.

But Godard's "Protestant upbringing" will not explain the obvious playfulness with which he frustrates our voyeurism, especially at the end of the scene: what could it be that Juliette, having proposed sex Italian style, would then refuse? Nor does it recognize that his reticence concerns the visual as much as the sexual. This sets him apart from the young man, whose ethnology of mirrors and cameras is pointedly comic.

Godard and Juliette's client differ in a still more consequential way. Godard's camera in 9.1 uses the pair of opposing mirrors in the room not simply to multiply the images of Juliette but, as it were, to propose that the image of her must be multifaceted.[3] The young man intervenes in this effort by removing one of the mirrors from the wall and putting it to a use of his own. In one sense this mirror belongs to the series of posters, which are (with one exception) hung at its height and thereby placed so as to fit into the slice of vertical space that the Techniscope frame renders. Its membership in this series is evidenced by its size and placement, and by the light rectangular trace it leaves on the wall after it is removed. When the young man repositions it, he produces an image of Juliette that belongs to the series in a second sense as well, namely because it displays her passive role in sexual relations. Godard's refusal to show this image, the image which belongs in the displaced mirror, is explicable not only as an expression of his Protestant upbringing but as a moral refusal to consent to, and reproduce, a view of Juliette's submissiveness. In this respect he differs not only from the young man but also from Juliette, who consents to the mirror, to a passive role in sexual relations, and to being seen.

Sequence 10

10.1 [Loud construction noise.]
(Pan arcing left, then hold.)

8.2″
35′08.0″

10.2 [Actual sound. This track, which consists of the woman's monologue and its attendant ambience, continues alone and uninterrupted until 10.12/10.13.]

WOMAN
She offered me   Elle m'a proposé

2.4″
35′10.4″

The cut 9.7/10.1 reprises 1.6/1.7: Juliette looking offscreen (left in the earlier case, right here), accompanied by quiet synchronized sound, followed by a low-angle shot of a crane and loud construction noise. Contrary to what Godard says in the earlier case about Juliette's turn of the head, here the gesture has obvious importance, since she is looking at something pointedly denied to our view. We know from 9.5 that the young man is sitting on the bed to her left and, when in 9.7 she glances briefly downward before replying to his question, we infer what it is she is looking at. Shot 10.1 replaces our view of this, and the cut therefore, though softened by the conceit about cranes and prostitutes, reads as yet another act of censorship.

The play on the word *grue* also comments on 10.2, a "master shot" (continued

10.3   (Pan right, then hold.)

sixty dollars a day to work in the Madeleine district.

trente mille francs par jour pour travailler dans le quartier de la Madeleine.

$$\frac{3.6''}{35'14.0''}$$

10.4

I don't know   Je sais

$$\frac{1.8''}{35'15.8'}$$

10.5   if you understand.   pas si vous vous rendez compte.

Uh, I   Euh, je

$$\frac{2.6''}{35'18.4''}$$

in 10.4, 10.6, and so forth) in which a woman tells us that although she is a trained secretary who speaks English and Italian, she cannot find a job because she is too old. Someone has offered her $60 a day to work in the Madeleine district, presumably as a prostitute. We take this, I think, to be documentary material: the woman does not look like an actress and her testimony has the ring of truth (in fact, it is drawn from quotations in *Le nouvel observateur*).

Shot 10.1, besides representing an act of censorship, is the first in a series of brief views of construction sites, cranes, new buildings, *grands ensembles,* and outdoor advertising signs that function as cutaways. The woman's speech continues over them (they can be described as cutaways chiefly for that reason), an unusual arrangement for this film. Also unusual is the rapidity of the montage: twelve shots in thirty-three seconds, three of them less than forty-eight frames long. To the woman's left in the master shot we see part of an old engraving with a red mat, which appears in the frame as a vertical stripe the color of the "Prisunic" letters in 10.3. Several of the cutaways are

10.6 am a secretary. I wor . . . I speak   suis secrétaire. Je trav . . . Je parle

2.0″
35′20.4″

10.7 English and Italian,   l'anglais et l'italien,

and   et

2.5″
35′22.9″

10.8 I couldn't find   je n'arrivais pas à trouver du

work   tra-

1.4″
35′24.3″

so framed as to have a strong vertical coinciding with this one, in one case (10.7) in a symmetrical position frame-right. This interlocking of forms between the master shot

10.9   because I'm too old.   vail parce que je suis trop vieille.

$$\frac{1.5''}{35'25.8''}$$

10.10

$$\frac{2.4''}{35'28.2''}$$

10.11

Again yesterday, at the Publicis agency,   **Encore hier, à Publicis, euh, ils**
uh, they $$\frac{3.9''}{35'32.1''}$$

10.12   told me that they didn't have anything for   m'ont dit qu'il n'y avait rien pour moi.
me.

and the cutaways, along with the intercutting itself, asserts—though, I think, unnecessarily and rather mechanically—a causal relation between the woman's experience and

1.2″
35′33.3″

10.13   [Very loud construction noise.]

20.0″
35′53.3″

10.14   [Silence.]

COMMENTARY 15
What is art? "That by which forms be-

Qu'est-ce que l'art? "Ce par quoi les formes de-

2.4″
35′55.7″

10.15   come style," someone said.

viennent style," a dit quelqu'un.

the new Paris.

Following this, the sequence returns to the issue of censorship. Shot 10.14, an apparent nonsequitur, shows the word "art" in mirror image in the same coloring and graphics as "beauty" in 9.6. Art too has been prostituted, censored. By whom? Commentary 15, which accompanies the shot, asks "What is art?" and answers: " 'That by which forms become style,' someone said." Godard has quoted this maxim before, in a review of *The Wrong Man* (*Godard on Godard,* p. 54); he knows very well that the "someone" who said it is André Malraux. Only a few months before shooting this film, in April 1966, he published his open letter to Malraux, vilifying him for banning

Now, style is man.   Or, le style, c'est l'homme.

$$\frac{3.5''}{35'59.2''}$$

10.16

Therefore, art is that by which forms be-   Donc, l'art est ce par quoi les formes de-
come   viennent

$$\frac{2.8''}{36'02.0''}$$

La religieuse. The conclusion here, that "art is that by which forms become human," comments ironically on the preceding montage, where the environment seems anything *but* human and the cutting labors to show the human consequences of the built "forms." It also comments on the two closeups of postcards, which it accompanies, inviting the question whether these are art or not. In one sense they seem less "human" than machine-made, though in another sense they do pass as art, since the forms have undeniably been appropriated by human beings. The image and text together wonder: how to humanize *these* forms? how to make art out of *this?* Thus they introduce a question taken up two scenes later in Commentary 23.

Sequence 11

11.1 | [Actual sound comes in at the cut, then fades up slightly.]

human.   **humaines.**

(Hands rinse hair.)

JULIETTE
I am looking at the wall, the objects.   Je regarde le mur, les objets.

Now. Never. There. For the moment . . . I   Maintenant. Jamais. Là. Provisoirement . . .
am looking outside.   je regarde dehors.

16.6″
36′18.5″

11.2

(Pause.)

MARIANNE
Say, you're really tan! Where have you   Dis donc, t'es vachement brune! Où tu as
been?   été?

This and Sequence 12 form a pair: here hair is washed and dried and there cars, thus framing the question behind Commentary 21: why do we take more attentive care of objects than of people?

The cut 10.16/11.1 slightly precedes the end of Commentary 15; to be precise, it falls near the beginning of the word "humaines" in the phrase "l'art est ce par quoi les formes deviennent humaines." In consequence, the image appears literally to act out the text, the still forms of 10.16 becoming the animate human hands and hair of 11.1. Thus Godard claims for his own art the aspiration that is expressed in Malraux's phrase and, as the tone of his attribution ("someone said") insinuates, to which he does not think Malraux is any longer entitled. At the same time, his scene does not represent this aspiration as fully achieved, for in 11.3, as the camera tracks backward before Juliette's friend Marianne (who is on her way to the telephone to arrange a rendezvous with a client), it reveals a column covered with postcards which, like those in 10.15 and 10.16, are at oblique angles. The intrusion of these postcards into the frame suggests the resistance this environment will offer to the artist's humanizing project.

Juliette's dialogue in 11.1 and 11.2 with her manicurist and friend, Marianne, is interlaced with more numerous bits of interior monologue than we have heard to this point. However, because the camera is behind Juliette, we cannot see which phrases she "speaks" and which she "thinks." In recording and delivery the two do not perceptibly differ. We identify those that seem exterior by their banality and by the fact that Marianne replies to them. We identify the interior ones by their content, which resembles that of Juliette's previous interior remarks (for example, her opening phrase, "I am looking at the wall" parallels that which begins Sequence 2: "What am I looking at?

JULIETTE
In Russia.

MARIANNE
Where?

JULIETTE
Silence. In Leningrad.

MARIANNE
Are the Russians nice?
(As Marianne does Juliette's nails, the
woman to the left begins to dye her hair.)

JULIETTE
Happiness. Oh, they're like everybody.

MARIANNE
I'm just asking.

JULIETTE
Well, they're likable. Some noises.

MARIANNE
Say, have you seen the Dupérets again?

JULIETTE
Yes, I saw them on my way past the Gare
Saint-Lazare. It's true, on the other hand,
that one never knows oneself.

MARIANNE
It's broken.

JULIETTE
Robert, Christophe. Blue spiral notebooks.

MARIANNE
And how are you doing?

JULIETTE
All right. Not to have to make love.

MARIANNE
You know, I like this better than the fac-
tory.

JULIETTE
Me too. I wouldn't like to work in a fac-
tory.

MARIANNE
Your children? How are your children?

JULIETTE
All right. What I say with words is never
what I say. All right, but they won't be-
have, you know. I wait. I look.

En Russie.

Où?

Silence. A Léningrad.

Ils sont gentils, les Russes?

Bonheur. Oh, ils sont comme tout le
monde.

Je te demande ça comme ça.

Mais ils sont sympathiques. Quelques
bruits.

Dis donc, t'as revu les Dupéret?

Oui, je les ai vus en passant gare Saint-Lazare. C'est vrai, d'autre part, qu'on ne se
connaît jamais.

Il est cassé.

Robert, Christophe. Des cahiers bleus à
spirales.

Et toi, ça va?

Ça va. Ne pas être obligée de faire l'amour.

Tu sais, j'aime mieux ça que l'usine.

Moi non plus, j'aimerais pas travailler à
l'usine.

Tes enfants? Tes enfants, ça va?

Ça va. Ce que je dis avec des mots n'est
jamais ce que je dis. Ça va, mais ils ne sont
pas sages, tu sais. J'attends. Je regarde.

The floor.") The contrast between the spoken and the thought explains Juliette's inexpressive countenance elsewhere not as the manifestation of an acting style but as the sign of a character whose interior life has no outlet. In 11.2 she offers what can be taken both as an acknowledgment of this and as a comment on the technique itself: "What I say with words is never what I say." In content some of what she says belongs clearly to her character ("Robert, Christophe"; "not to have to make love"), while some echoes Godard's own preoccupation with surfaces, objects, and noises: "I wait. I look" paraphrases the conclusion of Commentary 12, "I must look around me"; and "blue spiral notebooks" are what he uses for his script notes.[1]

The exterior dialogue also tests the boundaries of the fiction. When Marianne asks where Juliette has gotten her tan, Juliette gives the surprising reply "In Leningrad." Although we are told that Juliette is "of Russian extraction," it seems implausible that she, a Parisian working-class woman, would speak casually of so recent and expensive a trip.[2] Rather, her answer makes us think of Marina Vlady. A private joke that follows supports us in this. Marianne, played by an actress named Anny Duperey, asks if Juliette has seen the Dupérets again and Juliette replies that she saw them passing

MARIANNE
I'll put this on you.
(She holds up a bottle of nail polish.)

Je te mettrai celui-là.

JULIETTE
Yes, all right. My hair.
(A telephone rings.)
The telephone.

Ouais, d'accord. Mes cheveux.

Le téléphone.

1'30.4"
37'49.0"

11.3   [Actual sound, including the noise of hair dryers.]
(The telephone rings.)

MANAGERESS
Hello. Yes. Marianne, it's for you.

Allô. Oui. Marianne, c'est pour toi.

MARIANNE
Yes, I'm coming.

Oui, j'arrive.

(Marianne enters, coming toward the camera.)

(Pan left with her to the telephone.)
Hello. Yes.

Allô. Oui.

(In English:)
Oh, yes. Yes. Yes. Uh huh. Yes, yes. OK. OK.
(She hangs up. Pan left with her as she asks:)

Oh, yes. Yes. Yes. Uh huh. Yes, yes. OK. OK.

the Gare Saint-Lazare. These details support our inference in 11.5 that Paulette Cadjaris

Is Yvonne really not here?   Yvonne est vraiment pas là?
(Hold. Marianne goes away from the cam-
era toward the room from which she
emerged earlier in the shot.)

PAULETTE
No, no. She's sick.   Non, non. Elle est malade.
(Marianne turns around. The camera tracks
backward as she approaches.)

MARIANNE
Monsieur Michel!   Monsieur Michel!

(The telephone rings.)
Monsieur Michel!   Monsieur Michel!

MICHEL
Yes.   Oui.

MARIANNE
Do you mind if I leave half an hour earlier   Ça vous ennuie que je parte encore une
again this evening?   demi-heure plus tôt ce soir?

MICHEL
Well, just arrange it with Paulette.   Oh, ben, tu n'as qu'à t'arranger avec Pau-
                                                    lette.

MARIANNE
(Turns and crosses left out of the frame as
she says:)
Paulette!   Paulette!

PAULETTE
Yes.   Oui.

is the actual name of the woman we see speaking and that what she says is true in reality.

MARIANNE
Can't you   Tu peux pas me

                                                                        $\dfrac{1'18.3''}{39'07.2''}$

11.4   *fill in for me this evening?*   *remplacer ce soir?*

CUSTOMER
I'm very careful crossing streets. I think   Je suis très prudente pour traverser les rues.
about an accident before it can happen. And   Je pense à l'accident avant qu'il puisse ar-
that my life could stop there. Unemploy-   river. Et que ma vie s'arrête là. Le chômage.
ment. Sickness. Old age. Death, never. I   La maladie. La vieillesse. La mort, jamais. Je
have no plan for the future because the   n'ai pas de projet d'avenir, car l'horizon est
horizon is closed.   fermé.

PAULETTE
My name is Paulette Cadjaris.   *Je m'appelle Paulette Cadjaris.*

                                                                        $\dfrac{59.5''}{40'06.8''}$

11.5

(In the background Juliette and Marianne
cross toward us and rightward, exiting
frame right.)
I failed as a secretary-typist. No, I don't be-   J'ai echoué comme secrétaire-dactylo. Non,
lieve in the future. I go for walks. I don't   je ne crois pas à l'avenir. Je me promène. Je
like to be shut in. When I can, I do some   n'aime pas être enfermée. Quand je peux, je
reading. Yes, and I like very much to study   fais de la lecture. Oui, et j'aime beaucoup
people's character. I like walking,   étudier le caractère des gens. J'aime
                                                   marcher,

I must admit that I do not find Paulette Cadjaris's monologue very attractive. Like Juliette and the customer of 11.4 (whose thoughts resemble Juliette's), she is fed unheard lines and questions. But unlike the salesclerks in Sequence 6, she responds with a naive attempt at performance. The inadequacy of this performance, painfully evident in her delivery and gesture, especially at such points in the text as "les biographies" or "un arbre," parallels, and hence credits, her failure as a secretary-typist (it is precisely this connection that is missing in the case of the inept delivery of Madame Céline's text in *Une femme mariée*). To the extent that her story is factual, or rather to the extent that we believe it to be so, the shot is cruel to her (the situation is scarcely helped by the "pied-noir" accent that, like her name, identifies her as a French-Algerian). I do not mean to argue that Godard deliberately holds her up to ridicule (though the "dialogue with a consumer product" in *Masculine Feminine* shows him capable of this). My guess is that he is disconcerted by her warmth and trust and simply fails to manage the situation. Clearly, what he wants to do is ask: how to explain this life, these aspirations, this thinness? In isolation, his shot answers the question by repre-

(She raises her left hand in two brief upward gestures.)
climbing, bicycling, just for fun. Movies: two or three times a month. But not in the summer. The theater? I . . . I've never gone. But I'd like to very much. I prefer reading, biographies.

(She gestures upward with the index finger of her left hand.)
Studying people's life, their character, their work. Travel stories, ancient history, a tree. Later, when I'm married to François . . . What else have I done? A lot of ordinary things.

grimper, faire de la bicyclette, en amateur. Cinéma: deux ou trois fois par mois. Mais pas l'été. Au théâtre? Je . . . je ne suis jamais allée. Mais j'aimerais beaucoup. Je préfère la lecture, les biographies.

Étudier la vie des gens, leur caractère, leur travail. Les récits de voyage, l'histoire antique, un arbre. Plus tard, quand je serai mariée avec François . . . Qu'est-ce que j'ai fait d'autre? Un tas de choses banales.

1′41.3″
41′48.0″

senting her as a personal failure. In conjunction with 12.1, a long shot of a construction site, it repeats what Juliette twice proposes: that a landscape is like a face—in other words, that Paulette's sad smile at the end of 11.5 is a product of the same forces that we see literally "at work" in the shot that follows.

Sequence 12

12.1

[Silence.]

(Pause.)

<small>COMMENTARY 16</small>

More and more there is an intermingling of image and language.

Il y a de plus en plus interférence de l'image et du langage.

6.7″
41′54.7″

12.2

And at the extreme, one can say that to live in society today is almost to live in a

Et on peut dire à la limite que, vivre en société aujourd'hui, c'est quasiment

The second phrase of the Beethoven quartet, first heard following Juliette's line "Language is the house man lives in," begins again with Paulette's smile and continues over the cut 11.5/12.1. With this motif Godard indicates that language will be the central concern of the enormously complex scene that follows.

Toward the end of shot 12.1, Godard makes this concern explicit: "More and more there is an intermingling of image and language." Shot 12.2, which immediately follows, illustrates the sentence with a view of a service station attendant next to a sign reading "Achat Automobiles." The accompanying commentary, which explains that "to live in society today is almost to live in a giant comic strip," instructs us more specifically in how to read the shot: we are to understand that the attendant is speaking or thinking the words that appear next to him. We do not, of course, understand that this is true literally, as it is in the magazine drawings of Sequence 8. Rather, it is a claim like that made by the montage of Sequence 10 (the intercutting of the secretary's speech with shots of apartment complexes and advertising signs) or the cocktail party dialogue in *Pierrot le fou,* which consists of advertising copy. But in this instance Godard disclaims responsibility for relating the two elements: the image simply displays them in the same space, without contesting the notion that "society" has made what we see and that the director has merely taken a picture of it. The accompanying commentary makes the parallel argument that language has entered the image uninvited.

At the same time, the phrase "intermingling of image and language" is a strikingly accurate description of an often remarked tendency in Godard's style, manifested variously as a preoccupation with signs, advertising, and quotation, a fondness for intertitles, and a willingness to allow characters to talk at length—in general, a readiness to contradict the received opinion that says "show, don't tell." It is in this sense Godard who has framed and flattened 12.2 so as to make what we see into a giant comic strip. Thus he does, or at least repeats, what "society" does and in this way admits his partici-

giant comic strip. Yet

vivre dans une énorme bande dessinée. Pourtant, le

9.6″
42′04.3″

12.3

(Pan slightly left, then right with the Austin.)

language in itself is not sufficient to determine the image with precision.

langage, en tant que tel, ne suffit pas à déterminer l'image avec précision.

(Hold as the Austin exits frame right.)

4.6″
42′08.9″

12.4

For example . . .

Par exemple . . .

1.4″
42′10.3″

pation, not to say complicity, in it.

The following sentence of the commentary is especially difficult: "Yet language in itself is not sufficient to determine the image with precision." Shot 12.3 dramatizes this text: how indeed can language "determine" an image such as this one, which pans left and right with Juliette's rapidly moving Austin as it turns and enters the garage? Whose language does Godard mean? The example that the commentary indicates is "Achat Automobiles." Such language may penetrate the shots, but why should we suppose it to be sufficient to "determine" them? Thus the sentence can be taken to express Godard's confidence in the image, specifically in its power to resist definition by advertising phrases.

In one respect at least, the image is radically *unlike* a comic-strip panel. As we see even in 12.2, it cannot be simplified or schematized beyond a certain point; the infinity of details that it renders makes it proof against definition by the language it includes. At the same time, because of the illustrative relation between the shot and the commentary, we also understand that the language Godard is speaking of is his own (he wonders a few moments later how he should "show or say" what happened). As many writers on semiotics have argued, the image outruns even the thousand words that one can say about it. The relation of image and language in a film is, therefore, necessarily one of "intermingling": indeed, this scene has as its climax Godard's definition of himself as writer and painter. Why then does he qualify "langage" with the words "en tant que tel"? Loosely, they mean "in itself" or "by itself." More literally, they mean "language insofar as it is that," implying "language insofar as it is language and not something else." But what? A plausible answer might be "language insofar as it is such as we see in 12.2"; in other words, Godard is asking whether such instances as "Achat Automobiles" qualify as language at all. Both the question and the ironic tone in which it is asked are consistent with his complaint in Commentary 20 that the omnipresent signs make him "doubt language," as well as Juliette's conclusion in 6.4 that "a new language will have to be constructed."

Shots 12.4 and 12.5, which occur at the beginning and end of the phrase "Par exemple . . . ," are designated by it as examples of the sentence under discussion. The first of these shots shows a billboard with a cartoon-style drawing of a black car speeding screen-right. Against an orange background the word "protége" occurs three times—in yellow, light yellow, and white. The first two versions are partially cut off (either by the edge of the poster or the edge of the frame) and the third is complete. The head of a station attendant, probably Robert, crosses parallel to the poster in the direction opposite to the indicated movement of the car. His proximity to the wall establishes the extremely shallow depth of the shot, and the 1.4 seconds he takes to traverse the frame determine its length. The cut to 12.5 is graphically very intricate. Within the flat rectangle of the screen, the black cartoon auto is replaced by

12.5 [Very loud ambient sound, noise of machines.]

(Short pan right with the Austin, then hold as it parks. Juliette and Marianne get out and cross toward each other.)

12.4″
42′22.7″

12.6 [Silence.]

(The man who is in midframe at the cut crosses out frame right.)

COMMENTARY 17

For example, how to give an account of events? How to show or say that this afternoon, at about 4:10 P.M., Juliette and Marianne came into a garage at the Porte des Ternes where Juliette's husband works.

(On the last four words of the French a man crosses left, reaching midframe at the cut.)

Par exemple, comment rendre compte des événements? Comment montrer ou dire que cet après-midi-là, vers 16 h 10, Juliette et Marianne sont venues dans un garage de la porte des Ternes où travaille le mari de Juliette.

14.0″
42′36.7″

12.7 [Very loud ambient sound, noise of machines.]

Juliette's red Austin and the orange background by white. The result is a simultaneous lightening and animation of the image, an effect underlined by a straight cut from silence to loud ambient noise. Together, the image and sound suggest that 12.5 is the comic strip of 12.4 come to life.

In what sense does this exemplify the idea in the commentary? What precisely is it about the image that defies fixation by words? Shot 12.3 specifies that it is change and motion, and the cut 12.4/12.5 expands on this by animating the drawing and calling into question the definitive role of the word "protége." To change and motion the cut adds graphic design, the superimposition of forms within the rectangle, and color—that is, the meanings that accrue from the organization of the image as a surface.

With Commentary 17 the discussion shifts from image and language to image and narrative. Godard repeats the phrase "par exemple" (as "puisque" is repeated following 8.21), then gives his example in words rather than, as in 12.4 and 12.5, in images (a procedure that parallels the equivalence he proposes between "show" and "say"): "How to give an account of events? How to show or say that this afternoon, at about 4:10 P.M., Juliette and Marianne came into a garage at the Porte des Ternes where Juliette's husband works?" Here, as in Commentary 10 (where the time is also given to the minute), Godard invokes the "referential illusion," speaking of the fiction as if it were an actual event of which he must give an account ("rendre compte").[1]

Shot 12.6, which accompanies this commentary, offers a comic counterpart to its discussion of narrative. How to show or say what has happened between shots 12.4 and 12.6? In the latter the smashed front end of a real car replaces the drawn car speeding along; a mechanic, framed from the shoulders down, crossing rightward, replaces Robert, framed from the shoulders up, crossing leftward; a sign promising that "VIT assures pleasant, economical trips, without incidents" replaces the warning "protect." Together the shots develop the theme of the anonymous customer's interior monologue in 11.4: "I'm very careful crossing streets. I think about an accident before it can happen."[2] In 12.4, Robert rapidly crosses the frame in the opposite direction to the car speeding along behind him. The sign warns "protect." Toward the tail of 12.5, Marianne and Juliette get out of the red Austin and cross toward one another in front of it. In the depicted space they do not collide. But the red, yellow, and blue primary scheme to which their clothing contributes, like the cut 12.4/12.5, calls our attention to what is happening in the image plane. Here a "collision" does take place and issues in the smashed car of 12.6. In the comic-strip story, the warning "protect" has gone unheeded and VIT has not kept its promise.

(Juliette gets into the Austin. Pan right
with it as she drives it onto a turntable. An
attendant pushes it counterclockwise.

She gets out. Attendants guide the car
forward into the automatic car wash.)

$$\frac{34.4''}{43'11.1''}$$

12.8   [Silence.]

<small>COMMENTARY 18</small>
Sense and nonsense.
[Beep of car horn.]

Sens et non-sens.

$$\frac{1.6''}{43'12.7''}$$

12.9   [Silence.]

The relation of the phrase "sens et non-sens," which begins Commentary 18, to the accompanying shot, 12.8, involves a play on words: *sens,* which means both "sense" and "direction," is indicated by the yellow arrow painted on the ground and *non-sens* by the pair of feet walking in the direction opposite. The joke begins with the preceding shot, 12.7, in which Juliette drives her car onto a turntable, an attendant pushes it counterclockwise—that is, in the screen direction of the yellow arrow—then forward—in the screen direction of the feet. It also applies to the schemes of directional movement in the three shots preceding (12.4–12.6) and the "sense" those shots make thereby—that is, as a comic-strip story. The joke is that the two meanings, "sense" and "direction," are out of harmony: the "sense" of the image, exemplified in 12.4–12.6 by patterns of screen direction, is not all that we understand by "making sense," which includes, for example, reporting "exactly what happened" in the depicted space. Shot 12.7, the turning of the car, construed as an action in that space, thus plays a necessary part in narrating what happened when Juliette and Marianne arrived at Robert's garage at 4:10 P.M. But in this respect too, the sense of the sequence is threatened by nonsense, for, as we understand later, this "event" is out of its chronological place; it is properly the beginning of the car wash, which we do not see until 12.20, and as such does not belong before the fueling shown in 12.9.

Sens et non-sens is, furthermore, the title of a book by Maurice Merleau-Ponty. The allusion serves Godard as a means of invoking Merleau-Ponty's notion that *sens* is what is achieved via *non-sens* and that the struggle for sense—or, in Godard's terms, for "an account of events"—is an existential task proceeding from, and reflecting, an existential condition.[3] This notion assumes comic form in the feet that walk obliviously in the direction of nonsense. It also underlies the more serious directorial questions that follow: which words and images to use? where to put the camera? how loud to speak? But for the allusion, these would appear to concern only matters of technique. In context, however, the doubt that they reflect is clearly existential and this makes them, in Merleau-Ponty's terms, "nonsensical."

With 12.9 Godard's meditation on the relation of narrative to the film image

(An attendant opens the car door; Juliette says something to him that we do not hear. He closes the door.)

Yes, how to say exactly what happened?

(The attendant takes the nozzle from the pump and begins to fill the tank.)

To be sure, there is Juliette; there is her husband; there is the garage.

(Robert enters right and crouches by the car door. They talk, but we do not hear what they say.)

Oui, comment dire exactement ce qui s'est passé?

Bien sûr, il y a Juliette, il y a son mari, il y a le garage.

But is it really these words and these images that must be used?

(Robert glances at his watch. They keep talking.)

Are they the only ones? Are there not others? Am I speaking too loud? Am I watching from too far or too close?

(They kiss quickly.)

[At the instant that Robert's lips meet Juliette's, there is a short beep of a car horn and cut.]

Mais est-ce bien ces mots et ces images qu'il faut employer?

Sont-ils les seuls? Est-ce qu'il n'y en a pas d'autres? Est-ce que je parle trop fort? Est-ce que je regarde de trop loin ou de trop près?

$$\frac{18.0''}{43'30.7''}$$

12.10

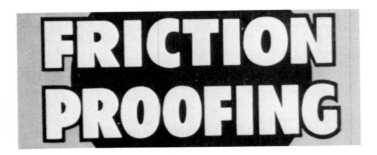

takes a new turn. On the one hand, the referential illusion is strengthened. We see Juliette at the wheel of the Austin while Godard wonders: "Oui, comment dire exactement ce qui s'est passé?" The question, while paraphrasing those of Commentary 17 (as the introductory "oui" acknowledges), slightly changes their emphasis: although "dire" is certainly a metonymy (hence a term of equivalence for "rendre compte" or "montrer ou dire"), it nonetheless suggests that what Godard is now trying to do is describe what he sees. An attendant opens and closes the car door on Juliette's side, apparently to ask her what she wants, then crosses behind the vehicle to fill the tank. As he does so, Godard says, "To be sure, there is Juliette; there is her husband; there is the garage," as if continuing to enumerate what he sees in the image. Then, unexpectedly, he asks: "But is it really these words and these images that must be used?" implying that he is now not simply describing the images but choosing them. At the same time, because his commentary occurs over the image—that is, after the filming—we understand his question to mean "Have I chosen the right image?" rather than "Which image should I choose?"

Shot 12.9 offers no narrative criterion by which to answer any of the questions Godard asks of it. Insofar as it includes all of the narrative elements that he enumerates—Juliette, her husband, the garage—it indeed reports "exactly what happened." Is he too close or too far? He could show the conversation between Juliette and Robert with equal clarity in a tighter framing, though this would have the effect of isolating it further from the background. On the other hand, the relation of the background action—the attendant filling the tank, the waiting cars—to the protagonists suggests other such relations possibly visible in a wider view. But since none of these functions in the narrative, the narrative gives no means of settling the question.

Despite the uncertainty expressed in the commentary, the shot is in no sense "undetermined." By asking whether he is too far or too close, Godard indirectly calls attention to the particular distance he has chosen. This choice is in some measure justified by the action, since it allows us to see that the transaction between Juliette and the attendant continues while she speaks with Robert. Still, this logic serves only to raise a further question, since the attendant, like the woman of 12.13, is an anonymous figure in the drama, an "extra," and the action that involves him has no narrative consequences. At the same time, the filling of the gas tank has at least one consequence of another sort, namely shot 12.32, the whirling figures on the pump. Whatever the logic that unites these details, it is not that of saying what happened, at least in the ordinary sense of the words. Rather, like the questions of the commentary, it sets the image and

[Three short beeps of a car horn, then a longer beep on the cut.]

3.8″
43′34.4″

12.11

[Short beep of car horn.]
   (The Austin comes down the street, turns screen left, and passes near the camera.)
   COMMENTARY 19
For example,   Par exemple,
[Short beep, then silence.]
   (Short pan left with the car begins.)
there are some   il y a des.

4.6″
43′39.0″

12.12

leaves and,   feuillages et
   (A zoom-out starts.)
although Juliette has nothing about her of a Faulkner heroine, . . . after all   bien que Juliette n'ait rien d'une héroine de Faulkner . . . et après tout
   (The zoom-out finishes. Hold:)

narrative into opposition and associates the director with the former.

Shots 12.12 through 12.14 constitute an answer to the question whether there are not other images "that must be used" in place of 12.9. The first of these begins tightly framed on green leaves, then zooms out to include a Mobil sign in the lower left corner; meanwhile, Godard speculates: "For example, there are some leaves and, although Juliette has nothing about her of a Faulkner heroine, after all they can well be dramatically equivalent to the leaves of wild palms."[4] Although the allusion itself is far-fetched, it serves to exemplify a system of meaning (of which the earlier allusion to Baudelaire is also an example) accessible in literature: this is what we understand by "valoir dramatiquement."

The possible relation between *The Wild Palms* and *2 ou 3 choses* has a precedent in the actual relation between the concluding tableaux of *Vivre sa vie* and Poe's "Oval Portrait." In the Poe story a man paints a woman's portrait; as he does so, the color drains from her face until, at the moment the picture is finished, she dies. As I recounted earlier, in Tableau 11 of the film a young man, whose voice is dubbed by Godard, reads a substantial excerpt from this story to Nana, who is played by Godard's wife, Anna Karina, then tells her: "It's our story; it's the story of a man who does his wife's portrait." Indeed, from this point onward, the story takes control of the film, furnishing all the explanation that there is of Nana's arbitrary death in Tableau 12.

What Godard is contemplating in Commentary 19 is, evidently, the elevation of a literary text to just such a controlling position. Although he does not explain why he rejects this possibility, the example of *Vivre sa vie* suggests that he does so as much because of the problems it raises regarding his own presence in the film as for its characterization of Juliette. (Nana, after all, is nothing like a Poe heroine.) For its part, *Vivre sa vie* has no terms but those of the narrative with which to register his presence, and this lack issues in a troubling contradiction, for, as the spectator knows, Nana is not the young man's "wife" or model (see Susan Sontag's essay "On Godard's *Vivre sa vie*" in Mussman, pp. 87–100). In *2 ou 3 choses,* Godard's explicit role is vastly more important; there is no question of subsuming it within the narrative, let alone within any single literary allusion. However, here too it is designated by the metaphor of the painter, supported in this case not by a literary text but by the evident care lavished on the composition and color of the image. *Vivre sa vie,* being in black and white,[5] necessarily gives this metaphor a more figurative status (despite the intertitles labeling the episodes "tableaux"), thereby undermining its power to "give an account" of why Nana dies.

they can well be dramatically equivalent to the leaves of wild palms. There is also another young

ils peuvent bien valoir dramatiquement ceux de palmiers sauvages. Il y a aussi une autre jeune

12.0″
43′51.0″

12.13

woman, of whom we shall know nothing. We shall not even know how to say so in all honesty.

femme, dont nous ne saurons rien. Nous ne saurons même pas comment le dire en toute honnêteté.

There is also a cloudy

Il y a aussi un ciel

7.3″
43′58.3″

12.14

sky—providing I turn my head

nuageux—à condition que je tourne la tête

instead of looking fixedly before me without moving—and inscriptions on the walls.

au lieu de regarder fixement devant moi sans bouger—et des inscriptions sur les murs.

7.7″
44′06.0″

The issue broached in 12.9 by means of a framing that includes the attendant fueling the car is addressed explicitly in 12.13, a shot that the commentary describes precisely: "There is also another young woman, of whom we shall know nothing. We shall not even know how to say so in all honesty." Although this young woman is placed in the frame in a way ordinarily reserved for the main characters (not, as in the case of the attendant, in the background), she in fact does not appear elsewhere in the film. The text specifies that it is not only the director, the first person singular, who will know nothing about her, but "we," the spectators. His inability to say this "in all honesty" jokes about the fact, unreported in the film, that the young woman is the second assistant director, Isabelle Pons. But why can he not report this? Of 1.5, a shot of that "other young woman," about whom we know two or three things, he is able to say: "This is Marina Vlady," and in 11.2 he contrives to mention a name like that of the actress playing Marianne. Indeed, we do know the sort of thing about the young woman of 12.13 that shot 1.6 reports about Juliette: the color of her hair and sweater, the expression on her face, the movements of her head. The sort of thing we do not know is what the narrative might tell us ("This is Juliette Janson; she lives here"). If we were in a position to get Godard's joke, we would understand that he knows something about her that neither the image nor the narrative can register. His text and image stress that we are not in this position. Not only are we ignorant of the specifics that the narrative might report, but the narrative does not even give us terms for stating this ignorance: that is, for recognizing the sorts of knowledge it promotes and suppresses. Including himself therefore among the spectators, the "we" of the text, Godard suggests that narrative itself, quite apart from the particularities of its execution, has a "problematic," a structure which has us think only of certain things as in need of, or capable of, explanation.

The following shot is similar in organization, framing, and scale, and, together with the commentary over it, offers a parallel argument about the image. We see a hazy blue sky, whereas Godard tells us: "There is also a cloudy sky—providing I turn my head instead of looking fixedly before me without moving." To understand this sentence we must envision the speaker as present within the real space of the filming; he is, for the moment, director rather than spectator. Our impulse to identify with him, to suppose that we too will see a cloudy segment of the sky if we turn our heads, is defeated by, and hence calls our attention to, our situation as spectators. Godard does not accommodate this impulse, as he might have, by inserting a shot showing the cloudy sky (12.29 demonstrates that such an insert is a stylistic possibility). In fact, he does just the opposite. After the phrase, "I turn my head," the station attendant in the shot, having finished lighting his cigarette, turns his head to look toward the camera, then, after the phrase "without moving," turns screen-right. Because, as elsewhere, we understand the commentary as "over" the image, we do not take his movements as responses to the director's words. But we do understand that he does what the director proposes to do and thus sharpens our consciousness that we are excluded from doing it, that we are bound to look fixedly ahead and to have our view limited by the edges of the frame. Of course, Godard has made the point before (most memorably in 1.5 and 1.6, where the motive was also a turn of the head) that the situation of the spectator differs from that of the director and actors. But here that point reflects on the film image, insisting that there are sorts of knowledge that it promotes and suppresses and that these differ from those of the narrative: for just as the narrative will not report "this is Isabelle Pons," so the image will not admit the approaching bad weather.[6]

12.15 | [Beeping of auto horn #1.]

(Pan left with the Austin: the continuation
of 12.11?)

1.8″
44′07.8″

12.16 | [Beeping of auto horn #2.]

(Pan right with the Austin: another take of
12.3?)

1.2″
44′09.0″

12.17 | [Beeping of auto horn #3.]

(Pan left with the Austin: another take of
12.15?)

2.2″
44′11.2″

These three alternatives—Charlotte Rittenmeyer (the heroine of *The Wild Palms*), Isabelle Pons, the cloudy sky—thus replace the enumeration of narrative elements in 12.9: Juliette, her husband, the garage. As they do so, they register a growing confusion about "how to say exactly what happened," one that issues in the vertigo of 12.15–12.18 (the Austin entering the service station), where screen directions ("sens et non-sens") abruptly switch, the action repeats in slightly different versions (each of which has a slightly different sound), and we are put, chronologically, back at the be-

12.18 [Beeping of auto horn #1.]

(Pan right with the Austin. Very brief hold
at the tail of the shot:)

1.3″
44′12.5″

12.19 [On the cut there is both a fast fade-out of
beeping to silence and the first word of the
commentary.]

(A zoom-out, starting at the cut.)
COMMENTARY 20
Why all these signs   **Pourquoi tous ces signes**

ginning: "Yes, how to say exactly what happened?"

In response, shot 12.19 begins by framing the letter "A" on a sign, zooms out decisively to reveal it as part of CAR, further to show RCARW, then back in to CAR, elegantly summing up several of the components of saying what happened: the intermingling of image and language, the insufficiency of language to determine the image, the doubt about which images and words to use. Here we never see the whole phrase but infer that it includes CARWASH, a word that functions as an intertitle introducing 12.20–12.26, in which the Austin is washed. The A by itself is, like zero, often Godard's term for a starting point: it has this sense both in an ABC sign in *Une femme mariée* and in 16.8 of *2 ou 3 choses,* a shot of BAB accompanied by the injunction "rediscover the b, a, ba of existence." In the present instance it signifies that the noise and confusion of 12.15–12.18 have driven the director to begin afresh. His second framing,

(The zoom-out stops.)

among us which end up by making me doubt lan-

(The zoom-out resumes.)

guage and sub-

(The zoom-out stops.)

parmi nous qui finissent par me faire douter du lan-

gage et qui me sub-

merge me in meanings, drowning the real in-

(A zoom-in starts.)

stead of disengaging it from the imaginary?

(On the last syllable of the French the zoom-in stops and a head in silhouette crosses leftward and downward.)

mergent de significations, en noyant le réel au

lieu de le dégager de l'imaginaire?

10.8″
44′23.3″

CAR, carries the sense of the English word (joining with the first to yield A CAR) and also the French sense of "because." The latter, being a conjunction, represents precisely the sort of linguistic coherence that his text despairs of.[7] In revealing—indeed creating—it, the framing does not *contradict* the text; rather it indicates how absent such linguistic links are, how much they must be searched for. The zooms dramatize this search. In addition, they act out the question "Am I watching from too far or too close?" For in the lettering we discover "sense" at one distance, one framing, but not at the others, a point Godard stresses at the tail of the shot by reinstating the framing CAR.

The meaning of these zooms inheres partly in their precisely drawn relation to the commentary. Because the zoom-out to the framing RCARW coincides with, and hence appears to illustrate, the phrase about doubting language, the zoom back in to CAR similarly appears to illustrate the process of disengagement that *its* accompanying phrase describes. However, what the zoom-in disengages is a word, sense, from a non-sensical cluster of letters, whereas the text speaks of disengaging "the real" from "the imaginary." Although these seem the wrong terms for what we see in the image, they accurately describe the distinction the film maintains between documentary and fiction as well as the role language plays in creating that distinction ("this is Marina Vlady"/"this is Juliette Janson"). But isn't it the case that the image is open *only* to "the real"? Godard's argument, I think, is that in today's society the visible has been riddled with language such as "VIT assures pleasant economical trips, without incidents," which invites legitimate doubt. His starting point as a filmmaker, therefore, is no longer something one might call "the real" but something that is already a comic strip, a story told by advertisements, hence suffused with the imaginary.

What exactly are the *signes* Godard is speaking of? The word *signe*, regarded as a term in semiotics, means a signifier plus a signified, an element in a sign system or *langage* (broadly defined). What we see in 12.19 is properly a *panneau*, though insofar as it signifies, it is also a *signe*. One might argue that insofar as the film image itself signifies, it presents to us as *signes* all the objects that it includes. The letters "RCARW" are thus not only part of one *signe,* but as framed constitute another. It is the latter that the text associates with a plethora of significations rather than, as in the case of the former, none (the letters do not spell anything). The various framings, singly and as a group, have a graphic authority, a precision as images (to which the decisiveness of the zooming contributes) that challenges the priority conferred by language on the framing CAR. The struggle between text and image dramatizes the insufficiency of language to "determine" the image and explains what Godard might mean by "doubting language." At the same time, the zooms return us to the issue raised in 12.14 (the station attendant and the unseen cloudy sky) concerning the spatial limits that the image imposes on our view. They demonstrate that the limits of a particular framing can be altered, but that this in itself is no guarantee of sense, which, as defined by language, occurs at a given scale and not a larger or smaller one. And as in 2.12, the zooming vividly implies a whole that it does not show.

Together the text and image of 12.19 make the point that language is not sufficient either as a criterion or model of signification, for the image produces significations at various (perhaps all) scales and "nonsense" at none. This fact raises a doubt about the very significance of scale, which deepens the existential doubt expressed in the question "Am I watching from too far or too close?" By this route the film returns to the problem of the degree to which "sense," or "the real," inheres in the visible at

12.20 [Loud actual sound of the car wash.]

(The car recedes through a water spray,
then through brushes.)

20.2″
44′43.4″

12.21 [Car motor revving.]

(Two attendants soap the car. Slow track
left with it. The attendant in the rear
pushes a button on the wall; the car stops,
the tracking stops. Hold.)
[Rapid fade-out to silence as the commentary starts.]
COMMENTARY 21
In the case of the image everything is
permitted, the best and the worst. In
front of me everyday good sense has
come to restore the broken step of my
reason. Objects exist,

A l'image, tout est permis, le meilleur et
le pire. Devant moi, le bon sens quotidien est venu rétablir la démarche brisée
de ma raison. Les objets existent

16.6″
45′00.0″

12.22 and if one gives to them a more
(Juliette looks up, offscreen left.)
attentive care than to people,
(Juliette smiles.)

et si on leur accorde un soin

plus attentif qu'aux personnes,

all. The doubt thus cast on the image and on its power to represent the real is something much less rhetorical for Godard than doubting language. Indeed, this doubt increases as his films grow more political. For if the visible world withholds and subverts the means of disengaging the real from the imaginary, then images of the world must do the same; their complicity is inevitable.[8]

Beginning with 12.21, the organizing principle of the image track undergoes a decisive change. Instead of wondering which elements belong in the narrative and presenting those that do out of their chronological order, Godard begins simply to follow the logic of "events," the sequential process of washing the car. His commentary identifies this logic with "everyday good sense," as distinct from the paradox "sense and nonsense." The text itself is quite abstruse. Because the opening sentence ("In the case of the image everything is permitted, the best and the worst") paraphrases Dostoevsky, we understand the connotations of "best" and "worst" as moral. Indeed, apart from Commentary 11 Godard's only previous use of the striking adjective "quotidien," which here qualifies "bon sens," is as the modifier of "morale" in Commentary 3. These connotations introduce a puzzling shift into the argument, which to this point has been preoccupied not with moral judgment but with sense.

A second problem in Commentary 21 is how to understand the relation of "in the case of the image" to "in front of me." The first of these phrases leads us to believe that 12.19 and 12.21 form a pair, the first citing reasons to distrust language and the second those to distrust the image. If this is so, then the relation of the two phrases is one of adversative asyndeton: in the image everything is permitted, *but* in front of me common sense intervenes. We then must understand Godard to mean not only that the image records everything of the world, the best and the worst, without discrimination, but also that in the *succession* of images everything is permitted. Specifically, shots 12.1–12.18 can, as we have seen, be cut together in chronological and narrative disorder without producing contradiction or nonsense or violating standards of what is bad and good. Indeed, these shots depend solely upon—and perhaps even exemplify—what Godard now describes as "la démarche brisée de ma raison" ("the broken step of my reason").

The opposition of the two phrases, "in the case of the image" and "in front of me," also draws out the ambiguity admitted both in the question "Am I watching from too far or too close?" and in the sentence about the cloudy sky: is the speaker before the image or on the scene? Here he removes the qualification, "providing I turn my head," which attends the latter possibility in 12.14; for now we must envision him watching the process of washing the car, which, according to his text, is in front of him, not in the image. This process—which is, I think, to be distinguished from the chain of events happening to the characters (in other words, the narrative)—is what intervenes to repair the broken step ("démarche") of his reasoning: we make so literal a connection between text and image because the car in its forward motion through the washing apparatus so literally describes a "démarche." In contrast to its turnings and abrupt direction changes earlier, its "sens et non-sens," its straight-forward path in 12.21 represents "le bon sens quotidien," where "sens" is taken to mean "direction."

As several commentators have pointed out, the passage beginning with the phrase "objects exist" and continuing through Commentary 22 reflects the influence of the poet Francis Ponge, specifically of his volume *Le parti pris des choses* (*Taking the Side of Things*). In this context, the word "object" is defined in opposition to "person" rather than, as in Sequence 8, to "subject." Hence it is synonymous with *chose*

$\dfrac{3.6''}{45'03.7''}$

12.23   it is precisely because they exist more than people.

c'est qu'ils existent justement plus que ces personnes.

(Pause. Marianne glances briefly at the camera, then back right.)

$\dfrac{13.8''}{45'17.4''}$

12.24   [Motor revving.]

(Attendants soap the car. The attendant in the rear pushes the button on the wall; the Austin moves left and the slow track left with it resumes.)

$\dfrac{10.0''}{45'27.5''}$

("thing") and is so used in Commentary 23. Ponge's influence extends at least through that commentary and appears in certain other details of the film as well, notably the series of extreme closeups. The views of the Pax box and the radio circuits in Sequence 2 are probably indebted to Ponge's book *Soap* and his poem "The Radio"; shot 18.2 is surely inspired by a poem entitled "La cigarette."

Because objects guarantee, or embody, "le bon sens quotidien,"[9] a more attentive care is given to the car than to the people, not only in the scene but in the image; this is how common sense repairs the "démarche brisée" of the image track, in particular 12.8, where the feet describe the scene's most literal "démarche" and the one whose "raison" is in most need of repair. In this way the commentary acknowledges the opposition between the unfolding of the narrative and the process of washing the car. While language and image cannot provide means to disengage the real from the imaginary, objects can. They are the real; therefore they exist more than the people we see in 12.22 and 12.23, especially insofar as these people are fictional characters. Thus Godard backs off, at least for the moment, from the terms of the fiction toward the more certain logic of spatial and temporal reality.

I find this part of the sequence, a sort of philosophical peripetaeia, both exciting and disappointing. What is there, after all, about common sense that holds out the promise of sustaining the narrator's reason? Undeniably, there is something affecting about Godard's return in 12.20–12.26 to staging and cutting a continuous scene, one in which something clearly happens—a car is washed and the "drowned" signification of 12.19 (CARWASH) is fished up and given artificial respiration—and in which all of the aesthetic and philosophical questions raised earlier yield to a simple physical ritual. From one perspective, that of trying to reconstitute a world, this is relevant and persuasive, particularly in its recognition that the world is, in the end, composed of material things. But from other perspectives, invoked with great precision earlier in the film, the car wash is something to be regarded critically, morally, politically; and the return to

12.25 | [Motor revving for seven frames, then rapid fade to silence as the commentary starts.]

COMMENTARY 22
Dead objects are always alive.
(Juliette looks off right, then at the camera.)

Les objets morts sont toujours vivants.

Living people are
(She looks down, then left.)
often already dead.

Les personnes vivantes sont

souvent déjà mortes.

$$\frac{7.4''}{45'34.9''}$$

12.26 | [Very loud noise of the car wash.]
(The car slowly approaches the camera.)
[Straight cut to silence.]

COMMENTARY 23
I am doing nothing other than searching for reasons to

Je ne fais rien d'autre que chercher des raisons de

$$\frac{16.2''}{45'51.1''}$$

this conventional organization seems too easy. Correspondingly, Commentary 22 appears too ready to indulge what I think of as a French taste for paradox: "Dead objects are always alive. Living people are often already dead." This statement is either opaque or false. Indeed, the accompanying shot of Juliette gives it the lie, as Juliette herself does later in the film (18.1): "To define oneself in a single word? Not yet dead!"

The segment starting at shot 12.26, the Austin emerging into the sunlight, is "the answer," the point at which the sequence consolidates the insights of common sense and tries to lay to rest the battery of preceding doubts and questions. The image demonstrates the sense in which dead objects are alive. At the same moment, Godard declares: "I am doing nothing other than searching for reasons to live happily." How are we to understand this? Apart from Commentary 11, he has neither spoken in such a confessional tone nor said anything about his own happiness. Neither has his film as a whole (unlike its companion, *Made in U.S.A.,* which begins with the words "Le bonheur, par exemple . . ."). Indeed, what he has been searching for in the minutes immediately preceding is "how to say exactly what happened." How, if at all, are these searches related?

To begin with, I think it is worth observing that the opening sentences of Commentary 23 resume the themes of Juliette's speech "I was the world . . . the world was

12.27   [Short, soft beep of car horn on the cut.]

live happily. And if,	**vivre heureux. Et si,**
[Short, soft beep on the previous word.]	
now, I push the analysis further,	**maintenant, je pousse plus loin l'analyse,**
[Long, soft beep on the previous syllable of the French, then silence.]	
I find	**je trouve**

$$\frac{5.1''}{45'56.1''}$$

12.28   (An attendant opens the car door; Juliette says something to him that we do not hear; he immediately closes the door, takes the nozzle from the gas pump and begins to fill the tank.)

that there is simply a reason for living because there is, first of all, memory and, secondly, the present	**qu'il y a simplement une raison de vivre parce qu'il y a d'abord le souvenir et, ensuite, le présent**

(Robert enters screen right and crouches by the car window. He and Juliette talk but we do not hear what they say.)

and the means for stopping to enjoy it—	**et la faculté de s'y arrêter pour en jouir—**

in other words,	**c'est-à-dire justement**

(Robert glances at his watch. They continue to talk.)

me": searching for a feeling, happiness, memory, and the importance of a remembered moment. In Commentary 23 memory comes first and "the present" second, putting the emphasis more nearly where it would be in the case of the film image, which "remembers" a moment (a fact stressed by Robert's glance at his watch in 12.28 and Godard's citation of the hour and minute in 12.6) yet appears to place it in the present. As if to illustrate this, shot 12.28 seems at first an exact repetition of 12.9 (in reality it is another take), yet it continues for nearly ten seconds past the point where the earlier shot ends. Just as the repetition explains the sentences about memory, the present, and the means for stopping to enjoy it, so the extension of the action fills out the vague

for having caught in passing a reason for living and for having kept it for several seconds after it has just

(They kiss. Robert gets up and exits right.)

been discovered in the midst of the unique circumstances surrounding it.

(Juliette turns left—presumably to Marianne offscreen—then turns back.)

The birth into the human world of the simplest things,

d'avoir attrapé au passage une raison de vivre et de l'avoir gardée quelques secondes après qu'elle vienne

d'être découverte au milieu des circonstances uniques qui l'entourent.

La naissance au monde humain des choses les plus simples,

$$\frac{27.7''}{46'23.8''}$$

12.29

(Robert walks away.)

their appropriation by the mind of man,

leur prise de possession par l'esprit de l'homme,

phrases about "having caught in passing a reason for living and . . . having kept it for several seconds after it has just been discovered in the midst of the unique circumstances surrounding it." The means ("faculté") for keeping something in this way are those of the film: to look at something ("regarder") is, as the dialogue in *Femme mariée* has it, "to keep it twice . . . because it is precious." Here what is kept includes not only the action that follows Juliette's and Robert's kiss in 12.28 but at least that which extends over the cut and into the next shot.

The cut 12.28/12.29 is remarkable for reasons that at first may not be obvious. It makes use of conventions of shooting and editing that to this point Godard has tended to avoid: the person looking (Juliette in 12.28) followed by what that person sees (Robert walking away in 12.29): shot/reverse shot. Moreover, 12.29 is a "deep focus" composition, where the action recedes and the space is measured by reference to objects at various planes: the windshield wiper, steering wheel, and rear-view mirror in the foreground, Robert in the middle ground, and the sign "Achat Automobiles" in the background. This too is something Godard has tended to avoid, preferring instead, as Haycock observes, to lay movement out laterally, to establish a dominant and controlling background plane, to place the camera parallel to it, and to use selective focus for closeups—in sum, to avoid enticing the eye into the spatial recession of the image.

This departure into a conventional figure of narrative rhetoric is partly explained by the commentary. The cut 12.28/12.29 exactly coincides with the end of the phrase "the birth into the human world of the simplest things," and the beginning of the next, "their appropriation by the mind of man," thus designating the point-of-view shot, 12.29, an illustration of the latter phrase. Now, it would seem that the Austin is one of the "things" Godard means and that 12.26, the shot of it slowly emerging into the daylight, precisely illustrates its "birth into the human world." Yet, by associating this text with 12.28, he insists that the human world is not to be represented by so disembodied, or subjectless, a view of objects. Rather, this birth is the occupation, the appropriation, by the camera of a human perspective, the point of view of Juliette. This does not signify that the narrator becomes Juliette or relinquishes his identity as the one responsible for the image and the action. At the same time, I do not think that, as Rothman proposes, there is a distinction to be made between the woman's view and the man's mind, for in Godard's sentence "de l'homme" is too clearly a synonym for "humain."[10]

In recent film theory the association of the image with a character's point of view is a topic of heated controversy. Daniel Dayan maintains that in classical narrative film the point-of-view shot promotes the illusion that the image is produced by a character, thus serving to deny how it is produced in reality. In his view, therefore, the figure has an ideological function. In reply, Rothman argues that the perceiving character by no means authorizes the point-of-view shot, which is an *unauthorized* appropriation of that character's gaze, and that the point-of-view figure, therefore, makes no statement about reality at all.[11]

I do not mean to enter into all the complexities of the controversy here. Yet I would maintain, at a minimum, that the logic on which the classical point-of-view shot depends is implicit, and that if it became explicit, we should no longer recognize it as classical. Thus it is crucial that, although the cut 12.28/12.29 makes use of the convention, that use is not a conventional one. Because Godard acknowledges earlier that it is he who chooses and orders the shots, we understand that it is he rather than Juliette who is explicitly responsible for 12.29. As for the cut itself, he makes its logic equally

(As Robert continues to walk, he turns
away, then looks back at Juliette, then turns
away again.)

a new world where men and things   un monde nouveau où les hommes à la
fois et les choses

$$\frac{5.7''}{46'29.5''}$$

explicit, describing it as a "taking of possession," an "appropriation." And in the larger context of the film, he makes it the exception rather than the rule. All of this implies that the cut does not so much equal as represent the appropriation spoken of in the commentary. Indeed, Godard's text makes clear that he is speaking about an ideal, not a reality or perhaps even a present possibility; it belongs not to the world we see but, as he says in 12.29, to "a new world," one that constitutes his "aim." In sum, the commentary portrays the cut as illustrating a *wish*. By the same token, the combination of text with images constitutes a sharp criticism of the conventional practice from which the cut derives and within which it has its conventional meaning. While this criticism does not go so far as Dayan in characterizing that meaning as a lie, it nonetheless has an undeniable ideological component.

The answer that Godard begins to articulate starting with 12.26 clearly derives from his earlier definition of art as "that by which forms become human." To the extent that this ideal remains such—in other words, that art is not reality—because of the gulf between subject and object, it has already been dealt with in the phenomenological terms of the café scene. What is new and remarkable here is the flirtation of Godard's answer with the terms of Marxism.

To begin with, the car-wash segment is not just an imagistic equivalent of "everyday good sense" but a work process of an industrial, mechanized sort, and Godard's lateral tracking shots of this production line (12.21 and 12.24) are strikingly similar to those of the initial sequence of his openly Marxist *British Sounds,* made two and a half years later. Shot 12.26 (the car emerging) vividly recalls the end of a production process, as if the birth into the human world involved manufacture rather than washing. The phrase "prise de possession" implies that the objects under discussion, as exemplified by the Austin, have been "alienated"—a word that in this context lacks the force it might have in existential philosophy. But because of the relation of the object to the human work done on it (work that, as we see in 12.26, intensifies its redness), we are put in mind of Marx's picture of the object alienated, literally taken away from the people who made it. In this way the image informs the vagueness of the text with a concrete sense of why objects are not in the "possession" of people; together the text and image propose a model for how they might be. Within this framework shot 12.29, despite the aura of longing surrounding it, is clearly marked as an unsatisfactory, false, and illusory way of taking possession: false because of the implied link between the point-of-view convention and the consumer society to which it belongs (Juliette, as 12.28 reminds us, *literally* possesses the car and, as we infer earlier, pays for it by prostitution) and illusory because of its denial of the material nature of the image. The shot contrasts with 12.31 (the closeup of the surface of the car), which not only designates "abstraction," the work of the painter, but also links the word "political" (the cut to 12.31 occurs just before this word) with an image that for the first and only time fills the screen with red.

It is essential, however, to add that Commentary 23 includes no single unambiguously Marxist term. It leaves the words "alienated" and "reified" unspoken. It characterizes the "prise de possession" as a mental act. And it springs the concluding emphasis on the political out of the air. In this context, then, what can it mean to define one's aim as "a new world where men and things will . . . know harmonious relations"? Everything in the sequence—and specifically the allusion here to the title of Sartre's essay on Ponge, "L'homme et les choses"—leads us to think of this as either an impossibility or a vision, that is, the very opposite of a policy. Isn't art the place where, as

12.30

will at one and the same time know harmonious relations: that is my aim. It is in the end

connaîtront des rapports harmonieux: voilà mon but. Il est finalement

$$\frac{5.7''}{46'35.2''}$$

12.31

(The sun glints through leaves reflected in the surface of the car.)
as much political as poetic.

autant politique que poétique.

And it explains, in any case, the rage of the expression. Whose? Mine: writer and painter.

Et il explique, en tout cas, la rage de l'expression. De qui? De moi: écrivain et peintre.

$$\frac{10.3''}{46'45.5''}$$

12.32

[Noise of counter (?), which fades down before the commentary starts.]

(During the shot the counter moves from 12,90 to 16,45.)

Malraux says, these "harmonious relations" exist, where forms become human?

Given the preoccupation of the sequence with the "poetic"—with objects, happiness, memory, the present, language, and narrative—it would be easy to overlook the fact that Godard never actually identifies himself as an artist, or even as a filmmaker. He is, rather, a "writer and painter." Of course he means by this to *define* filmmaker as the combination of writer and painter and thus to define film as the combination of text and image—a definition that the sequence undeniably earns for him. Yet a filmmaker is neither precisely in the position of the writer of literature nor is he literally a painter; he lacks many of the most potent means by which each is able to invent, or to claim to invent, "a new world."[12] All he has, after all, is the *old* world, the world that exists for this film as an object of criticism and the product of a particular policy. It is this world that we see in 12.29, just as in the shots preceding and following. Not even shot 12.31—the least distinct of all the film's images—succeeds in presenting an object unambiguously freed from its identity in that world. Godard acknowledges, even stresses, that identity by arriving at the closeup via the longer shot 12.30, which shows the same surface in its spatial context. Consequently, we are able not merely to infer but to *perceive* of 12.31 that it is a closeup of the car, not just a red field, not just an abstraction: it is something removed from its spatial context and energized with its own signification by cinematic means but (crucially) only in an identity that the image track acknowledges. In this way the cinematic figure is designated as such: Godard claims and accepts responsibility for the abstraction performed in 12.31, which is not only the abstraction of redness, representing the "rage" of his expression, but also that of the forms of the reflected leaves. The question "Whose?" that follows the phrase "the rage of the expression" wittily reminds us that "La rage de l'expression" is the title of a book by Ponge. The image 12.31 is thus "poetic" in several senses: first, because it illustrates Ponge's phrase; second, because it is expressionistic, an externalization (like 8.27–8.29) of a feeling; third, because it is indistinct and metaphorical; and finally, because it puts before us the allusion to Faulkner made earlier and reinvoked in 12.33, a scene of which it is literally the reflection.

What does Godard mean by "politique"? The word is explicated partly through its coincidence with a red field and partly through the *dégagement* of this surface from its spatial context. Although 12.31, the view of this field, might in isolation seem a poetic rather than a political gesture, it is important to recall that it belongs to a class of extreme closeups that occur throughout the film (the Pax box, the radio wiring, the coffee, the cigarette), in which the separation of the objects from their spatial context connotes an attitude of reflection and criticism. Moreover, 12.30 and (therefore) 12.31 are high-angle shots, unusual in the film's style and marked as such here by the paradigmatic relation of angles, 12.29 to 12.30: Juliette's point-of-view cut to—whose? Not a character's, for we are far from eye level in 12.30 and 12.31 and in the latter we are in impersonal proximity to the object. The text designates this view as "Godard's" ("Whose? Mine"). As such, it corresponds to the moment in Sequence 8 at which the narrator, also speaking over a high-angle shot (the coffee), most decisively occupies, or enters, the depicted space. To the extent that he again does so here, he implies a definition of the terms "political" and "poetic" (especially the latter) that links them to his exemption from the spatial, and therefore the physical, circumstances of his characters. From one perspective, this appears simply to rehearse the now familiar phenomenological distinction between his situation and theirs. From another, it seems to invoke the conventional definition of the artist's position as embodied, say, by the omniscient nar-

$$\frac{6.0''}{46'51.4''}$$

12.33 [Silence.]

(Slow zoom-in, starting on the cut.)

Should I have spoken of Juliette or of the leaves? Since in any case it is impossible really to do the two together, let us say that both were trembling gently at this beginning of the end of an October afternoon.

[After the commentary, the zoom-in continues for a moment in silence. When the zoom finishes and holds,

Fallait-il parler de Juliette ou des feuillages? Puisqu'il est impossible, de toute façon, de faire vraiment les deux ensemble, disons que tous les deux tremblaient doucement en ce début de fin d'après-midi d'octobre.

music enters and fades up.]

$$\frac{22.7''}{47'14.1''}$$

rator in prose fiction (*The Wild Palms*, for instance). This position entails a claim on Godard's part to a privileged access to knowledge and a place outside the world represented—not simply the fictional world, which in a conventional narrative film is the only one that there would be, but also the more inclusive, documentary world that this film calls "the Paris region"—in other words, the very society in which the director lives and works. This claim is a disturbing and problematical one, for it suggests the extent to which the sequence portrays the poetic and the political as opposed or reduces the latter to the former, that is, to a realm of personal signification, of subjectivity, exempt from the conditions that control the world of objects and people.

The two concluding shots, 12.32 and 12.33, in combination with Commentary 24, dispel any impression that the questions raised at the beginning of the sequence have been satisfactorily resolved. The first of these shows the franc counter on the gas pump (presumably the one that we see in 12.28); the cut to the second occurs just as the tally reaches 16,45 and the narrator finishes saying "Il est 16 h 45." In itself, this cleverness seems quite bizarre, either pointless or inexplicably pointed (time is money?). In context, however, the shot has a mysterious, rather electric aura (to which the coincidence contributes), created in part by the dramatic way that the extreme and amorphous abstraction of 12.31 yields to these precise quantities. The numbers start haltingly, then race ahead, as if the world they represent, the ordinary world of money and time, were coming to life again. This, more than the car wash, holds out the promise of restoring the broken step of the narrator's reason.

Shot 12.33, a zoom-in on the leaves, complements the earlier zoom-out, 12.12: its terminal closeup framing, together with its status as the only zoom-in of the film (excepting the tail of 12.19, the car-wash sign) makes it striking and climactic. The accompanying line, "Should I have spoken of Juliette or of the leaves?" asks whether the truth could have been told in either the narrative or extranarrative modes of the film and, as the sequence ends, returns us to the opening question: how to give an account of events? The commentary now rejects the possibility held out in 12.12 of finding a link within the narrative (via allusion to Faulkner): this is, we understand, why "it is impossible really to do the two together."

What do the leaves stand for? First, of course, for what is outside the purview of the narrative; also, for the world of Faulkner and allusion to it; finally, for the natural world, whose green so seldom intrudes that the pairing, Juliette versus the leaves, is justified as a choice. To my mind what is least satisfactory about this passage is the concluding sentence, the answer to the question of which subject to speak about: "let us say that both were trembling gently at this beginning of the end of an October afternoon."[13] The opening words designate this answer as a provisional one. It is a closing off, not a resolution, but it is literary and precious, especially because there is nothing made in the scene of Juliette's trembling gently.

Digression

The service station scene is, in my view, one of the richest and most beautiful in the cinema. Its every detail of imagery, phrase, and construction is brilliantly imagined and executed. It not only succeeds in mobilizing, elaborating, and advancing the entire complex of events and ideas developed throughout the first half of the film, but does so with precision, economy, and inventiveness. It is a dazzling achievement.

Even after many viewings, I cannot honestly say that I find anything that follows Sequence 12 remotely so good or interesting as it—or, for that matter, as a number of other sequences in the first half of the film. It appears that by this point the film has exhausted its repertoire of ideas and spent its energy. Sequences are now longer and fewer (I count 12 in the first half versus 6 in the second); shots are less numerous (155 versus 72); commentaries are fewer (24 versus 4) and tend to be much shorter. On the whole, the second half of the film, despite many strong details, is thin, flat, and rather boring. Ideas often seem muddled, and the writing and direction are sometimes shapeless and hesitant. In short, with the end of Sequence 12, the film loses its sense of forward movement.

Forward movement is, however, a notion that resists precise definition. In the case of most narrative films, it is—or at least derives from—the unfolding of the story. As the structure of Godard's films becomes less reliant on narrative, it comes to depend more obviously on a repertoire of elements that change as they recur and, in doing so, mark out a line of development. This repertoire—a mélange of quotations, slogans, tags, images, formal strategies, physical gestures, and habits of narration, which, to the audience acquainted with his work, together signify "Godard"—informs not only individual films but his work as a whole. Indeed, much of the interest and pleasure of watching a particular Godard film derives from its relationship with the others. As a consequence, the terms of any one work never seem definitive. This is not to say that Godard never gets a film right; rather, the recurring elements function as signs of the continuity of his thought and the changes as signs of reconsideration. His films thus constitute a picture of him thinking, a picture that extends, necessarily, from one work to the next.

In the first half of *2 ou 3 choses,* the sense of forward movement results from the struggle in one sequence toward defining a problem that is elaborated in a later one: the messages from the beyond, the possibility of talking together, *ensemble,* the barrier of subjectivity, the situation of the director, the nature of image and narrative, and so on. In Sequence 12 the summary text of Commentary 23 leads to a new perspective in a way that we recognize from the equally dense café scene, which at its conclusion promises an "apparition de la conscience." That promise, which the combination of text and image in 8.27–8.29 simultaneously fulfills and criticizes, is reformulated in Sequence 12, where (to put it schematically) the double meaning of the French word *conscience* becomes—or yields—the dichotomy *politique/poétique*. But at this very moment, the sequence backs off toward the comparatively feeble concluding sentences about Juliette and the leaves. Locally, these may be neither very damaging nor very consequential. Yet as the film unfolds from this point, it continues to back away: although Godard recognizes the compatibility of the *poétique* and the *politique* as problematical, he never addresses it in anything like the depth that he does, say, the problem of language or of talking together or of trying to imagine what the "apparition de la conscience" might be and look like. In other words, he never deals openly with the scene's incipient Marxism.

The weakness of the later sequences, I believe, stems from this: that the persona of the director, by claiming the exemption of the artist, protects himself from the sort of analysis and criticism he is making of the world. Significantly, he does not make such a claim at the beginning of the film, where he is simply a viewer regarding the image while accepting responsibility for having made it. That position, if not materialist, is at least consistent with materialism. So is the longing he expresses in Sequence 8 to insert himself within the world pictured and of which the picture is part. The melodramatic, transcendental terms on which he achieves this insertion may be open to question, but he gives evidence that he is aware of this and in Sequence 12 shows that he means to mount a reexamination of it: in other words, he indicates that the film will not be content with phenomenology.

The reexamination he conducts itself raises questions, however. He claims the titles "writer and painter" without the necessary qualification that they are metaphors and as such pose specific problems in describing his work as filmmaker. Like the placement of the camera in the accompanying shots, 12.30 and 12.31, they betray his impulse not just to remove himself from the space of the action but to exempt himself from its material conditions—that is, to represent himself as what he would earlier have called a "subject." This, I believe, is the end of any serious aspiration toward a *politique*. What remains includes, of course, the possibility of political opinions (for instance, opposition to the Vietnam War) but no possibility of a political being or of a consequent fulfillment of the recognition, partially achieved in many sequences, of the film as a sum of images and sounds—that is, as an object copresent in the material world of its producer and therefore itself open to a political definition. It is not that the film is explicitly denied this status. Rather, the consciousness of the filmmaker is exempted from it (does this amount to the same thing?) and placed in imagined (the terms of the film tempt me to say "illusory") community with Faulkner and Baudelaire. It is, I fear, from this vantage point that Godard speaks of Juliette and the leaves both trembling.

A passage Godard wrote in late 1963 on the American documentarist Richard Leacock casts a useful light on some of these problems:

By not separating cause and effect, by mixing the exception and the rule, Leacock and his crew do not take into account (and the cinema is nothing other than a rendering of accounts) the fact that their eye seeking images in the viewfinder is at once more and less than the recording apparatus used by that eye; yes, either more or less as the case may be (more with Welles, less with Hawks), but never merely the recording apparatus which, as the case may be, either remains a recorder or becomes a pen and paint-brush.[1]

This passage has three points in common with the commentaries of Sequence 12: the description of the filmmaker as writer and painter, the definition of the cinema as a "rendering of accounts" (*rendre compte*), and the importance in this rendering of the framing of images. In addition, it insists on a distinction about which Sequence 12 is silent: that between the eye and the camera. Of course, when Godard asks "Am I watching from too far or too close?" we understand that he is talking about the camera, and therefore about the framing of the shot; the attention he draws to the frame limits in the shots that follow confirms this understanding. Consequently, it is easy to overlook or to dismiss the fact that he does not actually *say* that he is speaking about the camera. Despite the preoccupation of *2 ou 3 choses,* and of Sequence 12 especially, with the problems of filmmaking, never once—with the possible exception of Commentary 26—does he either mention or show the camera, the recorder, or any part of the scene of production. In this regard his question about "the rage of the expression" (meaning both the compulsion to express himself and the rage expressed thereby) is a real one: "Whose?" And his answer, "Mine: writer and painter," accords with his silence elsewhere about the cinema: that is, it not only defines the filmmaker metaphorically but thereby displaces any definition that is more concrete.

Of course, there is nothing magical in the picture of a camera or the mention of one, and it would certainly spoil the tone of Commentary 23 to have it conclude: "De qui? De moi: cinéaste." At the same time I think it is relevant that, as Haycock points out, this is virtually the first of Godard's films in which the characters do not at some point go to the movies.[2] And it is equally relevant that in the films immediately following, Godard includes pictures of the camera. In *La chinoise* Jean-Pierre Leaud, after a declamatory statement, "We need violence," says (evidently to Godard), "You're laughing; you think I'm showing off for the camera: not at all!" whereupon Godard cuts to a reverse angle, showing the enormous camera. In Godard's contribution to *Far from Vietnam,* we see him delivering a monologue while standing next to a 35mm Mitchell. Paraphrasing Vertov, he titles this film *Camera-Eye,* which, in conjunction with the imagery, expresses a distinction as much as an identity. In light of this it cannot be surprising that his post-1968 filmmaking collective should be named "the Dziga Vertov Group" and that its films should, like Vertov's, take pains to show, and account for the role of, the apparatus.

Insofar as the commentaries of Sequence 12 in combination with 12.29 constitute a criticism (if an incidental one) of the conventional use of the point-of-view shot, that criticism has as its object the unqualified identification of the camera with the character's eye. As such, it applies to the numerous shots of *2 ou 3 choses* that effectively represent the *regard* of the director, who, in default of his explicit identification of himself as filmmaker, cannot be described as other than a character. This is certainly true of the shots of the coffee cup in Sequence 8—especially that associated with the injunction "I must look around me more than ever"; it is also true of 12.9, where Godard asks whether he is too near or too far, and of 12.30 and 12.31.

What defense can be made of the status of these shots? Do they need defense? Even if Dayan is wrong in arguing that the point-of-view figure makes a *false* statement about the origin of the image, it is difficult to deny that the figure makes *some* such statement. Therefore, it is not enough to say that in the commentaries of Sequence 12

Godard declares the origin of the images (and, by extension, the sounds). The question is *what* he declares about that origin. The images, he says, originate with him, the director. But who is he? Notably, he is not a person—or rather, a persona—who works, or, more precisely, who produces the sounds and images by working. I do not mean that Jean-Luc Godard does not work, but that the persona who speaks does not portray himself as someone who works in the same sense as, and with connections to, those who are shown working in the image—for instance, the attendants who wash Juliette's car.

How then *are* the sounds and images produced? Commentary 23 tells us: by the rage of expression. This, we understand, is a metaphor, a *poétique,* as is the phrase "writer and painter." In itself it invites no objection, but in the commanding position it assumes, it cuts off the root of a *politique,* in particular a *politique* that could include or subsume a *poétique.* Indeed, the stronger of the possibilities dramatized at the end of Sequence 12 is the reverse: a poetic, that is, personal, vision reaching out for the status of the political.

Another way of putting this is that the film is limited by its controlling metaphor, a society where all relationships are those of prostitution. As the film progresses, this metaphor bears an increasing burden. Certainly, it is inadequate as a description of what stands in the way of the "new world" or even as an explanation of the "comic strip" that society has become. It is not surprising therefore that in Sequence 12, in particular with the car wash, a new image displaces it and claims its position of centrality: this, significantly, is a work process. The "common sense" with which this process is associated makes it seem that another sort of displacement also occurs here, namely, of the metaphorical by the concrete. When, following this point, the film resumes the account of Juliette's day, it appears plainly to be retracing its steps, reinstating not only the terms of the narrative but the centrality that the narrative inevitably assigns to the metaphor of prostitution.

There is, of course, no internal reason that the film should not or could not have subjected the claim of the *poétique,* including the prostitution metaphor, to review, criticism, and qualification, just as it does the earlier ones—"apparition de la conscience," for example. The fact is simply that it *does* not, that it rests content with the position of Commentary 23, which, in the second half of the film, is challenged by nothing so vividly imagined or passionately stated. This position more closely resembles what Paul writes in his notebook toward the end of *Masculine Feminine*—"A philosopher is a man who pits his *conscience* against opinion"—than what Robert, the militant worker there, earlier quotes from Marx: "It is not men's *conscience* that determines their existence but their social existence that determines their *conscience."*

For all this, there is in Sequence 12 a deep ambivalence. How else are we to explain the views of the production line, the evocation of a new world where people and things are in harmonious relation, and the conclusive gesture of filling the screen with red? Where if not here does Godard locate the hope that prostitution and consumerism will be banished from their definitive place both in the film and in the society that the film depicts? But just as there is no internal reason that the film should go on to elaborate a criticism of the *poétique,* so there is none that it should attempt a more explicit address of Marxist ideas—except, perhaps, for two things: first, the feeling we have as viewers that it has no other place to go, given its concerns, its critical posture, and its apparent determination to track the issues it has raised to their source; and second, the direction taken by Godard's subsequent films, beginning in 1967 with his sympathetic view of the Marxist-Leninist students in *La chinoise* and his lament that he is "cut off from the working class" in *Far from Vietnam.*

Sequence 13

13.1

(A woman is getting into a cab; the young man in glasses of Sequence 8 goes to the door, speaks to her, then helps her out.)

[Music finishes. Silence.]
(He leads her off left.)

$$\frac{10.1''}{47'24.2''}$$

13.2 [Construction noise.]

In 13.1 a young woman is getting out of a cab on the Champs Elysées when the pimp of 5.5 and 8.4 goes to the door, speaks to her, then leads her off screen-left. Following

(The crane on the right turns screen right,
then dollies back; as it does so, the crane on
the left turns screen right.)

19.3″
47′43.5″

13.3 [Silence.]

(The truck on the left maneuvers into position.)

17.0″
48′00.5″

13.4 [Loud construction noise.]

6.5″
48′07.0″

13.5 [Starting at the cut the construction noise
fades down to a lower level.]

(A truck crosses left to right.)

are two shots of construction sites, then the book jacket reading "The Great Hope of the Twentieth Century," then another construction site.

[The construction noise cuts to silence.]

9.8″
48′16.9″

13.6 [Voice-over interview with ambient out-
door sounds.]
(Reflections in a window of children at
play.)
INTERVIEWER
How long have you been here?   Depuis combien de temps tu es là?
BOY
Me? Three years.   Moi? Depuis trois ans.
INTERVIEWER
Then where are you from?   Alors, tu viens d'où?
BOY
Algeria.   D'Algérie.
INTERVIEWER
Do you like it here better, uh . . . than   Tu te plais davantage, euh . . . qu'à
in Algiers?   Alger?
BOY
Oh,   Oh,

no.   non.
INTERVIEWER
(Repeating his answer:)
No.   Non.

12.4″
48′29.3″

The apartment complex and cyclone fence that we see reflected in a window in 13.6 are, presumably, products of both the construction and the Great Hope. At the bottom of the frame are reflections of children at play and on the sound track a boy, perhaps one of these children, is being interviewed.[1] He is Algerian, has been in France for three years but prefers Algiers. He has a brother and a sister. His father works in

13.7

(A breeze blows the plants.)
Do you have sisters? Brothers?   **Tu as des soeurs? Des frères?**
Boy
I have one sister and one brother.   **J'ai une soeur et un frère.**
Interviewer
What about your parents?   **Et tes parents?**
Boy
They're at home.   **Ils sont chez moi.**
Interviewer
What does your father do?   **Qu'est-ce que fait ton père?**
Boy
He   **Il**

$$\frac{8.8''}{48'38.0''}$$

13.8

is in aviation.   **est dans l'aviation.**
Interviewer
Your mother is . . . ?   **Ta mère est . . . ?**
Boy
My mother . . . She is . . . She doesn't   **Ma mère . . . Elle est . . . Elle travaille**

$$\frac{4.2''}{48'42.2''}$$

13.9   **work.**   **pas.**
[Ambient sound fades out to silence.]

aviation and his mother doesn't work. As the boy speaks, Godard cuts to a high-angle closeup of some weeds and grass, which we take to be part of the housing site. Propped against the plants are two color photographs of smiling couples, obviously models. The next shot, the word "idées," retrospectively confirms that the sound/image relationship has indicated a contradiction between reality and idea. The reality, which the boy's voice describes, is that of a working-class Algerian family, and the "idée" that displaces the ghostly, indistinct reflection of that reality (which is all that the image track admits of it) is the prosperous white couples that are so obviously unlike the boy's parents and siblings. This contradiction opens onto Juliette's meditation at the beginning of 14.3: "I was thinking of some things, but I don't know how they came into my thoughts." The account given here of how such things happen begins with

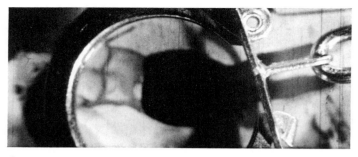

COMMENTARY 25

(During the first three words of the commentary a key ring lowers out of the frame and the camera refocuses on the postcard behind it.)

In this image three

Dans cette image se rejoignent

(The pants of the woman in the postcard begin to lower.)

civilizations meet:

les trois civilisations:

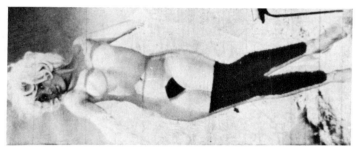

the civilization of leisure, the civilization of the key rings, and the civilization of the ass.

la civilisation des loisirs, la civilisation des porte-clés, et la civilisation du cul.

(Her pants now are gone and a black bra appears.)

And if, by chance,

Et si, par hasard,

13.4″
48′55.6″

13.10   you can't afford LSD,
buy a color television instead.

vous n'avez pas de quoi acheter du LSD, achetez donc la télévision en couleurs.

4.2″
48′59.8″

the color photographs and goes on to include the pornographic postcard (13.9) and "color television," all of which Godard labels "DROGUE" (13.10), "LSD."[2]

Significantly, the sequence opposes these drug images not to an *image* of the Algerian boy but to his *voice*. Shot 13.6 refers to him only in an indirect, general, and aestheticized way (the association of the mirror image with censorship in Sequence 9 obtains here also), as if the subject—or perhaps the documentary mode—were incompatible with the Techniscope image. The interview (the only one in the film that includes the interviewer's voice) recalls, in both style and content, those of *Le joli mai*, in which Marker's hand-held camera presents clear black-and-white images of many subjects like the one that Godard here omits. The comparison makes it plain that this omission reflects partly on the character of Godard's own imagery—wide-screen, color, tripod mounted. The sequence asks: Is this imagery so utterly unrelated to the color photographs of 13.7, which, as the Seuil/Avant-Scène script points out, are of the kind used in store displays to advertise brands of film? Or to the pornographic postcard, which, turned sideways as is the postcard in 2.12, fits the frame exactly and prefigures the action of 14.3? Does it therefore entirely escape the sarcasm directed at color television? Is it not in some sense also a drug?

Sequence 14

14.1 | [Actual sound.]

(Pan left with Juliette and Marianne as they emerge from an elevator.)

ELEVATOR OPERATOR

(Pointing left:)

It's there.   C'est là.

JULIETTE

Yes.   Ouais.

(Pan ends. Hold.)

MARIANNE

(As she crosses back to the mirror in the hotel hallway, she says to Juliette:)

So what did you think? You by yourself?   Mais dis donc, mais qu'est-ce que tu croyais? Tu seule?

(A bellboy crosses right to left.)

JULIETTE

Well, no. I thought it was thirty dollars, and for the whole night.   Mais non. Je croyais que c'était quinze mille et pour toute la nuit.

MARIANNE

Thirty dollars and for the whole night! You're crazy! Oh!   Quinze mille et pour toute la nuit! Tu es folle! Oh!

(Marianne combs her hair; Juliette arranges hers. Marianne crosses back toward the camera.)

In this second of the film's two prostitution scenes, much is made of color. When the American client, John Faubus, takes off his black-and-white striped robe, he reveals a T-shirt decorated with the American flag (14.3). In the frame with him are Juliette, wearing a yellow skirt and blue pullover, and Marianne, wearing a green skirt and red pullover. In the bathroom (14.4) a red-and-white striped robe hangs over the shower-

JULIETTE
(Looks off left through an open door. To
Marianne:)
I'm going in. It's open.   Je rentre. C'est ouvert.
MARIANNE
OK.   Oui, d'accord.
(Pan left with them as they go in.)

                                                                                    20.0″
                                                                                  49′19.8″

14.2 [Actual sound of the interior: doors open
       and close, women laugh.]

(The crane turns clockwise as the traffic cir-
culates counterclockwise.)

(Calling:)
Oh! . . . Oh!   *Oh! . . . Oh!*
JULIETTE
He isn't in.   *Il est pas là.*

                                                                                    11.5″
                                                                                  49′31.3″

14.3 [Actual sound.]
       (Marianne immediately disappears through
       a door. Pan left with Juliette.)

curtain pole and in the same frame we see Faubus in his T-shirt, doubled in the mirror, and Marianne in her red bra. The airline bags that the women put over their heads in 14.7 are red and blue respectively with white lettering.

These color schemes are part of the scene's strain of comic allegory, the theme of which is stated in Marianne's description of Faubus' T-shirt: "America über alles." Besides the T-shirt, the costumes and props of this allegory include the TWA and Pan

I was thinking of some things, but I don't know how they came into my thoughts.

(Marianne reappears through another door behind Juliette. Juliette to Marianne:)

Say, it's big here.

MARIANNE

Yeah.

(Pan left with Marianne. Juliette exits via the door through which Marianne appeared.)

JULIETTE

Ah! Is there another bathroom?

(Hold on Marianne as she stops.)

MARIANNE

(Calling:)

Oh! . . . Oh! . . . Johnny!

(Juliette reappears through another door, then Marianne exits through it. Pan left with Juliette.)

Johnny!

JULIETTE

Thought agrees with reality or puts it in doubt.

(She turns and moves rightward. Pan right with her.)

To put in doubt.

(The pan brings Marianne into the frame at the right. To her:)

But where is this guy of yours?

(Hold. They turn and look offscreen right. Marianne smiles. For the remainder of the sequence she and Faubus, as the right-hand column shows, speak sometimes in French and sometimes in English, while Juliette, except in the one instance noted, speaks French and appears not to understand much of what is said to her in English.)

Je pensais à des choses, mais je ne sais pas comment elles sont entrées dans ma pensée.

Dis donc, c'est grand ici.

Ouais.

Ah, y a encore une salle de bains?

Oh! . . . Oh! . . . Johnny!

Johnny!

La pensée s'accorde à la réalité, ou elle la met en doute.

Mettre en doute.

Mais où il est, ton type?

Am airline bags, the book of Ray Bradbury stories that Marianne is reading in 14.5, "the jeep and the napalm" that Faubus cites as examples of American inventions, his camera and light meter, the magazine photographs of the war in Vietnam, and *Life* magazine, from which some of them are taken. The action reproduces what Godard elsewhere claims is a sociological fact: that the women of the housing *ensembles* prosti-

MARIANNE
Hello.   Hello.

(She crosses out right.)

FAUBUS
Hello, Marianne. How are you? That your   *Hello, Marianne. How are you? That your*
girl friend?   *girl friend?*

MARIANNE
It est [sic] Juliette.   *It est [sic] Juliette.*

(Pan left with Juliette.)

FAUBUS
Hello.   *Hello.*

JULIETTE
(In English:)
Hello.   Hello.

(The pan picks up Faubus moving right.
Hold. Faubus lights Juliette's cigarette.)

FAUBUS
Marianne!   Marianne!

MARIANNE
(Enters right.)
Hm?   Hm?

FAUBUS
Here's a little present for you.   Here's a little present for you.

(He gives her money.)

And uh . . . undress yourself.   And uh . . . undress yourself.

(He takes off his robe.)

tute themselves "to Americans returned from Vietnam" (Seuil/Avant-Scène script, p. 16). The comedy and allegory arise from the way this action is staged. Faubus directs the women to undress, to put the airline bags over their heads, and to walk back and forth. As they do, Godard, by means of the cut 14.7/14.8, precisely compares their movements with those of a construction crane as it lifts and swings a bucket of cement (the comparison is prepared by the earlier parallel between the circling of the women at the head of 14.3 and that of the traffic and crane in 14.2). Besides restating the equivalence "prostitute/*grue*," the cut makes it seem that Faubus, whose voice continues over the shot ("Turn around . . . Show me your back"), commands this action as well. In other words, behind the prostitution and the building of the new Paris lie

MARIANNE
Yes.

FAUBUS
Make yourself comfortable.

JULIETTE
What did he say?
(He exits right.)

MARIANNE
(Showing Juliette the money:)
We undress here.

JULIETTE
(Taking her new pink dress out of a bag:)
I'll put it on to leave.

MARIANNE
(Taking the dress, looking at it:)
Listen, where did you get it?

JULIETTE
At Vogue's.

MARIANNE
Uh-huh. Not bad!
(She tosses the dress down. Juliette takes
off her raincoat as Marianne unbuttons her
sweater.)
Do you know Paco Rabane's dresses?

JULIETTE
No, what are they like?

MARIANNE
They're really neat. They're dresses made entirely of little plated spangles of color.

(She takes off her sweater. She is wearing a
red bra.)

JULIETTE
(Smiles.)
Oh really!

MARIANNE
(Laughs.)
Very funny. For going out, of course.
(She crosses right, out of the frame, as Juliette begins to unbutton her skirt. Marianne
tosses her sweater from offscreen right. Juliette catches it, while continuing to unbutton her skirt.)

Yes.

Make yourself comfortable.

Qu'est-ce qu'il a dit?

On se déshabille ici.

Je la mettrai pour partir.

Tiens, tu l'as eue où?

Chez Vogue.

Uh-huh. Pas mal!

Tu connais les robes de Paco Rabane?

Non, qu'est-ce que c'est?

C'est un truc vachement marrant. C'est des
robes entièrement en petites paillettes de
couleur métallisées.

Ah bon!

Très drôle. Pour sortir, évidemment.

1′24.5″
50′55.8″

American commands and American money.

But the scene is not so simple as this. Although Faubus has something in common with Belmondo's street-theater impersonation of an American general in *Pierrot,* he is not entirely a caricature. It is true that, to photograph the women, he uses an

14.4

(Marianne comes through the bathroom door, crosses in front of Faubus, who points a spot light meter at the camera.)

FAUBUS

My name is John Faubus. I'm a war correspondent in Saigon with the *Arkansas Daily*.

(He points the meter at Marianne, who is at the sink. Pan right with him.)

They're all crazy down there. So I got fed up with the atrocities and the bloodshed. So I came here to get some fresh air.

(He puts down the meter, picks up a camera, then hands Marianne a towel.)

I could speak French.

(To the camera:)

They're stupid and crazy down there. Well, a dead Vietcong costs the American treasury a million dollars. President Johnson could get himself twenty thousand girls like these two here for the same price.

(He puts his still camera to his eye.)

MARIANNE

I existed. That's all I knew.

(She turns and delivers the next line as she exits left, looking at the camera:)

My name is John Faubus. I'm a war correspondent in Saigon with the *Arkansas Daily*.

They're all crazy down there. So I got fed up with the atrocities and the bloodshed. So I came here to get some fresh air.

Je pourrais parler français.

Ils sont bêtes et fous là-bas. Alors, un Vietcong mort, ça coûte un million de dollars au Trésor américain. Le Président Johnson pourrait se payer vingt mille filles comme ces deux-là pour la même prix.

J'existais. C'est tout ce que je savais.

I couldn't have said anything else.

(Faubus takes her picture, then advances the film. Juliette enters, crosses right to the mirror above the sink. Faubus puts his camera, now upside down, to his eye, takes her picture, puts on his glasses, strokes her hair once, and exits left. Juliette turns her head to watch him go.)

Je pouvais pas dire autre chose.

expensive (and unnecessary) spot-reading light meter and a gimmicky camera (a Wide-lux), which, by means of a revolving lens and shutter, scans a field about 100 degrees across. But as I noted earlier, the image that the Widelux produces has proportions and perspective like those of Techniscope. Thus Godard is on the one hand joking about 'scope, which, like "the jeep and the napalm," is an American invention (at least in its 1953 incarnation—its 1927 French ancestor was never more than a historical curiosity), and on the other elaborating the question of the previous sequence about the extent to which his imagery is implicated in the politics he is criticizing.

Curiously, John Faubus is not played by an American. Is Godard acknowledging

FAUBUS
Would you like a cigarette?

Would you like a cigarette?

1'06.7"
52'02.5"

14.5 (He lights two cigarettes. Marianne is reading a French translation of *A Medicine for
Melancholy* by Ray Bradbury.)

MARIANNE
Yes.
Say, your T-shirt is America über alles.

Yes.
Dis donc, ton maillot, c'est America über
alles.

FAUBUS
(Handing her a cigarette:)
Yes, but it's they who invented the jeep
and the napalm.
(He lights her cigarette.)

Yes, but it's they who invented the jeep
and the napalm.

MARIANNE
(As she speaks, he reaches off left for a blue
airline bag, then a red one; he unzips them.)
Yes, the city is a construction in space. The
mobile elements of the city? I don't know.
The inhabitants. Yes, the mobile elements
are as important as the fixed elements.

Oui, la ville est une construction dans
l'espace. Les éléments mobiles de la cité? Je
sais pas. Les habitants. Oui, les éléments
mobiles sont aussi importants que les
éléments fixes.

42.4"
52'44.9"

14.6 *And even when it is ordinary, the spectacle of
the city can provoke a very special pleasure.*

*Et même quand c'est banal, le spectacle de la
ville peut provoquer un plaisir très spécial.*

JULIETTE
(In front of a window:)
No, no event is experienced by itself. One
always discovers that it is linked to what
surrounds it. It is perhaps because, very simply, I am the observer of this spectacle.

Non, aucun événement n'est vécu par lui-
même. On découvre toujours qu'il est lié à
ce qui l'entoure. C'est peut-être que, tout
simplement, l'observateur de ce spectacle,

this or simply making a mistake when he has him say, in reply to Marianne's observation that his T-shirt "is America über alles": "Yes, but it's they who invented the jeep and the napalm." Even if this *is* a slip, it reflects on the speaker's nationality and points to the oddity of the casting. American actors are easy enough to find in France. An American plays the role of the sailor who applauds Belmondo's impersonation in *Pierrot* (an interview with this man appears in Mussman, pp. 245–247) and elsewhere Godard uses Jack Palance, Jean Seberg, and Jane Fonda in American parts. Here, however, the "American" is Raoul Lévy, a Belgian, known as the producer of *And God Created Woman* and *Moderato Cantabile*. His English, though clear, is accented and unidiomatic (he says, "the nah-*palm*" rather than "*nay*-palm" without the article) and after a few lines, he gives it up: "Je pourrais parler français."

The casting of this role hints, I think, that quite apart from the private reference to the connections between Godard and Lévy (Godard appeared in Lévy's last picture, *The Defector*), Faubus and the director of *2 ou 3 choses* are not so entirely dissimilar as it might at first seem. Faubus may have the same last name as a segregationist governor of Arkansas, but his first name is the same as Godard's. Like Godard, he wears dark glasses. He is a correspondent, that is, a writer, and, with his Widelux, a "painter." He pays the women to undress,[1] to be seen but not to see; he directs their movements from offscreen; he photographs them in a format remarkable for its width. These similarities—like the title *Made in U.S.A.* and the dedication of that film "to Nick and Samuel, who taught me respect for image and sound"—acknowledge Godard's debt to the American cinema and his celebration of it as a critic. At the same time, because of the central place that the sequence gives to an attack on the American role in Vietnam, they comprise a self-criticism.[2]

At the beginning of the scene in the hotel room, Juliette wonders how things enter into her thoughts; at the end she declares: "Now I understand what the thought process is." The main thread of the scene is a series of meditations that connect these two points and that elaborate at least two answers to Juliette's question. First, insofar as her thoughts are her monologues, things enter into them through the unheard prompting of the director. Her lines contain much evidence of this, including numerous *oui*s and *non*s. There is other evidence as well. The first of the scene's two monologues is divided between the two women. Marianne begins it in 14.5 and Juliette continues in 14.6, although the division does not occur at the cut 14.5/14.6—rather, Marianne's part spills over into the shot of Juliette. Despite the change of speakers, it is necessary to think of what is said as one text, for Marianne at the conclusion of her part declares that "the spectacle of the city can provoke a very special pleasure" and Juliette toward the beginning of hers adds: "I am the observer of this spectacle." The division of this text underscores the message of the *oui*s and *non*s, denying that thoughts—or, at any rate, thoughts such as these—although "intérieurs," come from within. This point is further corroborated by the content of the meditation, which constitutes a reply to Commentary 23: "No event is experienced by itself. One always discovers that it is linked to what surrounds it . . . The image which arises from it [the

Each inhabitant

(She takes off her pullover.)

has had relations with certain parts of the
city. And with what? Oh, yes ... The
image which arises from it is bathed in
memories and meanings.

[The ambient noise begins slowly to in-
crease in volume.]

The physical clarity

(She switches a lamp on.)

of this image ...

(She switches the lamp off.)

Paris is a mysterious city,

(She switches the lamp on.)

c'est moi. Chaque habitant

a eu des rapports avec des parties definies de
la ville. Et avec quoi? Ah! oui ... L'image
qu'il en nait est baignée de souvenirs et de
significations.

La clarté physique

de cette image ...

Paris est une ville mystérieuse,

stifling,

(She switches the lamp off.)

natural.

FAUBUS

Why doesn't she come

(She switches the lamp on.)

over?

MARIANNE

Are you

(She switches the lamp off.)

coming, Juliette?

FAUBUS

Give her one too.

[The ambient noise lowers in volume.]

JULIETTE

(Switches the lamp on, then off.)

Why, what's happening? He's crazy!

asphyxiante,

naturelle.

Why doesn't she come

over?

Tu

viens, Juliette?

Give her one too.

Mais enfin, qu'est-ce qui se passe? Il est fou!
1'10.3"
53'55.1"

city] is bathed in memories and meanings." If this is not literally Godard speaking, it at least is Juliette speaking to Godard's concerns and in what we recognize as his vocabulary. But what "image" does she mean? Is this a generality? The text does not tell us and, lacking this information, we associate the word not only with the city imagery in the film as a whole but with the specific image we are watching: for the elliptical phrase "la clarté physique de cette image" aptly describes the change effected in the dark, backlit, silhouetted shot as Juliette turns the lamp on and off (*clarté* means both clarity and the light that brings this clarity about). One of the memories in which this

14.7 (Marianne is at right with the red TWA bag over her head. Juliette enters left.)

MARIANNE

Here, he likes it better when we don't look at him.

(Juliette puts the blue Pan Am bag over her head.)

Tiens, ça l'amuse plus quand on le regarde pas.

FAUBUS

OK, girls. You can start walking now. You can walk.

(Juliette crosses right, out of the frame, and Marianne left, out of the frame; then they cross through the frame in the opposite directions; they reenter, Marianne from the right, Juliette from the left.)

Marianne, you can stop.

(They stop.)

OK, girls. You can start walking now. Vous pouvez marcher.

Marianne, you can stop.

$$\frac{22.5''}{54'17.6''}$$

14.8 [Actual sound of interior; starting at the cut construction noise fades up, mixing with it.]

Turn around.

(A bucket lifts up and right, out of the frame.)

Turn around.

image is bathed is that of the scene in *Contempt* in which a lamp is also repeatedly and

No, not like this. Show me your back.
Show me your back.

(Pause. The bucket reappears in the upper left coming left and down. The crane at the right begins to turn clockwise.)

[The construction noise lowers in volume.]

Come this way, Marianne.

No, not like this. Show me your back.
Montrez-moi votre dos.

Come this way, Marianne.

29.8″
54′47.4″

14.9 | [Actual sound mixed with construction noise, which slowly fades down.]

(Marianne crosses right and toward the camera, out of the frame. Juliette crosses right, out of the frame.)

You can take it off now.

(Juliette enters right, crosses left.)

And you can tell your girl friend she can take it off also.

[Fade of construction noise finishes. This noise, now at a low level, continues, mixed with the actual sound of the interior.]

(Juliette stops.)

MARIANNE
You can take it off now.

(Juliette removes the bag from her head.)

FAUBUS
Will you join us, Juliette?

(Juliette looks off right, presumably at them.)

You can take it off now.

And you can tell your girl friend she can take it off also.

Tu peux l'enlever, maintenant.

Will you join us, Juliette?

MARIANNE
Come, Juliette.

JULIETTE
No, not that.

MARIANNE
It doesn't matter. I'm going to do it.

Viens, Juliette.

Non, pas ça.

Ça fait rien. Moi, je vais le faire.

idly switched on and off.

In the segment from 14.10 to 14.19 the sequence outlines a second way that

14.10

nothing more to say.   *nothing more to say.*
JULIETTE
It's a strange thing that one person,   *C'est une chose étrange qu'une personne*
                                                                        6.3″
                                                                        $\overline{55'14.5''}$

14.11

who is in Europe on August 17, 1966,   qui se trouve en Europe le 17 août 1966
(She looks off right, at the couple.)
can think of another who is in Asia.   puisse penser à une autre qui se trouve en
                                                     Asie.
(She looks down left, then back at them.)
Thinking, meaning to say: Penser, vouloir dire:
(She looks down left.)
these aren't activities like writing, running,   ce ne sont pas des activités comme écrire,
or eating,   courir, ou manger,
                                                                        23.9″
                                                                        $\overline{55'38.4''}$

things enter into Juliette's thought. She begins by saying: "It's a strange thing that one person, who is in Europe on August 17, 1966, can think of another who is in Asia." With her first phrase Godard shows a magazine photograph of Vietcong prisoners. This insert is the first of six, which at once represent her thoughts and constitute an explanation of how the person in Asia entered into them—namely, by photographs in maga-

14.12

no.   non.

$$\frac{3.1''}{55'41.5''}$$

14.13

They're interior.   C'est intérieur.
(She hums. As she does so, she looks to-
ward the couple, then away.)
If someone asks me to continue that song?   Si quelqu'un me demande de continuer
Yes, I could, I could continue. What kind   cette chanson? Oui, je pourrais, je pourrais
of process represents this . . . this knowl- continuer. Quelle sorte de processus
edge, that one can continue something? I   représente ce . . . ce savoir, que l'on peut
don't know.   continuer quelque chose? Je ne sais pas.

$$\frac{45.1''}{56'26.5''}$$

14.14

For example, I can think of someone who isn't   *Par exemple, je peux penser à quelqu'un qui*
here, imagine him,   *n'est pas ici, l'imaginer,*
(A slow tilt down begins.)

zines. Because some of these photographs are, as we see in 14.12, taken from an American magazine (Godard registers the often remarked irony of *Life*'s fascination with pictures of death) and are accompanied by text, they also represent a nonfictional

or else evoke him suddenly with a remark—	*ou alors l'évoquer brusquement par une remarque—*
(The tilt finishes. Hold. Pause in speech.)	
even	*même*
	14.4″
	56′41.0″

14.15

if he is dead.
(She looks frame right, toward the offscreen couple.)

s'il est mort.

For example, I declare "I'm hot."
(She resumes looking leftward.)
No, rather, "I'm impatient."
MARIANNE
America über alles!

Par exemple, je déclare "j'ai chaud."

Non, plutôt, "je suis impatiente."

America über alles!

	20.0″
	57′00.9″

14.16

[Actual sound of interior. A burst of "gunfire"—probably from a toy gun—coincides with the cut at the head of the shot.]

[A second burst of gunfire begins just before the cut at the tail and spills over into the head of the next shot.]

	3.4″
	57′04.3″

counterpart to the journalistic work of John Faubus. In 14.16–14.18 three of these inserts occur in sequence and with them an offscreen mechanical sound interrupted by

14.17

MARIANNE
America
über alles!
JULIETTE
Now
I understand what the thought process
is:
MARIANNE
America
über alles!

America
über alles!

Maintenant,
je comprends ce que c'est le processus de la
pensée:

America
über alles!

$\dfrac{4.0''}{57'08.3''}$

14.18 [A burst of "gunfire" on the cut at the
head of the shot.]

JULIETTE
  yes,   *oui,*

[A second burst of "gunfire" just before
the cut at the tail, spilling over into the
head of the next shot.]

$\dfrac{3.6''}{57'11.9''}$

Marianne's thrice-repeated phrase "America über alles." Although this sound is not certainly identifiable, it suggests both a toy machine gun such as Christophe's (17.2) and Faubus's camera, making his connection with the photographs a bit more explicit.

Although still photography is a logical term of comparison for the film image and functions as such earlier in the scene, I do not think it has this status here. The photographs represent the view of witnesses who, like Faubus, have seen "the atrocities and the bloodshed." From this Godard, like Juliette, is (as he says in *Camera-Eye*) "loin enfin." Formally, this fact is registered in the framing of the stills. They do not fit the Techniscope aperture as, for instance, the pornographic postcard (13.9) does. In 14.10 the frame is tilted; in 14.12 and 14.17 it includes text as well as image; in 14.18 it spans three photos; and in 14.14, it takes in the magazine picture only by means of a slow tilt downward.

Here as elsewhere, Godard tends to draw an absolute distinction between still photography and film. In *Pierrot le fou* (p. 36), Marianne Renoir, responding to a broadcast report of Vietcong losses, says something which indicates the basis of that distinction:

We know nothing. They just say 115 dead. It's like photographs. They've always fascinated me. You see a still photograph of some man or other, with a caption underneath. He was a coward perhaps, or pretty smart. But at that precise instant when the photograph was taken, no one can say what he actually is, and what he was thinking exactly—about his wife maybe, or his mistress, his past, his future, or basketball. One never knows.

What Marianne Renoir says here applies to the photographs in Sequence 14. Even though we cannot know what the people in those photographs are thinking, we do know Juliette's thoughts and know them, moreover, partly through the inserted photographs. It is with respect to the possibility of such knowledge that film and photography differ.

Having said this, I must add that I find the actual substance of Juliette's meditations rather confusing. For example, in 14.6 she says: "Each inhabitant has had relations with certain parts of the city. And with what? Oh, yes . . ." By this I understand that she does not hear the last of the phrases Godard gives her through the hidden earphone; he repeats it and this time she catches it ("Oh, yes"), but instead of repeating it aloud, she goes on to the next sentence. Or, to take a later instance (14.15): of what is "I declare 'I'm hot'" an "example"? The large number of such loose ends, repetitions, ellipses, and non sequiturs that run through the scene make it long and trying. The most consequential of these occur at the end. When in 14.17 Juliette concludes that she now understands what the thought process is, we barely hear her, for while she is speaking, Marianne is repeating the phrase "America über alles" and the toy gun

14.19 [Actual sound continues.]

an effort of the imagination ... the examination of real objects.

un effort d'imagination ... l'examen d'objets réels.

(She looks offscreen right, toward Marianne and Faubus, then back.)

To say something, to mean to say something:

Dire quelque chose, vouloir dire quelque chose:

(She looks offscreen right.)

yes, maybe these are expressions of the life of the muscles

oui, peut-être ce sont les formulations de la vie musculaire

(She looks down.)

and nerves.

et nerveuse.

(She looks toward the camera.)

For example, I say, "I'm going to look for Robert at the Elysées-Marbeuf."

Par exemple, je dis, "je vais aller chercher Robert à l'Elysées-Marbeuf."

(She looks down.)

And now I try to think it without words,

Et, maintenant, j'essai de le penser sans paroles,

(She looks at the camera for five frames before the cut.)

46.0″
57′57.9″

is firing. And when, at the head of 14.19, she tells us what her understanding is, she fails to enunciate clearly. The Seuil/Avant-Scène script renders this crucial line, probably on the basis of the producer's dialogue transcription, as follows: "C'est de substituer un effort d'imagination à l'examen d'objets réels" ("It is substituting an effort of the imagination for the examination of real objects"). But all that one can actually make out in the shot is "un effort d'imagination . . . l'examen d'objets réels." If we credit the Seuil/Avant-Scène script, the image track represents this thought process quite literally. As she speaks, Juliette repeatedly glances offscreen right, presumably at the couple on the bed. For a view of this sexual act, these "real objects" (as opposed to the "subject," Juliette), the image track substitutes the still photographs, the "effort of the imagination" by which a person in Europe can think of another in Asia. Given what the spectator actually hears, however, the line means that the real object is what is shown in the photographs; hence it argues that thought can have a real object even if that object is not present. In either case it is important that the magazines from which the photographs are taken, unlike the copy of *Lui* in Sequence 8, are themselves not shown in the real space of the scene. Their presence in the image track is, therefore, as in the case of the book jackets, implicitly the doing of the filmmaker.

In light of all this, the last cut in the sequence is particularly confusing. Juliette, having defined the thought process and related it to "the life of the muscles and nerves," now gives us what she proposes to be an "example": "I say 'I'm going to look for Robert at the Elysées-Marbeuf.' And now I try to think it without words, neither aloud nor to myself." After "without words," she pauses and looks at the camera and on this look the image track cuts to Robert at the Elysées-Marbeuf (15.1). This cut has a precedent. A few moments earlier Juliette gave another example of her ability to "think of someone who isn't here, imagine him, or else evoke him suddenly with a remark," during which we see 14.14, a famous still of a bloody Vietnamese prisoner. But in this case I do not take it that she is in the position of the director or that the image track is under her command. Therefore the cut to 15.1 is especially perplexing: for not only does it ask us without preparation to accept her as controlling the image track but it confuses the essential distinctions between still photographs and the film image, hence between the roles of Faubus and Godard, and the carefully drawn account of the agency by which the photographs appear in the image track. Is this anything more than a tricky way to cut to the new sequence? The possibility that it is not contributes to the feeling that the film is running out of energy.

Sequence 15

15.1   [Actual sound, including pinball noise.]

neither aloud nor to myself.	*ni à voix haute, ni à voix basse.*
YOUNG WOMAN	
Are you waiting for someone?	Vous attendez quelqu'un?
ROBERT	
Yes, my wife. What about you?	Oui, ma femme. Et vous?
YOUNG WOMAN	
I'm waiting for someone, but I don't know if he is going to come. Is it her you're writing to?	Moi, j'attends quelqu'un, mais je ne sais pas s'il va venir. C'est à elle que vous écrivez?
ROBERT	
No, it's for myself.	Non, c'est pour moi.
YOUNG WOMAN	
Do you have a match?	Vous avez du feu?
(Girl and Ivanoff enter, cross left behind the pinball player and around toward the camera, then out of frame left.)	
Thank you. Too bad it's raining.	Merci. Dommage, il pleut.
ROBERT	
Yes.	Oui.
BOUVARD	
"It was, most happily, not this way under the direction of Comrade Lenin."	*"Il n'en fut pas ainsi, fort heureusement, sous la direction du camarade Lénine."*

1′08.9″
59′06.8″

This is not only the longest scene in the film (almost fourteen minutes) but in my opinion the weakest. Its main thread, the dialogue of Robert and the young woman, is meandering and sophistic, and the actress, Juliet Berto, makes the writing seem weaker than it is by her nervous and mannered delivery. The four-minute exchange between Ivanoff and the teenage girl who questions him never gets to the point: she says she wants his advice, he asks "Why me?" and they get so sidetracked by his question that they never get back to hers. As for Bouvard and Pécuchet, we infer after a few moments what they are doing and don't need to listen to them go on for nearly three minutes. All of this is aggravated by rather unattractive images—long, held views of the speakers with distracting material in the background—*découpage* that emphasizes the tedium by dividing the dialogue of Robert and the young woman into three segments and that of Bouvard and Pécuchet into two, and a sound track in which lines are often barely audible because of the acoustical harshness of the room and the deafening game of pinball that a stout woman is playing just inches behind Robert and the young woman.

Scenes comparable to this one both in character and in position occur elsewhere in Godard's work. I think, for instance, of the long scene in Patricia's room in *Breath-*

(Each quotation comes from a different book. Bouvard chooses the books at random from the piles in front of him. Pécuchet writes down what Bouvard reads aloud.)

"Recycled rubber: recycled rubber is obtained by making rubber objects undergo special treatments." "Leon Pellet, moving, trucking, excursions. 108 rue Joubert-Phillips, near the cemetery. Telephone 295."

"Any man, any time, anywhere. Claudel and Danny got into the yellow sedan while Jessie was running across the yard."
"The water of the fountains flows heavy as a dog's mouth. The rose frightens me; it never laughs." " 'Purify thyself, stranger.' 'I shall enter pure,' said Dimitrios. With the end of her hair dipped in the water, the young woman guarding the gate wet first his eyelids, then his lips and fingers."
"In the heart of the most beautiful Pyrénées, the department of the Hautes-Pyrénées offers the most varied choice: 24, rue du Quatre-September, Paris 2ᵉ. Telephone 742-21-34." " 'I still do not know what means will be employed to prevent the impulsive acts of madmen.' Nikita Khrushchev."

"Caucciù rigenerato: si ottene il caucciù rigenerato faciendo subire speciali tratamenti agli objecti di caucciù." "Léon Pellet, déménagements, transports, excursions. 108 rue Joubert-Phillips, près du cimetière. Téléphone 295."
"Any man, any time, anywhere. Claudel and Danny got into the yellow sedan while Jessie was running across the yard."
"L'eau des fontaines coule grave comme la bouche d'un chien. La rose m'intimide; elle ne rit jamais." " 'Purifie-toi, étranger.' 'J'entrerai pur,' dit Démétrios. Du bout des ses cheveux trempés dans l'eau, la jeune gardienne de la porte lui mouilla d'abord les paupières, puis les lèvres et les doigts."
"Au coeur des plus belles Pyrénées, le département des Hautes-Pyrénées offre le choix le plus varié: 24 rue du Quatre-Septembre, Paris 2ᵉ. Téléphone 742-21-34."
" 'J'ignore encore quels seront les moyens employés pour prévenir les coups de tête des aliénés.' Nikita Khrouchtchev."

1'38.8"
60'45.5"

less, the overlong dialogue between Nana and the philosopher in *Vivre sa vie,* the post-card sequence in *Les carabiniers,* the dialogue between Robert and Catherine in the kitchen in *Masculine Feminine,* and the grandfather's monologue in *Numéro deux.* Other examples could be cited as well. Their pattern reflects, I think, both Godard's habit of writing as he is shooting and what Suzanne Schiffman describes as his "constant fear of ending up making a film too short."[1] It is understandable that, given his working methods, his creative energy should sometimes give out—especially when he approaches the end of a project. What is not so understandable is why he does not minimize the effect of this exhaustion by cutting. Problem solving of this sort is evidently foreign to his sensibility. To quote Schiffman again (*Focus on Godard,* p. 48):

Godard is the only director who never shoots a sequence from more than one angle. He takes the shot, and that's it—he goes on to the next one. He edits in the same manner, almost end to end; he doesn't make twenty different shots in order to have twenty different solutions. He has only one solution. During the editing, he reinvents certain solutions.

If the results of this method are, as in the case of Sequence 15, not especially successful, they can seem on the one hand inexplicably passive—"the work of a lazy man," as Schiffman says of *Les carabiniers* (which she likes, nonetheless)—and on the other hostile toward the audience. To those inclined to return this hostility, instances such as these appear to define, and therefore to discredit, the whole. They support the common

" 'I'll go work in Paris in a year or two,' she said modestly. It was as if Mrs. Calendar had had the power to make her play a part."

ROBERT
You have nothing else to tell me?

YOUNG WOMAN
No, not especially. What about you?

ROBERT
What about me? Do you want me to tell you what I'm doing?

YOUNG WOMAN
You told me a few minutes ago: you're writing.

ROBERT
Yes, I'm writing. But it's very special. I get messages from the beyond. Yes, I saw a film where there was a guy who did that: Orphée.
(She glances at the camera.)
Tell me again what you told me a few minutes ago about the rain.

YOUNG WOMAN
I liked the rain very much.

ROBERT
No, you didn't tell me that.

YOUNG WOMAN
You think I didn't tell you that?

ROBERT
You told me . . .

YOUNG WOMAN
. . . that the rain made me sad. Is that it?

ROBERT
You don't find that a banal thing to say?

YOUNG WOMAN
No, it isn't banal, because the . . . the rain

" 'J'irai travailler à Paris dans un an ou deux,' dit-elle modestement. C'était comme si Mrs. Calendar avait eu le pouvoir de lui faire jouer un rôle."

Vous n'avez rien d'autre à me dire?

Non, pas spécialement. Et vous?

Et moi? Vous voulez que je vous dise ce que je suis en train de faire?

Vous me l'avez dit tout à l'heure: vous êtes en train d'écrire.

Oui, j'écris. Mais c'est très spécial. Je capte les messages de l'au-delà. Oui, j'ai vu un film où il y avait un type qui faisait ça: Orphée.

Redites-moi ce que vous m'avez dit tout à l'heure à propos de la pluie.

J'aimais bien la pluie.

Non, vous m'avez pas dit ça.

Vous croyez que je vous ai pas dit ça?

Vous m'avez dit . . .

. . . dit que la pluie, ça me rendait triste. C'est ça?

Vous ne trouvez pas que c'est banal à dire?

Non, c'est pas banal, parce que la . . . la

complaints that Godard's films are full of endless and pointless talk between people in cafés, that nothing happens, that they are taken up with empty and pretentious intellectualizing. If, as in the present case, such complaints contain some truth, they still are not a sufficient response to the hard questions that Godard is struggling to address.

In 15.1 a young woman sitting next to Robert strikes up a conversation with

doesn't make everybody sad.

ROBERT
Tell me something else that you find interesting. I find that in the movies one doesn't succeed in really talking. That is what I'd like to do with you.

YOUNG WOMAN
You want to really talk with me?

ROBERT
Only because you are unknown to me. I like very much talking with the Unknown.

YOUNG WOMAN
Well then, talk.

ROBERT
Do you know what talking is?

YOUNG WOMAN
Talking is saying words.

ROBERT
And what is saying words?

YOUNG WOMAN
Saying words? It's talking, to say silly or very fine things.

ROBERT
For example, the two of us—how could we talk together? But, but . . . but really talk, involving ourselves totally.

YOUNG WOMAN
Well, take an interesting subject and talk, discuss that subject.

(She glances at the camera.)

ROBERT
Good, well then, we are going to talk about sex.

YOUNG WOMAN
Always sex.

ROBERT
Are you afraid?

YOUNG WOMAN
Absolutely not.

ROBERT
I believe you are afraid.

YOUNG WOMAN
As you wish . . . I tell you that I'm not afraid. Why should I be afraid?

ROBERT
Well, why is it that sex always scares people?

pluie ne rend pas triste tout le monde.

Dites-moi quelque chose d'autre que vous trouvez intéressant. Moi, je trouve qu'au cinéma on n'arrive pas à parler vraiment. C'est ce que je voudrais faire avec vous.

Vous voulez parler vraiment avec moi?

Seulement parce que vous êtes une inconnue. J'aime bien parler avec l'Inconnu.

Eh bien, parlez.

Est-ce que vous savez ce que c'est que parler?

Parler, c'est dire des mots.

Et dire des mots, qu'est-ce que c'est?

Dire des mots? C'est parler, pour dire des bêtises ou des choses très bien.

Par exemple, tous les deux—comment est-ce qu'on pourrait parler ensemble? Mais, mais . . . mais vraiment parler, en nous engageant totalement.

Eh bien, prendre un sujet intéressant et parler, discuter sur ce sujet.

Bon, eh bien, on va parler du sexe.

Toujours le sexe.

Vous avez peur?

Absolument pas.

Moi, je crois que vous avez peur.

Si vous voulez . . . Je vous dis que j'ai pas peur. Pourquoi est-ce que j'aurais peur?

Mais pourquoi est-ce que le sexe fait toujours

him and in 15.3 he invites her to tell him something she finds interesting: "I find that in the movies one doesn't succeed in really talking. That is what I'd like to do with you." Why? Because she is a stranger, "une inconnue," and he likes to talk "avec l'Inconnu"—a joke about the messages which, as he has just told her, he receives from "l'au-delà." He asks: "How could we talk together . . . really talk, involving ourselves totally?" Thus the film not only returns to the issue of talking together, but, because of the surprising acknowledgment that Robert and the young woman are "in the movies" ("au cinéma"), *acknowledges* this return, as if setting out an explicit task of review and revision. With respect to this task, Robert is Godard's surrogate. The subject he chooses for the experiment of "talking together" is the ostensible subject of the film, namely sex ("Toujours le sexe," the young woman says, faintly annoyed). The way in

YOUNG WOMAN
But it doesn't scare me.

ROBERT
For example, I'm going to ask you to say a sentence; I'm sure you're going to refuse.

YOUNG WOMAN
Say it.
(She glances at the camera.)

ROBERT
But are you going to say it? Do you promise?

YOUNG WOMAN
That depends on what the sentence is—if it pleases me or if it doesn't please me, if it is intelligent or not.

ROBERT
You see, you're afraid.

YOUNG WOMAN
Well no, I'm not afraid; it isn't a question of fear.

ROBERT
Good, all right . . . I'm going to say it for you: "My sex is placed between my legs." Go on, repeat it.

YOUNG WOMAN
I'm not in school.

ROBERT
All the same, you told me that . . . that . . . that you're not afraid of sex.

YOUNG WOMAN
No, I'm not afraid.

ROBERT
Well, say that sentence.

YOUNG WOMAN
Why say that sentence? It's absurd.

ROBERT
It's as simple as lighting a cigarette.

YOUNG WOMAN
Oh, no. If I light a cigarette, it's because mine has gone out or because I want to smoke, but to say something so banal and obvious isn't worth the trouble.

ROBERT
No. But still, you have a sex just as you have eyes, shoulders.

peur aux gens?

Mais, moi, il me fait pas peur.

Par exemple, je vais vous demander de dire une phrase; je suis sûr que vous allez refuser.

Dites-la.

Mais vous allez la dire? vous promettez?

Ça dépend quelle est la phrase—si elle me plaît ou si elle me plaît pas, si elle est intelligente ou pas.

Vous voyez que vous avez peur.

Ben non, j'ai pas peur; c'est pas une question de peur.

Bon, ben . . . je vais vous la dire: "mon sexe est placé entre mes jambes." Allez, répétez.

Je suis pas à l'école.

Quand même, vous m'avez dit que . . . que . . . que vous n'avez pas peur du sexe.

Non, je n'ai pas peur.

Alors, dites cette phrase.

Pourquoi dire cette phrase? C'est absurde.

C'est aussi simple que d'allumer une cigarette.

Ben non, si j'allume une cigarette, c'est que la mienne est éteinte ou que j'ai envie de fumer, mais dire une évidence si banale, c'est pas la peine.

Non. Mais enfin, vous avez un sexe comme vous avez des yeux, des épaules.

which he proposes that they talk about it is consistent not so much with his ambition of complete self-involvement as with a directorial role: from offscreen he asks her to repeat ("répétez") the sentence "My sex is placed between my legs" (compare the epigraph of the Seuil/Avant-Scène script: "When one lifts the city's skirts, one sees its sex"). This sentence is, of course, a version of Juliette's line in 9.4, which we recognize as "repeated" (*répéter* also means "to rehearse") after the offscreen director: "He is going to put his sex between my legs." But the young woman, unlike Juliette, has no "passive side" and refuses to say what Robert asks her to: she protests that she is not at school and that the phrase is "absurd." Given Robert's physical resemblance to Godard,

YOUNG WOMAN
Well, yes!

Eh ben oui!

ROBERT
Why is it that we can't talk about it?

Pourquoi est-ce qu'on ne peut pas en parler?

YOUNG WOMAN
Because I don't talk about my eyes, I don't talk about my shoulders, I don't talk about my sex, and that's it!

Parce que je parle pas de mes yeux, je parle pas de mes épaules, je parle pas de mon sexe, et c'est tout!

ROBERT
You're wrong. Your eyes are very pretty.

Vous avez tort. Ils sont très jolis, vos yeux.

YOUNG WOMAN
I don't give a damn.

Je m'en fous.

ROBERT
You have a very pretty mouth too.

Vous avez une très jolie bouche aussi.

YOUNG WOMAN
As if I cared.

Je m'en fiche.

ROBERT
Look, that guy there, facing us, isn't he the Nobel Prize winner?

Tiens, le type qui est là, en face, c'est pas le prix Nobel?

YOUNG WOMAN
(She looks offscreen left.)
Ivanoff? Could be.

Ivanoff? Peut-être.

ROBERT
In any case it looks a lot

En tout cas, il lui ressem-

like him.

ble beaucoup.

4'31.3"
65'16.8"

his declaration that he and the young woman are "au cinéma," and his attempt to direct her, it would be difficult not to construe her refusal as a self-criticism on the part of the director.

At the beginning of this shot, as at the end of 15.1, Robert is writing in his notebook. He explains to the young woman: "I'm writing. But it's very special. I get messages from the beyond. Yes, I saw a film where there was a guy who did that: *Orphée.*" For Orpheus, as for Robert, the source of these messages is the radio. In Cocteau's film, the messages include news (like the Saigon-Washington transmission that Robert monitors) and verses such as "a glass of water lights up the world" and "the bird sings with its fingers," written and broadcast from the *au-delà* by the dead young poet Cégeste ("ses gestes"?). When in 15.9 and 15.11 we glimpse what Robert is writing, we see that it too refers to poetry: Aloysius Bertrand and "Gaspard de la Nuit." In these shots we recognize the handwriting, red felt pen, and crosshatched paper of Ferdinand's journal in *Pierrot le fou,* which I assume to be actually Godard's own blue spiral notebook. If Robert resembles Orpheus in the source and content of his writing, he is also, then, like him in representing the filmmaker, who is in both cases a "writer and painter."[2] Significantly, our view of Robert's page shows his pen crossing out words: "venu" in 15.9 and "calme" in 15.11: that is, he is canceling and revising—a gesture related to the authorial self-criticism constituted by the young woman's refusal to repeat his sentence.

Writing is also a theme of the other two parts of the sequence. Ivanoff is a fictional Nobel Prize–winning author, who, at the start of 15.4, signs a copy of his book

GIRL
What will the morality of communism be?

IVANOFF
I think that it will be the same thing as now.
(He autographs his book.)
GIRL
Yes, but what does that mean?
IVANOFF
Looking out for one another, working for one's country, loving it, loving the arts, science . . .
GIRL
Then what will the difference be?
IVANOFF
With communism, that will be easier to explain.
GIRL
Ah, yes. I understand. It's money. It's a very . . . it's a very great evil, because you begin to steal without noticing it.

(He gives her the autographed book. A waiter enters right and serves him beer and her coke.)
May I ask you another question?
IVANOFF
Yes indeed.
GIRL
Should one be honest with oneself?

IVANOFF
At your age, absolutely.
GIRL
And at yours, then?
IVANOFF
At my age? Uh . . . as much as possible.
GIRL
No, no. Always.
IVANOFF
It's true. One must always be attentive, feel the intoxication of life.

Qu'est-ce que ce sera la morale du communisme?

Je pense que ce sera la même chose que maintenant.

Oui, mais c'est-à-dire?

Faire attention les uns aux autres, travailler pour son pays, l'aimer, aimer les arts, la science . . .

Alors, quelle sera la différence?

Avec le communisme, ce sera plus facile à expliquer.

Ah! oui. Je comprends. C'est l'argent. C'est un bien . . . c'est un bien grand mal, parce que on commence à voler sans s'en apercevoir.

Je peux vous poser encore une question?

Oui, oui.

Est-ce qu'il faut être honnête avec soi-même?

A votre âge, absolument.

Et au vôtre, alors?

A mon âge? Euh . . . autant que possible.

Non, non. Toujours.

C'est vrai. Il faut toujours être attentif, sentir l'ivresse de la vie.
                                          1'33.7"
                                          66'50.5"

for the girl with whom he has entered. Sitting, she begins a series of three questions. First: "What will the morality of communism be?" (Ivanoff is wearing a red shirt.) In a sense, the question belongs to Godard, who in 12.31 has alluded to revolution, then in Sequence 14 harshly criticized the United States for its role in Vietnam, and now, as it were, considers the alternative. The comic evasiveness of Ivanoff's reply also belongs to Godard: "With communism, that will be easier to explain." Next, she asks whether

15.5

GIRL
May I ask you another question?

IVANOFF
Of course.

GIRL
Does poetry educate, or is it only decoration?

IVANOFF
Well, everything that decorates life is education.

GIRL
You spoke of intoxication a minute ago—is that beer or vodka?

IVANOFF
Neither. Without anything.

GIRL
I've never tried either one. What is the intoxication of life?

IVANOFF
I think you ... you know what it is.

GIRL
Me? Oh, no, no. I'm often depressed, you know. I cry; it's something to be ashamed of. Don't you have the time to talk to me about it for a moment?

IVANOFF
But of course.

GIRL
Actually, it would be better in writing ... Oh, but in writing it would be even more impossible than now. Could you not look at me, because I'm ashamed of what I'm going to say, yet it's absolutely necessary that I say it to you? You are the only person who can advise me.

IVANOFF
Why me?

Je peux vous poser encore une question?

Bien sûr.

La poésie forme, ou bien est-ce qu'elle décore seulement?

Et bien, tout ce qui décore la vie est une formation.

Vous avez parlé d'une ivresse tout à l'heure—c'est la bière ou la vodka?

Ni l'une, ni l'autre. Sans rien.

J'ai jamais essayé ni l'une, ni l'autre. Qu'est-ce que c'est, l'ivresse de la vie?

Je crois que vous ... vous savez ce que c'est.

Moi? Oh! non, non. Moi, j'ai souvent le cafard, vous savez. Je pleure, c'est une honte. Vous n'avez pas le temps de m'en parler un moment?

Mais si.

Remarquez, vaudrait mieux le faire par écrit ... Oh! mais par écrit, ça irait encore plus mal que maintenant. Est-ce que vous pouvez ne pas me regarder, parce que j'ai honte de ce que je vais dire, mais il faut absolument que je vous le dise? Vous êtes le seul qui pouvez me conseiller.

Pourquoi moi?

poetry educates or only decorates. He replies: "Well, everything that decorates life is education."[3] When, finally, she asks for advice, she is unable to answer his challenge

GIRL
I don't know.   Je sais pas.

1′11.0″
68′01.5″

15.6

IVANOFF
Why me?   Pourquoi moi?

GIRL
I don't know.   *Je sais pas.*

IVANOFF
Don't you have friends? Teachers? Parents?   Vous n'avez pas de camarades? de maîtres?
                                                             de parents?

GIRL
Yes, I do.   *Si, j'en ai.*

IVANOFF
They aren't bad people, are they?   Ce ne sont pas de mauvaises gens?

GIRL
No, there are some who are good.   *Non, il y en a qui sont bons.*

IVANOFF
And intelligent?   Et intelligents?

GIRL
Yes, intelligent.   *Oui, intelligents.*

IVANOFF
Then why me? Have you read my books?   Alors pourquoi moi? Vous avez lu mes
                                                             livres?

GIRL
They explain them to us in class, but as for   *On nous les explique en classe, mais pour ce qui*
reading them, I haven't read very much.   *est de les lire, j'ai pas beaucoup lu.*

IVANOFF
Then you don't find it strange that it's me   Alors vous ne trouvez pas que c'est étrange
precisely that you want to   que ce soit à moi justement que vous vou-
                                                             lez

1′01.2″
69′02.6″

15.7   *talk to?*   *parler?*

"Why me?" She has not read his books; she has not read much at all. In the end she

GIRL
I thought that you were more courageous.

IVANOFF
It perhaps isn't a question of courage but of competence.

GIRL
Oh well then, it's better in writing. I'm going to leave.

(She turns her head and looks off left.)

Je croyais que vous étiez plus courageux.

Il ne s'agit peut-être pas de courage, mais de compétence.

Ben alors, il vaut mieux par écrit. Je vais m'en aller.

YOUNG WOMAN
And you—what have you

Et vous, qu'est-ce que vous

26.3″
69′28.9″

15.8

done all day long, since you're so terrific?

ROBERT
This morning I worked.

avez fait toute la journée, puisque vous êtes si fort?

Ce matin, j'ai travaillé.

does not ask her question, concluding that it would be better to write it.

On this remark Godard cuts to a one-shot of Robert writing (15.8), while the young woman offscreen questions him—a parallel to the one-shot (15.3) in which he questions her. Both interrogations reprise material from Sequence 6, specifically Juliette's meditation on the naming of colors. The young woman asks where Robert has

YOUNG WOMAN	
Where?	*Où ça?*
ROBERT	
My garage.	Mon garage.
YOUNG WOMAN	
Is it yours?	*Il est à vous?*
ROBERT	
No, it isn't mine.	Non, il est pas à moi.
YOUNG WOMAN	
Then why do you say "my"?	*Alors, pourquoi vous dites "mon"?*
ROBERT	
At the garage. You're right.	Au garage. Vous avez raison.

20.4″
69′49.3″

15.9

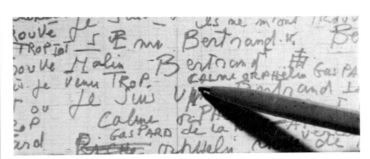

(A pen crosses out the word "venu.")

YOUNG WOMAN
No, but you're not listening to what I'm saying.   *Non, mais vous n'écoutez pas ce que je dis.*

3.9″
69′53.2″

15.10

ROBERT
Yes I am.   Si.

YOUNG WOMAN
No. How do you know it's a garage? Are you   *Non. Comment vous savez que c'est un garage?*
sure they didn't get the name wrong? Might it   *Vous êtes sûr qu'on ne s'est pas trompé de nom?*
be a swimming pool or a hotel?   *Que ça soit une piscine ou un hôtel?*

worked during the day. "My garage," he replies. Why does he say "my" if it isn't his? "At the garage. You're right," he admits, and Godard cuts to 15.9, his pen, in a parallel admission of error, crossing out the word "venu." The young woman presses her case: "How do you know it's a garage? Are you sure they didn't get the name wrong? Might it be a swimming pool or a hotel?" His answer is that things bear a certain

ROBERT
Ah! It's possible, yes. It could also be called   Ah! C'est possible, oui. Ça pourrait s'ap-
                                                     peler aussi

                                                                                    18.4″
                                                                                  70′11.6″

15.11   something else, yes.   autre chose, oui.

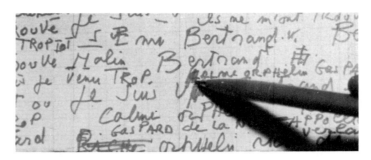

(A pen crosses out the word "calme.")

YOUNG WOMAN
Good. Exactly. What is it that causes things to   Bon. Ben justement. Qu'est-ce qui fait que les
bear a certain name?   choses portent un certain nom?

ROBERT
It's because one gives it to them.   C'est parce qu'on les leur donne.

YOUNG WOMAN
And   Et

                                                                                    10.1″
                                                                                  70′21.7″

15.12   who gives it to them?   qui leur donne?

Since you know people so well, do you know   Puisque vous connaissez si bien le monde, est-ce
yourself?   que vous vous connaissez vous-même?

ROBERT
Not very well, no!   Pas très bien, non!

BOUVARD
"Gilbert's face was slightly tensed.   "Le visage de Gilbert s'était légèrement crispé.
(Robert looks off left, possibly toward Bou-
vard.)

name "because one gives it to them." "Who gives it to them?" she asks; "Since you know people so well, do you know yourself?" His admission that he doesn't hints at further self-criticism on the director's part.

But what has her question about his self-knowledge to do with what precedes it? And what is Godard's purpose in rephrasing Juliette's earlier speculation about color names? The only answer I can suggest is the political point made by insisting that the garage is not in fact "his" and the girl's question to Ivanoff about morality under communism. I do not find this answer entirely convincing, particularly because it does not

	Martine perceived this	Martine s'en aperçut	13.8" 70'35.4"
15.13	and she blushed."	et elle rougit."	

"If the Hungarian success, established by dualism,
(A waiter enters, delivers food, exits.)
is an internal event, the birth of Italy and Germany interests Europe, especially Napoleon III."
WAITER
After the egg with mayonnaise, what will it be, Monsieur

"Si le succès des Hongrois, consacré par le dualisme,

est un événement intérieur, la naissance de l'Italie et de l'Allemagne intéresse l'Europe, plus spécialement Napoléon III."

Après l'oeuf mayonnaise, qu'est-ce que ce sera, Monsieur

13.6"
70'49.0"

15.14   *Bouvard?*
BOUVARD
Another egg with mayonnaise and a chocolate mousse.

Bouvard?

Un autre oeuf mayonnaise et une mousse au chocolat.

(Pécuchet is chewing.)
"In spite of myself, the fingers of both my hands fidgeted wildly. 'It's done, he's going to talk,' said a voice. The water stopped running; they

"Malgré moi, les doigts de mes deux mains s'agitèrent follement. 'Ça y est, il va parler,' dit une voix. L'eau s'arrêta de couler; on m'enleva

explain why the garage shouldn't be called a swimming pool or a hotel.

With shots 15.13 and 15.14 we return to Bouvard and Pécuchet, who, as in 15.2, are seated amid piles of books. Pécuchet busily writes, while Bouvard selects volumes at random and reads a few sentences aloud from each. The result is, as we hear, a perfectly meaningless hodgepodge of murder mysteries, political history, spy stories (including some sentences about water torture of the kind shown in *Le petit soldat* and *Pierrot*), travelogues, philosophy, and telephone numbers, in French, English, and Italian. Clearly, this is a joke about Godard's habits and methods,[4] particularly about the fondness he shares with other New Wave directors for quotation. In an interview published in December 1962 he said:

Our first films were all *films de cinéphile*—the work of film enthusiasts. One can make use of what one has already seen in the cinema to make deliberate references. This was true of me in particular. I thought in terms of purely cinematographic attitudes. For some shots I referred to scenes I remembered from Preminger, Cukor, etc. And the character played by Jean Seberg [in *Breathless*] was a continuation of her role in *Bonjour Tristesse*. I could have taken the last shot of Preminger's film and started after dissolving to a title, 'Three Years Later.' This is much the same sort of thing as my taste for quotation, which I still retain. Why should we be reproached for it? People in life quote as they please, so we have the right to quote as we please. Therefore I show people quoting, merely making sure that they quote what pleases me. In the notes I make of anything that might be of use for a film, I will add a quote from Dostoievsky if I like it. Why not? If you want to say something, there is only one solution, say it.[5]

Among the quotations in the present segment is that of the names of the two characters, taken from Flaubert's unfinished novel, *Bouvard et Pécuchet*. In Flaubert these characters, two stolid burghers, set about mastering one subject after another—agriculture, biology, anatomy, and so on—by reading books. They do not really understand what they read and their projects invariably end in disaster. The identity of Godard's characters is revealed, in the fashion of a punch line, near the end of the scene: a waiter, asking them what more they want to eat, addresses them by name. Bouvard orders another hard-boiled egg and a chocolate mousse. Pécuchet is already at work on

took the rag off of me. I breathed. In the shadows I saw the lieutenants and the captain, with cigarettes in their mouths,
(Pécuchet eats something.)
hit my belly with all their might to make it expel the absorbed water."
"However, thought is not only like a search and question directed
at not-thinking ... an adventure ..."
WAITER
And you, Monsieur Pécuchet, what do you want after the hard-boiled eggs?
PÉCUCHET
(Toward offscreen right:)
Me—
a "mystère."
BOUVARD
"Thought is in essence ..."
WAITER
There is no "mystère"!
BOUVARD
"... demanded by being.
(Pécuchet looks toward the waiter out of frame right, then out of frame left toward Bouvard.)
Thought is,
(Pécuchet looks at the camera and keeps looking at it.)

as thought, linked to the coming of being—being insofar as it is the unknown. Already being is destined for thought. Being is, insofar as it is the destination of thought ..."

de chiffon. Je respirais. Dans l'ombre, je voyais les lieutenants et le capitaine, cigarette aux lèvres,

frapper à tour de bras sur mon ventre pour me faire rejeter l'eau absorbée."
"Toutefois la pensée n'est pas seulement comme recherche et question dirigée
sur le non-penser ... une aventure ..."
Et vous, qu'est-ce que vous voulez, Monsieur Pécuchet, après les oeufs durs?

Moi,
un mystère.

"La pensée est dans son essence ..."

Y a pas de mystère!

"... revendiquée par l'être.

La pensée est,

comme pensée, liée à la venue de l'être—à l'être en tant qu'il est l'inconnu. Déjà l'être s'est destiné à la pensée. L'être est, en tant que le destin de la pensée ..."
53.6"
71'42.6"

a plate of French fries, sausages, and hard-boiled eggs when the waiter asks him what he wants for dessert. He replies "a *mystère*," which is a kind of cake. While Bouvard continues reading aloud, the waiter calls out "There is no *mystère*," whereupon Pécuchet stares astonished at the camera for a very long moment before the cut to 16.1. Part of the joke consists in the rotund figure of Pécuchet and the big meal he is consuming. Another part is the judgment "there is no 'mystery,' " following the transcription of all these bits of text. And still another part is that the dialogue is itself a quotation. In Chabrol's *Les bonnes femmes,* a not very well educated young woman is about to meet the more educated parents of her fiancé, who instructs her to manage the situation by repeating a few remarks about Michelangelo (an uncomprehending quotation like those here) and ordering a *mystère.* She does the first and when she tries to do the second, the waiter tells her "il n'y a pas de mystère," whereupon she is speechless, her instructions having run out. As for Pécuchet, *he* may be speechless in part because he perceives that "real life," where, as Godard tells us, people quote as they please, has itself turned into a quotation.

Even on first viewing, it is obvious that the theme of this sequence is writing. What may not be so obvious is that all three parts of it end in failures: the young woman will not speak Robert's line; Ivanoff will not hear the girl's question; and the two men are revealed to be Bouvard and Pécuchet, archetypes of incompetence. Insofar as the sequence constitutes a reflection by the film on its own methods—the method of direction, the process of asking questions, the reliance on quotation—the burden of this reflection is critical. This, I take it, is the beginning of the process which at the end of the film Godard describes as going back to zero.

Sequence 16

16.1   [Silence.]

[Midway through the shot, a straight cut
to dialogue.]

BLACK WOMAN

Well, are you coming? You know very well that   *Alors, tu viens? Tu sais bien que j'ai pas que*
I have other things   *ça*

$$\frac{5.4''}{71'48.0''}$$

16.2   [Actual sound.]

    to do!   *à faire!*

(She enters through a door, crosses left out
of the frame, reenters left. Pan right and tilt
up with her.)

Hurry up!   Dépêche-toi!

(A black man enters as she takes off her
pullover and crosses toward the camera.)

The book title *Sociology of the Novel* (16.1) applies as much to what precedes it as to what follows—namely, a West Indian couple preparing to make love in a basement of

(She crosses out of the frame at lower left.
He crosses a step right and looks off
through the door.)

BLACK MAN

(To her:)

Why not there?   Pourquoi pas là?

BLACK WOMAN

Don't you see? There isn't room!   *Tu vois bien? Y a plus de place!*

(He follows her off, removing his coat as he
goes.)

15.1″
72′03.1″

16.3   [The sound of the previous shot continues
for two or three seconds, then a straight
cut to silence.]

(The red car on the right slowly pulls up to
the pump.)
[As the driver gets out, actual sound of the
following shot, loud traffic noise, fades up.]

24.7″
72′27.8″

the *grand ensemble* (16.2). This shot dramatizes a sentence in the Vimenet article and closes off the series concerned with immigrants. The action appears to be an example of something—but what? Are the man and woman lovers? Or are they, as her opening line suggests, client and prostitute? Why are they in the basement? In what sense is this the "sociology of the novel"?

Following is a ghostly, exquisitely composed shot of a gas station, 16.3 (the comparison of action and color—red in particular—at the cut 16.2/16.3, along with the spilling of the sound of 16.2 into the head of 16.3, makes 16.3 seem a joke about the man in 16.2 getting "serviced"), then two shots (actually two takes) of Juliette's Aus-

16.4

(Hold until the Austin emerges from behind the bushes, then pan right with it
down the road. As it turns right, its turn
signal flashing, and drives past the camera,
Juliette and Robert are visible inside.)

15.1″
72′42.9″

16.5 [At the cut a very fast fade to silence.]

(Hold until the Austin emerges from behind the bushes, then pan right with it
down the road. As it begins its right turn,
the commentary starts.)

COMMENTARY 26

**There is no need of fortuitous events in
order to photograph and kill people.**

(The Austin drives, as before, past the camera. The cut at the tail occurs earlier in the
action than in the case of the preceding
shot.)

**Il n'y a pas besoin d'événements fortuits
pour photographier et tuer le monde.**

tin speeding along and making the turn to the service road that leads to the apartment complex (16.4 and 16.5), a clerk in a Prisunic supermarket (16.6), and finally the Austin receding into the roads of the *ensemble* (16.7). This group of shots has a foreboding, almost apocalyptic tone, resulting from the contrast of the preternatural silence and sunlight of 16.3 with the violent traffic noise and overcast sky of 16.4, the replay of this action in silence (16.5), then the abrupt, aggressively loud, and threatening super-

12.3″
72′55.2″

16.6 [Very loud ambient sound of a supermarket.]

(Groceries move past the clerk as she rings them up. She glances twice at the camera.)

6.9″
73′02.1″

16.7 [Loud sound of car motor rapidly diminishing in volume.]

(The car recedes into the apartment complex.)

10.5″
73′12.6″

16.8 [The sound of the previous shot continues at a low level.]

market ambience with its Musak and bargain announcements (16.6) and the tilted framing and rifle-like recession of the whining motor in 16.7. In this context the quite ordinary smile of the supermarket clerk and the cartoon cat in the poster behind her take on a sinister, grotesque air, and the dizzying camera tilt in the following shot makes it seem that the world is coming unhinged.

The silence of 16.5 (the second take of the speeding Austin) cues the single, cryptic sentence of Commentary 26: "There is no need of fortuitous events in order to photograph and kill people." Does the accompanying image, with its hint of an impending accident like those in *Orphée,* exemplify a fortuitous event? Insofar as it does, it brings to mind the accident, also involving a small red car, that kills two of the principals at the end of *Contempt,* as well as the arbitrary deaths that conclude several other Godard films, notably *Masculine Feminine* and *Vivre sa vie.* In this reading "fortuitous events" means something like "narrative events" and the sentence thus seems a precursor to the title that ends *Weekend:* "Fin de conte, fin de cinéma."

Godard's phrasing in Commentary 26 specifies that even without the fortuitous events of narrative, to photograph *le monde* is still to kill it. What can this mean? Partly, I think, it is a statement of the received idea that photography is an aggressive act. English, for instance, speaks of "taking" someone's picture and identifies filming with "shooting" (which in French is *tourner,* "turning," a carryover from the days when cameras were hand-cranked). This idea informs Godard's characterization of photography in Sequence 14. Indeed, the copula "photograph and kill" precisely describes the association of "machine-gun fire" with the still photographs of 14.16–14.18. As if to confirm this, the tilted frame of 14.10 recurs in 16.7 (this is perhaps what Godard means in *Camera-Eye* by promising to allow Vietnam to invade Paris).

This explanation does not account for the generality claimed by Godard's phrasing. The association of the still photographs with the gunfire in 14.16–14.18 is specific in that both gunner and photographer are, if not the American John Faubus, then at least American (in this connection the doubt cast on Faubus's nationality is significant). Is the association "photograph and kill" meant of photography in general? Does it preserve the distinction drawn in Sequence 14 between still photography (*photographier*) and film (*filmer*)? Here Godard does not resolve these questions so much as designate their importance in the shots and scenes that follow. The power of the camera to "shoot down" can be felt in the immediately following picture of the Prisunic cashier and the projectile sound accompanying the next, the receding automobile. It is dramatized explicitly when in 17.2 Christophe returns the camera's "shooting" by firing

(Very short hold, then pan left.)

COMMENTARY 27

To rediscover the b, a, ba of existence.   **Retrouver le b, a, ba de l'existence.**

(Short hold.)

2.3″
73′14.9″

16.9 [Actual sound throughout; at the head of the shot outdoor ambient noise fades up quickly, mixing with the actual sound.]

JULIETTE

... nor when. I remember only that it happened. Maybe that isn't important.

... ni quand. Je me souviens seulement que c'est arrivé. Peut-être que ça n'a pas d'importance.

It was while I was walking with the guy from the Metro who was taking me to the

C'était pendant que je marchais avec le type du métro qui m'emmenait à l'hôtel. C'était

his toy gun at it and in a more complex way by the 360-degree pan of 16.9.

Shot 16.8 shows part of a sign, framing the letters "AB," then, after a short pan left, "BA." Godard's accompanying phrase, "to rediscover the b, a, ba of existence," explains what we see as a progression from the alphabetical ("b, a") to the syllabic ("ba"). The metaphor thus constituted recalls that of the car-wash sign (12.19) but is logically anterior to it, being—in the vocabulary of linguistics—"distinctive" rather than "significative." The linguistic basis of this metaphor in turn recalls, and is in turn logically anterior to, Juliette's paradigm "je, me, moi." This retreat from the paradigm to the word, the word to the syllable, and the syllable to the letter corresponds to the movement backward in the alphabet in 16.8. Both dramatize the commitment of this part of the film to revision, review, and return toward "zero."

As one of the film's numerous shots of parts of signs, 16.8 is remarkable for cutting off the process of our reading at an earlier point, before we have glimpsed the "drowning" significations (as in the CARWASH sign) of the letters alone, of the words and nonwords they form, of the whole that the image implies but does not (will not? cannot?) show. Here no letters stand isolated, no words are formed, no whole is implied. But as in Juliette's progression "je, me, moi, tout le monde," we sense the link between these elements of "existence" and the whole of the "monde" she again speaks of in 16.9; moreover, we understand that getting from one to the other, though possible, is problematical.

The existence of the link between the elements and the whole is asserted by the pans in shots 16.8 and 16.9, between which the difference is perhaps less consequential than it appears on first viewing. In 16.8 the pan left is short and stops soon; instead of giving a greater sense of the whole (whatever that may be), it intensifies the fragmentariness and puzzle. At the same time, it represents a turning point—or rather, a return to a point from which to start—a genuine, if tiny, movement from letter to syllable. (Is this the beginning of the "new language" which, as Juliette says in 6.4, "will have

hotel. It was a funny feeling. I thought about it all day long. The feeling of my connections with the world.

(She looks up, then around right. The camera begins a 360-degree pan right.)

All of a sudden, I had the impression that I was the world

un drôle de sentiment. J'y ai pensé toute la journée. Le sentiment de mes liens avec le monde.

Tout à coup, j'ai eu l'impression que j'étais le monde

and that the world was me. It would take pages and pages to describe that. Or volumes and volumes.

et que le monde était moi. Il faudrait des pages et des pages pour décrire ça. Ou des volumes et des volumes.

The landscape is

(She reappears in the frame.)

similar to a face.

(The pan finishes. Hold.)

It was tempting to say: "I simply see a face with a peculiar expression." But . . . that doesn't mean that it's an extraordinary expression or that you will try to describe it. Perhaps one wants to say, uh . . . : "It's this, it's that. She looks like Chekov's Natasha,

(She smiles.)

Le paysage, c'est

pareil qu'un visage.

On était tenté de dire: "je vois simplement un visage avec une expression particulière." Mais . . . ça veut pas dire que c'est une expression extraordinaire ni que vous allez essayer de la décrire. Peut-être on a envie de dire, euh. . . : "c'est ceci, c'est cela. Elle ressemble à Natacha de Tchékov,

to be constructed"?) In 16.9 the pan right purports to illustrate Juliette's "liens avec le monde," her "connections with the world," moving from her through a 360-degree inspection of the *grand ensemble* (here all that there is of "le monde"). The shot is large-scale, the pan (inherently an inclusive and sweeping figure in Techniscope) long and, within its terms, complete, even a designation of completeness. Insofar as there is a parallel between the two pans, it affirms the continuity of the elemental links between "b, a" and "ba" with Juliette's "liens avec le monde" and (therefore) with their grammatical articulation: "je, me, moi."

While the pan in 16.9 may signify completeness (a definitive inventory of *liens*), the shot itself has the air of being quite empty. Empty of what? To begin with, as Cavell points out, of us. Juliette is talking to us, but when the camera turns around, it "turns out" we are not there. Although this is of course inevitable in such a pan, it is not inevitable that a pan should be used to make the point. To see this, we have only to think of how Godard deals with the issue in other films of the period. In *Pierrot le fou,* Anna Karina turns to the camera while Belmondo is driving and speaks to it; when he asks to whom she is speaking she replies: "Les spectateurs." In *La chinoise,* when Jean-Pierre Léaud denies the influence of the camera, Godard, as I recounted earlier, cuts to a shot of it. In 16.9 there is, opposite Juliette's *regard,* neither camera nor spectators. Secondly, the shot is empty of any sort of thing not present in the initial framing of Juliette: the pan turns up nothing but more buildings, more windows, more walls; as it progresses, we recognize that we are seeing nothing new, that the meaning of "liens" is diminished, not enriched. It points toward environmental or sociological terms of explanation, but winds up conveying some doubt about where to locate these terms. Out there? We have, after all, seen the *grand ensemble* before. The pan across it therefore carries an interrogatory inflection: *Are* these the *liens? Is* this the *monde? Are*

[Ambient noise, including children's voices, begins a crescendo.]

or else she's the sister of Flaherty's Nanook."

[The crescendo finishes; the noise remains at a high level.]

But it would seem more accurate to say: "One cannot describe this with words." At the same time, it seems to me that the expression on my face must represent something, something that can be separated from the general outline—I mean, uh . . .
from the kind of outline that forms it.

[Automobile horns cover the three preceding words.]

Yes. It was as if it were possible to say at the outset: "This face has a peculiar expression . . ." And then . . . And then? In fact, it's this one. For example, fatigue . . .

ou alors c'est la soeur de Nanouk de Flaherty."

Mais, il serait plus juste de dire: "on ne peut pas décrire cela avec des mots." Pourtant il me semble que l'expression de mon visage doit représenter quelque chose, quelque chose qui peut être détaché du dessin général—je veux dire, euh . . .
de l'espèce de forme dessinée qui le forme.

Oui. C'était comme si c'était possible de dire d'abord: "ce visage a une expression particulière . . ." Et ensuite . . . Et ensuite? En fait, c'est celle-ci. Par exemple, la fatigue . . .

2'55.0"
76'10.0"

16.10 [Voice over, sounds of children at play in the background.]

OLD WOMAN
I used to live in the 16th Arrondisse-

Je demeurais dans le XVIᵉ. Et puis notre

the terms of explanation those of the visible?

Once the pan is completed and returns to Juliette, her text mirrors the emptiness of it. First, her reflections become increasingly fragmentary, going from topic to topic, until finally their connectedness vanishes altogether: we have no means of knowing for certain what "fatigue" is an "example" of. Second, she lapses into inaudibility, overwhelmed by the ambient noise that cuts her "lien" with us. Finally, her "lien" with the director, to whom she is obviously listening, also starts to fail: when she cocks her head and says "And then . . . And then?" we infer—partly on the basis of Godard's willful intensification of the noise track a moment before—that she is simply having trouble hearing him.

Juliette's text in 16.9 begins as a paraphrase of her earlier speech "I was the world and . . . the world was me." As such, it both invites us to reconsider what she previously said and at the same time makes the claim that the film has revised, and gone forward from, the terms that speech implies. This strategy, though daring, feels more than a bit desperate; it is as if, amid the confusion, cul-de-sacs, and repetitions of the film's second half, Godard were recognizing the need for a clear, simple yardstick in order to show not only *how* the film has advanced but *that* it has. This would perhaps not be the case if the inaudibility, lost words, and fragments that blur the end of the text did not occur just as Juliette is extending and elaborating what she said earlier, adding what appears to be crucial new material.

Despite this, several important elements of the revision are clear. First, Juliette's speech is addressed to the camera, synchronized with the image rather than over it. Thus Godard abandons, even denies, the earlier claim that the image renders Juliette's subjectivity. The address, interrupted as it is by the lengthy pan, relates to the film's developing concern with the camera axis, the locus of the camera's power "to photograph and kill." She reports a feeling, but the feeling does not control the organization of the sequence. Rather it becomes a text, a testimony, identified as such by the film. Second, and more importantly, this text is referred to physical surroundings very different from those of 8.27–8.29. These vastly alter the meaning of her word "monde," which no longer signifies a sunlit, tree-lined street, a rhythm, a scene packed with metaphoric resonances, but the gray concrete environment of the *grand ensemble*. Her connections with this world have nothing to do with a transcendental experience of integration but with the simple fact that this is where she lives. The emphasis placed on this fact derives, I think, from Godard's quest "to rediscover the b, a, ba of existence" as well as from his repudiation of "fortuitous events." Because of it, the "feeling" that Juliette reports is designated as an idea that would originate in such a setting—one might even say, in the illusions that such a setting encourages and depends on. It is, in the vocabulary of the film, an "idée" (16.14). As a result, her text becomes less lyrical, more open this time to banal detail such as: "It was while I was walking with the guy from the Metro who was taking me to the hotel" (the "remembered" images, 8.27–8.29, fail to show him). In short, Juliette reinstates the connection made in the double sense of "elle" in the film's title, a connection that to this point has been almost exclusively the director's responsibility.

There is another way in which Juliette has encroached upon the director's position here. The camera begins its pan in 16.9 only when prompted by her glance screen-right after the phrase "The feeling of my connections with the world," as if the demonstration of these connections was now also her responsibility. This too is a revision. For if 16.9 declares, like Commentary 2, that "she lives here," then the pan asserts that

ment. And then our apartment was sold. They stuck us here.

appartement a été vendu. On nous a collés ici.

6.5″
76′16.5″

16.11 [Bombardment noise.]

It's not at all the same, is it!   C'est pas tout à fait pareil, hein!
(The shot begins with Robert one-third of the distance from the right side of the frame. He crosses leftward, stops, lights a cigarette.)
JULIETTE
What are we going to do?   Qu'est-ce qu'on va faire?
(Juliette enters right, crosses leftward. By the last frame of the shot she is where Robert was in the first frame:)

9.6″
76′26.1″

16.12

the turning of her head *has* importance, the importance of direction (in both senses of the word). Indeed, she introduces her speech with the qualification "Maybe that isn't important." Moreover, the phrase with which she in turn introduces the pan and announces what it will illustrate echoes the content and vocabulary of the director's own declaration in Commentary 9 that he is examining "the life of the city and its inhabitants and the links [*liens*] that unite them." In recognizing the parallel between the pans of 16.8 and 16.9, we must also recognize the parallel between the speeches that set them in motion and hence between the speakers, Godard and Juliette. This, I think, is what makes it seem right when a few lines later she lets down her character mask and makes a face in admitting—in the third person, as if quoting the director—that she looks like "Chekov's Natasha"—virtually the only moment in the film when an adult actor seems natural in the ordinary way we understand that word.

Many of the remaining shots of the sequence relate to its concern with revision. Shot 16.12 repeats the action of 16.11: Juliette follows Robert's entry into the frame ("Free Entry," as the previous shot has it), and when she gets to where he was at the head of the shot, Godard cuts to 16.12, literally replacing her with him and replaying the action, this time beyond what is shown at the tail of 16.11. In the background of this rather too clever ballet is a wall of tattered posters. The only one of these that is intact reads "Peace in Vietnam: let us act, let us demand." The similarity between the framing of these shots and that at the head and tail of 16.9 argues that the description of Juliette's "monde" must include Vietnam. The bombardment sounds that accompany the shots support our inference that Juliette's question "What are we going to do?" refers at least partly to the poster (only partly because it is also the beginning of a dialogue continued in 17.3). Robert's answer, judging by the cut that precedes it (16.11/16.12) as well as by many other details in this part of the film (especially the

(When the shot begins, Robert is exactly in the position Juliette reached in the last frame of the previous shot. He crosses leftward.)

ROBERT

We'll start over again.   On recommencera.

(He stops, as before, and lights a cigarette. Juliette enters right, crosses leftward, takes the cigarette from his mouth as she passes him, and exits left. Hold.)

[About one second before the shot ends there is a straight cut to the sound of the next shots: a voice-over interview with the sounds of children at play in the background.]

12.0″
76′38.1″

16.13

CHILDREN

Ah! me too, hm! We have a lot of fun here; we have a lot of fun; it's a laugh.   Ah! moi aussi, hein! On se marre bien là; on se marre bien; on rigole bien.

3.4″
76′41.5″

16.14

But there isn't much to play with.   Mais y a peu de jeux.

3.2″
76′44.7″

concluding line of the script), is also Godard's: "We'll start over again."

As for the other repetitions: the bombardment noise with 16.11 and 16.12 repeats that of 2.5–2.9; shot 16.13 repeats 4.4, the woman's face reflected in the window; and 16.14 is "idées" again. With 16.14 are snatches of interviews with children like that of the Algerian boy in Sequence 13, where this shot also occurs. Shots 16.15,

16.15

There. They should put in some things to play with. Down there, there are only some ladders, but you break a

Voilà. Ils devraient mettre des jeux. Là-bas, y a que des échelles, mais on se casse une

3.4″
76′48.1″

16.16

leg.
(Laughter.)
That's it. There used to be a

jambe.

C'est ça. Y'avait un

2.8″
76′50.9″

16.17

merry-go-round, but they took it away. There used to be swings, but they aren't there any more.

manège, mais ils l'ont enlevé. Y'avait des balançoires, mais elles sont plus là.

3.4″
76′54.3″

16.17, and 16.18 resemble those used as cutaways in the secretary's speech in Sequence 10, and with 16.10 we have a testimony like hers about a "free entry" into this environment: "I used to live in the 16th Arrondissement. And then our apartment was sold. They stuck us here. It's not at all the same, is it!" The children also complain: there is nothing to do here, there ought to be a playground. "The landscape is similar

Yeah, we have lots of fun. You have to find something to do.

Ouais, on se marre bien. Faudrait trouver quelque chose à faire.

$$\frac{5.7''}{77'00.0''}$$

to a face," Juliette proposes at the conclusion of the pan in 16.9. She speculates that although what you see in a face cannot be described with words, still it must represent something. If you can say that her face shows fatigue, then these voices report at least part of what can be said about the meaning of the landscape that resembles it.

Sequence 17

17.1 [The sound of the previous shot continues for six frames, then actual sound fades up.]

(Juliette and Robert enter a hallway through a door and cross right to their apartment door. Pan left with them, then hold.)

JULIETTE
OK, you go look for the children.   Bon, tu vas chercher les enfants.

ROBERT
OK, OK.   Bon, bon.

(He turns and crosses out left.)

JULIETTE
(To him as he is going:)
And the key?   Et la clé?

ROBERT
OK, OK.   *Bon, bon.*

JULIETTE
(Catches sight of Christophe sitting on the steps, smiles.)
So there you are.   Tiens, tu es là, toi.

(Pan right and tilt down with her as she sits beside him, gives him a kiss.)
What are you doing?   Qu'est-ce que tu fais?

CHRISTOPHE
I'm doing my homework.   Je fais mes devoirs.

In 17.1 Christophe and Juliette read aloud—at tedious and unnecessary length, I think—the composition he is writing as a homework assignment. The theme of this

JULIETTE
What's it about?

CHRISTOPHE
Friendship. I'll read it to you.

JULIETTE
Yes.

CHRISTOPHE
"This year in the new school they have put all us boys and girls together; this is why we belong to a mixed class.

(As he reads, Juliette takes her notebook and pen from her handbag.)
"Yes and no, friendship between girls and boys is possible and desirable. Yes, because certain girls are very nice, very honest. Maryse, Martine, Ghislaine, Roseline. With these girls, we have calm conversations.

(Juliette writes something down, then puts her notebook away.)
" 'Hello kid,' I say to Claudie. 'Hello,' she answers, 'how are you?' Then we begin to talk until we don't agree. 'Quiet,' he says. 'Yes, but that's what you said to me.'

" 'Calm down.' In this case, I give in and we go on talking. Here it—this friendship—is desirabl . . . able, since the girls are nice. With Maryse and Roseline we have con . . . we have more serious conversations. 'What answer did you find for the problem?' asked Roseline, uh . . . uh . . . 'H . . .' "

JULIETTE
Wait.
(She takes his notebook; he picks up a

C'est sur quoi?

La camaraderie. Je vais te le lire.

Oui.

"Cette année, dans le nouveau lycée, on nous a tous réunis garçons et filles; ce qui fait que nous appartenons à une classe mixte.

"Oui et non, la camaraderie entre filles et garçons est possible et souhaitable. Oui, parce que certaines filles sont très gentilles, très franches. Maryse, Martine, Ghislaine, Roseline. Avec ces filles, nous avons des dialogues calmes.

" 'Bonjour kid,' dis-je à Claudie. 'Bonjour,' répond-elle, 'ça va?' Ensuite, nous nous mettons à parler jusqu'à ce que nous ne soyons pas d'accord. 'Silence,' dit-il. 'Oui, mais tu m'as dit ça.'

" 'Calme-toi.' Dans ce cas j'acquiesce et nous continuons à parler. Ici, elle—cette camaraderie—est souhaitabl . . . able, les filles étant gentilles. Avec Maryse et Roseline, nous avons des con . . . nous avons des conversations plus sérieuses. 'Combien as-tu trouvé au problème?' demanda Roseline, euh . . . euh . . . 'H . . .' "

Attends.

composition—whether friendship between boys and girls is possible and desirable—and its account of the difficulties boys and girls have in talking together of course resemble themes of the film as a whole and of the dialogue between Robert and the young woman in the Elysées-Marbeuf in particular. When Juliette leaves to go into the apart-

plastic tommy gun.)

" 'H'OB = AOB.' 'No.

$$A'OB = \frac{AOB'}{2}.'$$

(Robert approaches the apartment door with Solange, who is whining. Christophe aims his gun at Juliette.)

" 'OK, whatever you like!'

(Juliette waves to Solange. Christophe aims his gun at Solange.)

"There too, this friendship is possible and desirable. No, because certain other girls are mean, have a shifty look . . ."

ROBERT

(As he and Solange enter the apartment:)

Juliette, are you coming?

JULIETTE

Yes, yes.

". . . those who wear glasses. In this case, we do not talk calmly; we argue. 'Oh!' she goes, 'you're impossible.' "

I have to get up.

(She gives him the notebook and gets up.)

CHRISTOPHE

Please, mama, may I go on?

JULIETTE

OK.

(She goes off into the apartment.)

CHRISTOPHE

Wait.

" 'Brrr!' she goes, 'you're impossible.' I don't say anything but I give her a kick. She throws a ball at my face and it stops there because the teacher punishes her. In this case friendship is not possible and not desirable. I'd rather be in the electric chair with my feet in a glass of water.

" 'H'OB = AOB.' 'Non.

$$A'OB = \frac{AOB'}{2}.'$$

" 'Bon, comme tu veux!'

"Là aussi, cette camaraderie est possible et souhaitable. Non, parce que certaines autres sont méchantes, ont le regard fuyant . . ."

Juliette, tu viens?

Oui, oui.

". . . celles qui ont des lunettes. Dans ce cas, nous ne conversons pas calmement; on se dispute. 'Ah!' fait-elle, 'tu es impossible.' "

Il faut me lever.

Je peux continuer, maman, s'il te plaît?

Bon.

Attends.

" 'Brrr!' fait-elle, 'tu es impossible.' Je ne dis rien, mais je lui donne un coup de pied. Elle me lance une boule sur la figure et ça s'arrête là, parce que le professeur la punie. Dans ce cas, le camaraderie n'est pas possible et pas souhaitable. Je préférerais être sur la chaise électrique, les pieds dans un verre d'eau.

2'19.5″
79'19.6″

17.2

"These mean and nice girls are, all the same, clean and on the whole nice—that's what calms me down a bit."

"Ces méchantes et gentilles filles sont, quand même, propres et dans l'ensemble gentilles, ce qui me calme un peu."

ment, Christophe asks whether he can continue alone, and soon after he begins Godard cuts to a closer shot of him (17.2). To whom is he now reading? To himself, we as-

(He puts the notebook down, picks up his
plastic gun and shoots it twice at the camera.)

25.4″
79′45.0″

17.3 [The sound of the gun at the tail of the
previous shot spills over into the first
twelve frames, then actual sound.]

(As Juliette puts something down on the
table out of frame bottom, Robert enters
left and crosses rightward to her.)

ROBERT
Ouf! we've arrived!

Ouf! on est arrivé!

(He puts something down and goes out the
way he came in.)

JULIETTE
Arrived where?

Arrivé où?

(She unpacks the groceries: a loaf of bread,
boxes, and so on.)

ROBERT
Home.

Chez nous.

JULIETTE
And afterward, what are we going to do?

Et après, qu'est-ce qu'on va faire?

ROBERT
Sleep. What's gotten into you?

Dormir. Qu'est-ce qui te prend?

sume, until at the end of the shot he puts down his notebook, picks up his plastic tommy gun, and fires it twice—directly at the camera. This is a disturbing moment, not least because it is unpleasant to be shot at with a plastic machine gun. In one sense Christophe is firing at the camera, making us aware that it has been shooting (photographing and killing?) him. But we also feel that he is shooting us, the audience of his reading, contradicting without reason the hopes he has held out for friendship.

The dialogue between Robert and Juliette in the kitchen (17.3) continues that of 16.11 and 16.12, even quoting it verbatim: "What are we going to do?" "We'll start

JULIETTE
And afterward?   Et après?

ROBERT
(Appears briefly through the doorway cross-
ing leftward.)
We'll wake up.   *On se réveillera.*

JULIETTE
And afterward?   Et après?

ROBERT
Same thing. We'll start over again.   *Pareil. On recommencera.*
(She opens the cabinet and puts away the
boxes.)
We'll work. We'll eat.   *On travaillera. On mangera.*

JULIETTE
And afterward?   Et après?

ROBERT
(Enters, faces her, takes off his dark
glasses.)
I don't know.   Je sais pas.
(He puts on clear glasses.)

Die.   Mourir.

JULIETTE
And   Et

                                                                        43.6″
                                                                        80′28.6″

17.4   [Quiet ambience continues from the previ-
       ous shot, including soft tapping—perhaps
       the noise of eyeglasses being folded.]
           afterward?   *après?*

over again." Vietnam is thus in the background of the daily cycle of activities that Robert lists, a cycle that is also the organizing principle of the film's narrative line: come home, sleep, wake up, work, eat. Robert rehearses this list in response to Juliette's repeated question, "And afterward?" and when she insists on it (on the wall behind her is a 1966 calendar), he finally concedes: "I don't know. Die." Once more she asks "And afterward?" and Godard substitutes for Robert's reply the view we had in

(The numbers advance, at first slowly, then faster, from 00,00 to 01,15.)

$$\frac{6.4''}{80'35.0''}$$

17.5 [Actual sound.]

CHRISTOPHE

(Dives in from left onto the bed.)

Mama, please, may I play a little longer or read?

JULIETTE

Yes, yes.

CHRISTOPHE

Thank you, mama.

JULIETTE

(As she speaks, Christophe jumps on the bed and sings.)

What is it to know something?

(Calls out:)

Robert, bring me Solange, please.

(To the camera:)

Maman, s'il te plaît, est-ce que je peux jouer un petit peu ou lire?

Oui, oui.

Merci, maman.

Savoir quelque chose, c'est quoi?

Robert, amène-moi Solange, s'il te plaît.

To show my eyes. I know they're my eyes because I see with them. I know they're not my knees or some other thing because I've been told that.

Montrer mes yeux. Je sais que ce sont mes yeux parce que je vois avec. Je sais que ce ne sont pas mes genoux ou autre chose, parce qu'on me l'a dit.

12.32 of the franc counter on the gasoline pump, now at zero and hesitantly starting, then racing ahead to 01,15.

This shot has a complex meaning. Undeniably, the zero signifies the "logical and mysterious" day of death and the subsequent progression of figures, the afterlife. Behind this signification lies not only the syntagmatic placement of the shot as the answer to Juliette's final question, but the association made in 12.32 of the moving figures with passing time ("16 h 45"). In addition, the shot touches on the theme of returning to zero; like 16.13, it is one of the numerous repetitions and revisions of the film's second half, and moreover it is one that, like 16.8, outlines a retreat: 12.32 begins with the counter at 12,90 and 17.4 at 00,00. This retreat anticipates the concluding words of the film about being reduced to zero and having to begin again from there.

Amid this metaphoric density it is perhaps easy to forget that what the shot literally shows is, as the context of 12.32 stresses, a money counter in motion, representing the act of spending and consuming. As such, it confers a retrospective importance on the seemingly incidental fact that as Juliette asks her questions she is putting away newly bought groceries. The counter, as it were, measures the expense that these represent, which in turn marks and measures the daily cycle that Robert describes. The reference made by the moving figures to death and the afterlife is, therefore, an ironic one. Death is not, or is not only, the existential fact defined in Sequence 8 by the attributes "logical and mysterious," but the metaphoric term for a condition with a social and economic cause (as, for example, in the sentence "Living people are often already dead"). This permits us to say that it is not only because Marina Vlady is following Brecht's dicta that Juliette does not look very animated. The film acknowledges this condition as other than normal when in 16.9 she smiles, then insists that the expression on her face "must represent something" and when at the beginning of Sequence 18 she tells us: "To define oneself in a single word? Not yet dead!"

As Juliette puts the children to bed in 17.5, she speculates on what it means to know something. In doing so, she recapitulates two questions implied in Sequence 6: how does one perceive, and how does one name what is perceived? In 6.6 she reports that she knows her sweater is blue because she sees that it is. Saying this, as she explains, depends on not confusing blue with green. In the present case, the implied questions concern the means rather than the objects of her vision. Yet she knows what her eyes are in just the way she knows the color of her sweater, "because I see with them." As for the names of these organs, she declares: "I know they're not my knees or some other thing because I've been told that." This answer repeats what Robert tells the young woman in 15.11: things bear a certain name because one gives it to them. In its relation to these earlier texts, Juliette's monologue is clearly part of Godard's efforts

(To Christophe:)
Stay still a bit, listen!

CHRISTOPHE
Yes, mama.

JULIETTE
(To the camera:)
How would it be if I hadn't been told that?
And to live then . . .

(Robert enters from left, carrying Solange,
who is crying. He hands her to Juliette and
kisses her as she says:)

SOLANGE
Where is papa?

JULIETTE
(Holding Solange:)
He's not here. Listen;
(Robert exits left, carrying Christophe's
gun.)

we're going to sleep now. Don't you . . .
don't you want to go to sleep with Christophe?

Reste tranquille un peu, écoute!

Oui, maman.

Comment ce serait si on me l'avait pas dit?
Et vivre alors . . .

Où il est papa?

Il est pas là. Ecoute;

on va faire dodo maintenant. Tu veux pas
. . . tu veux pas faire dodo avec Christophe?

1′07.2″
81′42.2″

17.6 [Solange's cries continue over the cut, then
actual sound.]

ROBERT

(He is seated at his shortwave radio. He
puts on his earphones, opens his notebook,
uncaps his red pen.)
If Hitler came, I'd shoot him down. How
can I say that? Because I'd wait for him.

(During the preceding sentence, Robert
picks up Christophe's toy tommy gun and
aims it toward the kitchen.)

Si Hitler arrivait, je lui tirerais dessus. Comment je peux dire ça? Parce que je l'attendrais.

at review and revision. But it is not so clear where her remarks lead or that they differ substantially from what was said before.

Robert, seated at his shortwave radio in 17.6, takes up the thread of Juliette's

And as soon as he comes in, I shoot him down.
(He fires, puts the gun down, turns to look at the camera,

then turns back to his radio and notebook.)
No, I don't know where he is.
(He writes.)
When I don't know, I imagine.
(He writes.)
How do I manage to imagine something when I don't know where it is?
(He writes, adjusts a knob on the short-wave radio. He looks at the camera.)
No, I don't know if he still exists.
(He turns back toward his radio.)
Yes, maybe I am confusing reality and thought.
(He looks at the camera.)
Yes, yes, I'd be tempted to say that.
(He turns away, writes.)
That since there do not always exist real objects that can guarantee the truth . . .

(He looks at the camera, then away.)
the truth of our thoughts, what we think is not the real,
(Juliette enters screen right from the kitchen. She is framed so that we see her body but not her face.)
it's a phantom of the real.

Et dès qu'il entre, je lui tire dessus.

Non, je ne sais pas où il est.

Quand je ne sais pas, j'imagine.

Comment je fais pour imaginer quelque chose quand je ne sais pas où elle est?

Non, je ne sais pas s'il existe encore.

Oui, peut-être que je confonds la réalité et la pensée.

Oui, oui, je serais tenté de dire ça.

Que puisque il n'existe pas toujours d'objets réels qui puissent garantir la vérité . . .

la vérité de nos pensées, ce n'est pas le réel que nous pensons,

c'est un fantôme du réel.

speculation: "If Hitler came, I'd shoot him down ... No, I don't know where he is. When I don't know, I imagine." When in 14.14 Juliette imagines an absent person, one who indeed might be dead, Godard shows a photograph of a Vietnamese, and when in 14.19 she thinks of another absent person, Robert, Godard renders this thought as a cut. Consequently, the subject of Robert's meditation, being a continuation of hers, appears in some rather obscure sense to be the cinema. For example, his question "How do I manage to imagine something when I don't know where it is?" makes sense asked of cinema but not of thought. We can of course have a mental image of something—Hitler, in Robert's example—without knowing where it is, but to make a film image we need more. Is cinema knowing or imagining? Reality or thought? If it were not for Juliette's speculation in Sequence 14, we should be tempted to assume the former, but especially in the second half of the film Godard has been at pains to show how the film image is implicated in "idées." Robert puts this as follows: "Yes, maybe I am confusing reality and thought," and his concluding definition of thought as "a phantom of the real" not only reflects that confusion but aptly defines film as well.

What is Robert's relation to Godard here? I have argued that in Sequence 15 Robert begins to function as Godard's surrogate, his *semblable* and stand-in questioner. Insofar as Robert's present remarks constitute a meditation on film, he continues to play that role here. He is, after all, wearing earphones and, as in Sequence 15, writing in a notebook. On the other hand, he is, for the only time in the film, obviously responding to unheard questions and statements. He repeatedly turns to address his answers directly to the camera, as he does not in the similar shots of Sequence 2. If he is Godard's delegate, how can it be that he is so unmistakably talking to someone whom we can understand only to be Godard?

To begin with, his headphones, in combination with his looks toward the camera, finally acknowledge what Marina Vlady reports about Godard's use of microphone and earphone, confirming what we must infer about the *oui*s and *non*s throughout the film. The spoken text, like that which Robert is writing in his notebook, originates in the *au-delà*, that is, the "beyond" to be found behind the camera. This, in context, is more than either a joke or a further acknowledgment of directorial method. There is, as Robert proposes in 15.3, a resemblance between himself and another guy in the movies who gets messages from the beyond, namely Orpheus. Given what constitutes the beyond in this case, Robert's address to it suggests an analogy between the camera and Cocteau's mirror. Cinema itself, one might say, is such a mirror, the mirror through which the poet passes.

As Robert says "a phantom of the real," Juliette enters from the kitchen. In reference to her very substantial body, his phrase is funny. Juliette registers this by asking

JULIETTE
What?

ROBERT
(To Juliette:)
Not sure.

JULIETTE
It's done, the children are asleep.
(She exits right.)

ROBERT
Oh good!

Quoi?

Pas sûr.

Ça y est, les enfants dorment.

Ah bon!

2'00.7''
83'42.8''

"What?" He looks at her fixedly and says "Not sure." Although we understand that he is replying to something he hears in his headphones, not to her, his remark is nonetheless an absurd non sequitur. Since he has been speaking to Godard's concerns, namely the cinema, it seems that here he speaks very much for Godard, and that, outside the terms of the narrative, of speaking together, he is speaking not *to* but *of* her (if with some irony), fixing the point of Godard's retrenchment from the two or three things he knows about her: just as she retreats a moment later to the self-definition "not yet dead," so he does to the summary "not sure."

Sequence 18

18.1

[Actual sound.]

JULIETTE

(To the camera:)

To define oneself in a single word?   Se définir en un seul mot?

Not yet dead!   Pas encore mort!

(She picks up a book and turns the pages,
reads:)

"The man of promise rates higher in practi-   "L'homme d'avenir a une intelligence pra-
cal intelligence than most people. This in-   tique supérieure à celle de la plupart des
telligence also encompasses judgment and   gens. Cette intelligence comprend aussi la
breadth of information.   faculté de jugement et l'étendue des infor-
                                                     mations.

(Robert enters screen left, sits on the bed,
and begins to undress.)

"Richardson, Bellows, Henry, and Co.   "Richardson, Bellows, Henry, et Cie, ont
found among 2,589 people working for cli-   trouvé parmi deux mille cinq cent quatre-
ent companies that the managers and execu-   vingt-neuf employés travaillant pour les

Shot 18.1, the last belonging to the narrative, makes parting reference to several of the film's *systèmes*. Juliette's blue cardigan, Robert's white T-shirt, and their red blanket form the tricolor, as do the letters of the concluding title, "FIN" (18.5). Here, as elsewhere, the colors signify France and the United States. Accordingly, Robert is reading an American book, Vance Packard's *Pyramid Climbers* and Juliette a French magazine, *Elle* (!). She reads aloud passages from each, his on work and career, hers on love. His describes the social hierarchy of business (reminding us of her remark in 9.4 on his

tives had an average score of 84, the supervisors and foremen averaged 78, and the mechanics and operators averaged 74. The man of promise is self-confident but not aggressively so." Is it you who underlined that?

ROBERT
Yes.

JULIETTE
"The man of promise is willing to admit his problems and mistakes. Such a man is not afraid to say: 'I don't know.' It is felt that only the emotionally secure person can admit failure." No, there I don't agree.

ROBERT
You have only to read something else if you don't like that!
(He takes the book from her.)

JULIETTE
(Picks up a magazine and thumbs through it. Looking at a page she says:)
Do you know the difference between true and false love?

ROBERT
No. What?
(He gets into bed.)

JULIETTE
The false is when I become myself again; the true is when I change,
(Looking up:)
or when the person who is loved has changed.

ROBERT
(Turning the pages of his book:)
You find I've changed? No, you know, I'm tired, that's all.
(He puts on his glasses and reads.)

JULIETTE
(To him:)
No, not you. Me. I've changed, at the same time I'm becoming myself again; then

sociétés qui forment leur clientèle une note en intelligence pratique de quatre-vingt-quatre points chez les directeurs et les cadres, de soixante-dix-huit points chez les contrôleurs et les contremaîtres, et de soixante-quatorze points chez les mécaniciens et manoeuvres. L'homme d'avenir a confiance en lui, mais sans agressivité." C'est toi qui as souligné ça?

Oui.

"L'homme d'avenir est prêt à admettre ses problèmes et à reconnaître ses fautes. Un tel homme ne crait pas de dire: 'Je ne sais pas.' On a le sentiment que seules les personnes sûres d'elles peuvent admettre un échec." Non, ça, je suis pas d'accord.

T'as qu'à lire autre chose si ça te plaît pas!

Tu sais la différence qu'il y a entre l'amour vrai et le faux?

Non. Quoi?

Le faux c'est quand je reviens à moi; le vrai c'est quand je change,

ou que le personne aimé a changé.

Tu trouves que j'ai changé? Non, tu sais, je suis fatigué, c'est tout.

Non, pas toi. Moi. J'ai changé, en même temps je reviens à moi; alors qu'est-ce que

lack of ambition) and the man of promise who "is not afraid to say 'I don't know.' "
Hers tells how to distinguish true from false love (she being in bed, we assume she is
comparing Robert to her clients), but she protests that she meets both criteria: "then

what's that?   c'est?

ROBERT
I don't know.   Je sais pas.

JULIETTE
OK, since you don't know, give me a ciga- Bon, puisque tu sais pas, donne-moi une
rette.   cigarette.

(He gives her a cigarette and she lights it.)

2′13.0″
85′55.8″

18.2 | [Silence.]

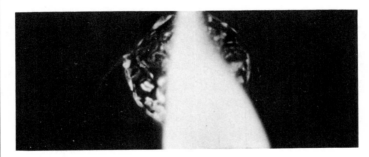

(The match flame withdraws; the tobacco
glows.)

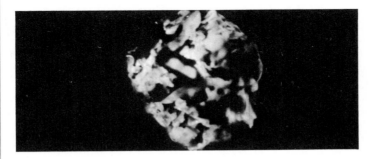

COMMENTARY 28
I listen to the commercials   **J'écoute la publicité**
(The glow dies out.)
on my transistor radio.   **sur mon transistor.**

what's that?" He, being a man of promise, replies: "Je sais pas": he does not even know this one thing about *elle*. She says: "OK, since you don't know, give me a cigarette."

Shot 18.2, the cigarette and match, is the last of the film's series of extreme closeups. The black background of the shot takes the series a step further, contradicting the evidence of the dialogue and matched-action cut 18.1/18.2 that the cigarette is Juliette's. But further in what direction? That, I think, represented by 18.4, the still life of consumer items (which, incidentally, includes several packs of cigarettes). The other shots in the series—even that of the Pax box—have no element that challenges our understanding that the spatial surroundings are missing simply because of the proximity of the camera. In fact, the sequence of 12.30 and 12.31 affirms that this understanding is correct. On this principle the black background of 18.2 would signify the darkness of the room. Yet, as the matched action at 18.1/18.2 specifies, no one has turned out the lights.

The image 18.2, then, is strictly neither a part of the fiction nor an alternative (such as the various "documentary" shots or the franc counter when it recurs) but an outright negation of it. The flaring of the match and the repeated fading and rekindling of the tobacco become, when set off against the black and combined with Commentary 28 ("Thanks to E, SS, O, I set out calmly on the road of dreams"), an image not only of forgetful gratification but of conflagration; it is a means by which the forgetting is obstructed and the things that Esso would banish from our minds are present after all. In connoting these things, the image draws on the association of Vietnam and bombardment noise with the act of lighting a cigarette in 16.11 and 16.12 and with cigarette smoke in 2.6 and 2.8. But just where are these things "present"? The black background will not allow that it is in the room. Accordingly, Godard's report that he is taking the road of dreams not only adds to, but contradicts, our understanding that it is Robert and Juliette who are taking such a road. Apart from the intimation that the cigarette, like the coffee cup earlier, is his, he puts himself into their place in his text but not in the image. If it can be said that in the commentaries of Sequence 8 he enters what is represented as the characters' space, then it also can be said that in the relation of the present commentary to 18.1 and 18.2 he deprives them of it. Indeed, we should not be prepared either to accept or even to understand what Godard says in this commentary were it not for the preceding occasions on which Juliette and Robert have spoken and acted for *him*. Our understanding must be that, within the terms of his text, going to bed and dreaming are what I should call metaphors (ironic ones at

(The tobacco glows.)
Thanks to E, SS, O,   Grâce à E, SS, O,
(The glow dies.)
I set out calmly on the road of dreams   je pars tranquille sur la route du rêve
(During the previous five words the to-
bacco glows, then the glow dies.)
and I forget the rest.   et j'oublie le reste.
I forget Hiroshima,   J'oublie Hiroshima,
I forget Auschwitz,   j'oublie Auschwitz,
I forget   j'oublie
(The tobacco glows again.)
Budapest,   Budapest,

18.5″
86′14.3″

18.3

I forget Vietnam,   j'oublie le Vietnam,
I forget the minimum wage,   j'oublie le S.M.I.G.,
I forget the housing crisis, I forget the   j'oublie la crise du logement, j'oublie la
famine in India.   famine aux Indes.

7.6″
86′22.0″

that) and what the film proceeds to call "idées" (18.3), and that their association with 18.2 has the effect of including the space depicted in that shot among their number.

What exactly are these "idées"? In the four times that the rubric occurs in the film (2.11, 13.8, 16.14, 18.3) it is always conjoined with an image that shows or refers to the *grand ensemble* and in three of these with postcard or advertising photos. As the name of the book series, it repeats the argument quoted in the Seuil/Avant-Scène preface (pp. 16–17) that the paperbacks and the *grands ensembles* are expressions of the same culture and politics. In context, the relation of these elements is more specific; it includes the suggestion that the *grands ensembles* and the "class politics" they represent are connected, in the fashion of infrastructure to superstructure, to the *idées* (or more precisely, to the ideology) that emerge from them. This ideology is inscribed not only in images—the postcard and advertising photographs to which the label "idées" is affixed—but in sounds as well, specifically in the two radio messages from the *au-delà*: the Saigon-Washington transmission that Robert intercepts in Sequence 2 and the commercials that Godard, taking Robert's place in this respect too, hears on his transistor portable. The exactness with which the cut 18.2/18.3 is placed in relation to the accompanying text specifies that it is the particular intersection of these commercials with Vietnam that calls forth the word "idées" and confers on it the connotation "ideology." This label also applies to what we see at the head of 18.4, the package of Hollywood chewing gum before a postcard of a smiling couple. These are *idées* that are the special concern of the director. His phrase here, "I've forgotten everything," not only summarizes the foregoing list but renders, with sharp irony, the effect of the image that it accompanies.

It is with respect to the identification of this material as ideology that Godard's rhetorical assumption of Robert's and Juliette's place is of special importance. Throughout the film the speaker of the commentaries is, as I have tried to show, an observer—a director, a poet, a painter, someone who, as an artist, claims exemption from the material conditions of the world he depicts. The text of Commentary 28—in particular, the metaphors of sleep and dreaming, and the picture of the speaker as radio listener—changes this portrayal significantly. In this text he for the first time speaks as a resident of the *grands ensembles,* going to bed in place of, or perhaps in solidarity with, his characters, and acknowledging that he is a victim of advertisements just as he has shown them to be. His admission of the power of such advertisements to make him forget Vietnam and Auschwitz is quite another thing than declaring, as he does in Sequence 12, that they make him doubt language. At the same time, the Hollywood chewing gum assures us that this change entails no denial of his special role and concerns as director. The import of the change can be put as follows: that he, living in what he calls "society today," is thereby in the position of a resident in the *grands ensembles*—in other words, that the *grands ensembles* are terms that define "la vie moderne." By this route he succeeds in acknowledging the inclusion of himself and his work as director in the society so defined. This is the beginning, if an abortive one, of a politics.

It is not surprising therefore that Commentary 28, despite its literal sense, is anything but a statement of defeat. The repeated "I forget" is, of course, a rhetorical figure, namely *praeteritio,* the enumeration of things that the speaker insists he is omitting.[1] Through this figure Godard expresses what I think is a justified confidence that his film has not on the whole acceded to Esso or taken "the road of dreams," but has made particular and determined efforts to remember Auschwitz and Vietnam. Thus he

I've forgotten

(A slow zoom-out starts.)

everything except that, since I am reduced to zero, it's from there that I shall
have to set out again.

J'ai tout

oublié, sauf que, puisqu'on me ramène à
zéro, c'est de là qu'il faudra repartir.

provides a sharply critical perspective on the image that he labels "Hollywood chewing gum." If this image allows a joke about his preoccupation as critic and director with American films, it also—and more importantly—resolves the worries that attend the very similar photographs in 13.7, affirming that his own imagery and his own couple are not, in the end, very much like these.

The unlikeness of the two couples is also argued in the color scheme: at the head of 18.4 the man is in red, the woman in blue, with the yellow chewing gum package filling out the painter's primaries and thus engaging the film's opposition of these to the tricolor, which, as I noted, is the scheme of 18.1, Robert and Juliette in bed. The zoom-out that follows the initial framing in 18.4 connotes renunciation of this primary palette and hence of the role of painter.[2] It also puts the Hollywood image "in its place," which is not the context of other images, least of all *Godard's* images, but that of consumer products: detergents, cigarettes, crackers, and, appropriately, transistor radios, the particular agents of this political forgetfulness. The zoom as a figure has the inherent effect of stressing the central place that the Hollywood image occupies within that context; thus it underlines the significance of associating that image with the summary phrase "I've forgotten everything."

But shot 18.4 does more than recognize that Hollywood pictures are, or have a central place among, consumer products. On the one hand, it asks whether the same is not true of all film images, particularly those in color and 'scope, in other words, those of the feature film. On the other, it *opposes* the image of Hollywood gum, puts it *out there,* "shoots" it, and does so with all the connotations of potent resistance that these latter sequences have given to the camera axis and to compositional frontality: the address to the camera, the machine-gun noise and the Vietnam photos, "to photograph and kill," shooting the toy gun, Hitler.

The relation of text and image in 18.4 differs in several important respects from anything that has preceded it in the film. As in the passage on the Pax Americana in 2.9, a link is drawn between global political issues and detergents. The shot itself resembles an advertisement—for example, this one:

As such it represents Godard's pretended forgetting. Together with the text, it frames the question of how to see these products, these familiar artifacts of urban life, politi-

(Silence as the zoom continues, then stops:)

cally—that is, in relation to Hiroshima, Auschwitz, Budapest, Vietnam, the minimum wage, the housing crisis, the famine in India.

The answer, insofar as there is one and as it advances the answers developed through the film, has two ingredients. First, the objects are arranged so as to remind us, as the zoom progresses, of the layout of the *grand ensemble,* as if to say: "These must be seen to resemble that." This resemblance is not so much to the *grand ensemble* in the abstract as to the high-angle view of it in 2.13, where it is presented as an example of "class politics." Secondly, this arrangement is the terminal point of the film's series of extreme closeups. In the earlier cases what surrounds the objects is excluded by the frame limits; in 18.2, the glowing cigarette, the surround is replaced by blackness, erased. What we see at the head of 18.4 appears to belong to this series. We discover with the zoom-out that the chewing gum (along with the postcard) is one of a number of such objects that have been literally displaced and put against a *new* background (in this connection the zoom-out represents a reversal of the progression from 12.30 to 12.31). It is less important, I think, that this background is grass or that it is green than that it resembles the background of 13.7 (for example).

The similarity so indicated between the photographs in 13.7 and the one at the head of 18.4 calls attention to a significant difference: in the earlier case we can believe that the photographs are found as and where they are; in fact, the context encourages us to believe that they are part of the litter around the *grand ensemble.* It is impossible to believe any such thing either of the picture at the head of 18.4 or of any of the other objects revealed by the zoom-out. The shot strongly implies precisely what we see in this production still:

This act of arrangement may be said to answer the action of 17.3, Juliette's unpacking of the groceries: whereas she puts them in their place, Godard, so to speak, takes them out of it (in fact, the blue box of Lustucru noodles she puts in the cabinet reappears in the lower left corner of 18.4). If we were to consider 18.4 in isolation, we might be tempted to describe this displacement as surrealist, that is, conforming to an aesthetic program: the items do not *belong* on the grass and look absurd there (just as they do on Monsieur Gérard's table in 5.1). But in context, it has a quite different sense, calling attention to the unseen but nonetheless real agency of the arranger, the director.

By this means Godard again declares that it is he who is making, and accepting responsibility for, the image and its argument.

The substance of this declaration, however, differs significantly from what is implied by such earlier questions as "Am I watching from too far or too close?" or "Should I have spoken of Juliette or of the leaves?" The basis of those questions is what I have called the referential illusion, the pretense that there is a world, including both fiction and nonfiction, which exists utterly independent of the director and of which he must give an account—selecting, framing, sequencing, but not overtly *arranging*, at least not if this means reconstructing the spatial relation of things. The arrangement evidenced in 18.4 is, therefore, a stylistic departure and, partly for this reason, has the aura of finality. The difference between it and what precedes it outlines an argument: namely, that to pierce through what is opaque about the visible, language by itself, *pensées*, even montage, will not suffice. Some much stronger intervention is necessary. And in this consists the real opposition between 18.4 and the Hollywood picture that it displays.

If 18.4 is literally a closeup, the *ensemble* of consumer products is just as literally a model for a high-angle long shot. We might describe this long shot as the establishing view missing from Sequence 1. In this case its deferral until the very last moment of the film would signify how much one must do to achieve such a view. Yet insofar as 18.4 is a closeup, it also signifies (so to speak) the *absence* of the long shot that it mimics, as if to confirm the film's distrust of the claims inevitably borne by overviews of this kind. In this respect it has a special relation to the film's only high-angle view of the *grand ensemble*, 2.13. Indeed, shots 18.3 and 18.4 exactly parallel the progression from 2.11 to 2.13: both series begin with the title "idées," cut to a mass-produced picture, zoom out to reveal the position of that picture on grass, and conclude with a long-shot of an *ensemble*. The differences are only that in the earlier case the zoom arrives at a view of the actual *grand ensemble*, not a "model," and does so via a cut (2.12/2.13). The connotations of negation and erasure given to that view by the pleonastic pan leftward indicate its unsatisfactoriness. The later case is in these respects a revision. The replacement of the *grand ensemble* by the model of it made with consumer products corroborates the inference I drew earlier about the opacity of the *found* and the political need to oppose it with the *arranged*. It also has clearly to do with the filmmaker's trajectory toward zero, toward "the b, a, ba of existence."

More important, perhaps, than the substance of this revision is its character. The relation of the two series is, I would argue, genuinely dialectical: shot 18.4 combines the elements of 2.12 (the grass and photos) and 2.13 (the *grand ensemble*), fusing them not with a cut that uses movement to mask a spatial discontinuity but with a zoom that discloses a spatial continuity achieved by frank arrangement. To this space we can accurately apply the description "synthesized." Its stylistic realization, besides resolving the conflict between watching from too close or too far, does something to explain the confidence of Godard's concluding sentence: "I've forgotten everything except that, since I am reduced to zero, it's from there that I shall have to set out again." Because the zoom is prompted by the words "I am reduced to zero," it appears to illustrate them: to be reduced to zero is to begin to see the house one lives in as constituted by consumer products. Indeed, the shot as a whole not only renders this vision but indicates stylistically—that is, by reference to its dialectical ancestry—what it will mean for Godard as a filmmaker to set out again from this place (in the nuance "*re*partir" he recalls "je pars tranquille," implying that the way down is decidedly not the way up). In-

(The image fades, but not to black; hold:)

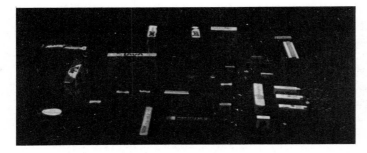

(Pause.)

27.9″
86′49.9″

18.5

[Fade-out of music.]

3.0″
86′52.9″

sofar as the zoom itself represents this act of redeparture, Hollywood chewing gum is the zero from which it recedes. For Godard this is, as he indicates in his final word *repartir,* a *second* departure, one that connotes rejection rather than derivation.

By the same token, the zoom and text together retrospectively identify the movement "inward" (in both the physical and psychological senses of the word) from 12.30 to 12.31 as a movement *toward* zero. This judgment also applies to the ideas associated with 12.31, the rage of expression that conjoins the political and poetic while relinquishing a clear view of objects. If "zero" is an authentic starting point, it is also a long way from a world in which things (such as we see in 18.4) will know harmonious relations with people. In a similar way, Commentary 28 as a whole, with its mixture of confidence, defeat, and realism, can be understood as a revision of that which accompanies shots 2.11–2.12, the misjudged claim to speak for eight million people yielding to the more modest determination not to forget Auschwitz and Vietnam.

After the zoom and commentary finish, the image, for the only time in the film, fades. Yet before the fade reaches black, it unexpectedly stops (just as the final musical fragment stops at the dominant, rather than proceeding all the way to the tonic), allowing the scene to remain for several seconds in a faint backlight that eliminates details and emphasizes shapes. The effect is a little like that which is produced when in 14.6 Juliette, also backlit, switches off the lamp. Lacking what she there calls "physical clarity," the image in these few seconds succeeds in evoking many things: a more compelling ambiguity of scale, a more vivid similarity of the consumer products to the apartment buildings, the intractability of the visible, the struggle against the welter of detail in the image, the need to abstract, and even the coming of night. Setting out from zero, then, will involve seeing in simpler terms, combating, as Juliette does, the power of the image to render detail and with it perhaps the camera's power to photograph and kill.

I must add that I find the political position of Commentary 28 rather confused. Godard groups Auschwitz with Budapest and India in a way that seems to repudiate terms like left and right or "class politics." With what does he propose to replace them? What, after all, *does* it mean to remember Hiroshima, the housing crisis, the famine in India? This, I believe, is a legitimate question, and the political confusion—or rather, vagueness—of Commentary 28 appears in how little idea it gives of either what an answer might be or how to go about finding one. The resistance it pledges to the blandishments of Esso seems inexplicably mild for a film that begins by speaking so knowingly about "the natural tendencies of big capitalism." So, in addition to the confidence of the image, there is in the text the feeling of truly being reduced from two or three things to zero, and, as the impersonal phrasing, "on me ramène à zéro," concedes, not knowing how or by whom.

Finally, I should note that the phrase "at zero" alludes to a book in the *idées* series called *Gauche: année zéro* (Paris: Gallimard, 1964) and thus has a specifically political overtone. It resembles the concluding phrases of other Godard films of this period: the citation of the same book at the conclusion of *Made in U.S.A.,* the recognition at the end of *La chinoise* of being at the beginning of a long march, the cross-words "end of story, end of cinema" that close *Weekend.* Like these, it conveys the sense of being defeated, put back, but also put back on the track. Toward the beginning of *Le gai savoir,* Emile (great grandson of Rousseau) declares: "On va repartir à zéro" ("We are going to set out again from zero"), and Patricia (daughter of Lumumba) replies: "Non, avant de repartir, il faut y aller. On va retourner à zéro." ("No, before setting out

again, it is necessary to go there. We are going to return to zero.") Significantly, Godard gave his next film the title *One Plus One*. Seven years afterward, in 1975, he called a film *Numéro deux,* and one year after that he subtitled a series of television programs 6 × 2. Seen in this perspective, the items of Commentary 28—Vietnam, Budapest, Hiroshima—do not seem to indicate a specific political position so much as to specify that the lack signified by *zéro* is political in character; it is the lack of a coherent politics. It is this problem that animates Godard's work from this point until the events of May 1968 and the Marxism-Leninism of *Un film comme les autres* and *British Sounds.*

Notes

Sequence 0

1 Christian Metz, *Language and Cinema*, tr. Donna Jean Umiker-Sebeok (The Hague: Mouton, 1974), pp. 74–79.

2 *The World Viewed* (New York: Viking Press, 1971), p. 23. Gilberto Perez makes the same point in "The Narrative Sequence," *Hudson Review,* 30 (1977), 82.

3 "Grands ensembles et Vietnam," included in the prefatory texts to Jean-Luc Godard, *2 ou 3 choses que je sais d'elle* (Paris: Seuil/Avant-Scène, 1971), pp. 16–17, hereafter cited as "Seuil/Avant-Scène script" in order to distinguish it from the film. The translation is mine.

Sequence 1

1 *Film Form,* ed. and trans. Jay Leyda (New York: Harcourt, Brace, and World, 1944), p. 49.

2 While there are many indications that the voice-over commentator speaks in the persona of the director of the film (for instance, in Commentary 17 he ponders a directorial decision), there is no internal evidence that the lines of this persona are spoken by Jean-Luc Godard. Indeed, there are not even any credits to inform us that Godard is the director. Nonetheless, partly because of the widespread consciousness of the film *auteur,* which Godard as critic helped create, we certainly know who directed this film. The very absence of credits implies that Godard takes it for granted that we know. In order to follow the film, we must see it as a *Godard* film, replete with his concerns, his stylistic strategies, and allusions to his previous work. In the same way, I think, we infer without being told that the commentator's voice is actually that of Godard. Those who recognize the *Vivre sa vie* poster on the wall in 5.1 will probably also recognize his voice, which is heard in several of the films made before 1966, notably *Band of Outsiders* and *Vivre sa vie,* and nearly all of those made after. Such spectators will also be aware that in *Contempt* Fritz Lang plays himself, a film director, and in *Masculine Feminine* Brigitte Bardot appears as herself, an actress. Accordingly, when in the present case we are told that the woman in 1.5 is Marina Vlady, an actress, it is natural that we should think of the man who tells us this, the director, as Jean-Luc Godard. The nonprofessional delivery of the commentaries functions as a sign that this speaker is not an actor and is not, therefore, assuming a role.

Having said this, I must also acknowledge that no interpretative problem would be raised by failing to conclude that "the part of director" is spoken by the film's actual director. In this respect, the present case differs from that of *Vivre sa vie,* where Godard dubs that part of the unnamed young man who, having read to Nana an excerpt from Edgar Allan Poe's "Oval Portrait," tells her: "It's our story; it's the story of a man who does his wife's portrait." Since the character who ostensibly delivers the line is not speaking to "his wife," there is no way of understanding the line in the absence of knowledge that originates outside the film, namely that (1) the actress who plays Nana is Godard's wife, Anna Karina, and (2) the voice we are hearing is in fact Godard's.

3 Only from the Seuil/Avant-Scène script, p. 21, do we know what this sentence is and that it has been censored.

4 In an excerpt from his diary published in *Cahiers du cinéma* (November 1966), Godard writes:

I made a mistake about the sound engineers for the mixing of my last films. I have engaged Maumont for *Made in U.S.A.* and Bonfanti for *2 ou 3 choses,* instead of doing the opposite. Let me explain. One can consider mixed sound in two ways. Either as a new sound, which it is a question of capturing, of recording, as in the case of shooting the picture. Or as a known sound, therefore a sound to reproduce, exploiting to the maximum the quality of the reproduction. For reproducing a sound, and transferring it from magnetic to optical while mixing several tracks, that is, making a single sound out of several, Maumont is the strongest, and his skill and his ear have no equal in Europe, especially with the elements prepared by Nenny. But if on the other hand it is a question simply of capturing the sounds of another world that fall on you, that is, of making several sounds with only one track, that is, of never considering a sound as definitive, but quite variable, that is, above all of mixing relations and not objects, and of knowing, for example, that there are certain noises and certain musics that begin to exist only when they are saturated—in that case, the youth of Antoine Bonfanti outstrips the wisdom of Maumont, and the heart of one the knowledge of the other. That explains why, through my fault (for it is necessary to harmonize the techniques with the subject, the microphone as well as the lens), the sound of *Made in U.S.A.* might be betrayed by the reproduction, and that of *2 ou 3 choses* by the recording.

The translation I have quoted differs slightly from that reprinted in *Jean-Luc Godard: A Critical Anthology,* ed. Toby Mussman (New York: E. P. Dutton and Co., 1968), p. 297—hereafter cited as "Mussman."

5 Noël Burch, *Theory of Film Practice* (New York: Praeger, 1973), pp. 17–31.

6 In an interview reprinted in *The New Wave,* ed. Peter Graham (London: Martin Secker and Warburg; New York: Doubleday and Co., 1968), p. 100, François Truffaut recalls:

It remains to be seen why it was that certain films, such as *Une Femme Est Une Femme,* didn't get across to the public. As far as this film is concerned, I would say that one can reach one's audience in almost any conceivable way, but not by assaulting their basic peace of mind. If one plays around with the sound-track and the images in too unusual a way, people start objecting—it is a normal reaction. They ripped up the seats at Nice because they thought the projection booth was not properly equipped. Of course one could explain things to people through articles, but in those cinemas where the film was put on the audiences were taken by surprise. Godard went too far for them in the sound-mixing. When the girl comes out of the cafe, there's suddenly no sound, just complete silence. Straight away people think the projector has broken down. Although, of course, those spectators in Nice were not civilised—one simply does not knife cinema seats.

7 *Brecht on Theatre,* ed. and trans. John Willett (New York: Hill and Wang, 1964), pp. 138, 142.

8 Seuil/Avant-Scène script, p. 120. Godard has used this method before, for example in *Pierrot le fou* and in Madame Céline's speech in *Une femme mariée.* See James Blue, "Excerpt from an Interview with Richard Grenier and Jean-Luc Godard" in Mussman, pp. 245–253.

9 A list of the often remarked Brechtian elements in Godard's work before 1967 might include: the musical style and ironic tone of *Les carabiniers,* the intertitles of *Vivre sa vie* and *Masculine Feminine,* the picture of the cinema apparatus in *Contempt,* the episodes of street theater in *Pierrot le fou,* the arbitrary denouements of *Contempt* and *Masculine Feminine,* and the general fascination with gangsters, prostitutes, and America. Most striking, however, is the acting style, in which the actors do not transform themselves wholly into their characters, but sometimes recite texts and address the audience directly. In *La chinoise* (1967) Jean-Pierre Léaud acknowledges this debt by facing a blackboard covered with the names of dramatists and slowly erasing them until only Brecht's is left. None of this, however, should discount the crucial ways in which Godard differs from Brecht or what this difference owes to the dissimilarities between film and theater. Brecht's own writing about film and filmmaking does not go very far in proposing what a "Brechtian" film might be, and Godard, for his part, repeatedly expresses distaste for the theater and for the theatrical in film. Although many of his films "distance" the audience, they do not specifically produce Brecht's "alienation effect." And until *2 ou 3 choses,* they have none of Brecht's clarity of political purpose.

10   I have discussed this in "The Role of Theory in Films and Novels," *New Literary History,* 3 (Spring 1972), 551–554.

11   In an article reprinted in *Masculine Feminine: A Film by Jean-Luc Godard,* ed. Robert Hughes (New York: Grove Press, 1969), pp. 227–228, Philippe Labro reports:

> Godard speaks to his actor:
> "Let's start over; pay a little attention now . . . What is it you can't say? If you can't say it, don't say it . . . You are absolutely not thinking, not for a second, about what you're saying . . . You lighted your cigarette; I didn't tell you to do that in this shot. You can't do just any old thing, just because we film the way amateurs do!"
> These last words (the key words) are pronounced with one of the rare smiles (half sardonic, half affectionate) of the long evening. Then, seeing that Léaud is still chagrined because he didn't do the right thing, he says, kindly and calmly:
> "Don't think of anything, don't think of anything, do as I do, keep your head empty, it's the secret of being relaxed."

12   "The Imaginary Signifier," *Screen* (Summer 1975), 44–45.

13   "The Fiction Film and Its Spectator: A Metapsychological Study," *New Literary History,* 8 (Autumn 1976), 95.

14   "An Introduction to the Structural Analysis of Narrative," *New Literary History,* 6 (Winter 1975), 244–245.

15   *Brecht on Theatre,* p. 138.

16   "Radical Ideology in the Cinema: An Essay on Jean-Luc Godard," honors thesis, Harvard College, 1971, pp. 69–70.

17   Published in *Nouvel observateur* and reprinted in *Godard on Godard,* ed. Jean Narboni and Tom Milne (London: Martin Secker and Warburg; New York: Viking Press, 1972), pp. 237–238. In a later *Nouvel observateur* article, Godard writes: "When faced by a choice between dictatorship by money and by political censorship, I prefer the former" (Mussman, p. 278).

18   Mussman, p. 275. Two years later, parts of the text of *Le gai savoir,* which resemble the suppressed sentence of Commentary 3, were censored. The film itself was originally commissioned by French television, then refused for broadcast, a scenario repeated by South London Weekend Television in the case of *British Sounds* and by Italian television (R.A.I.) in the case of *Struggles in Italy.*

19   *Godard on Godard,* pp. 238–239.

20   Mussman, p. 282. Godard carries out this project in *Numéro deux.*

21   Mussman, p. 296.

22   I am indebted here to Nicholas K. Browne's analysis of Sequence 12 in "Defense and Desire: Reading Structures of Dis-Locaton in Godard's *2 ou 3 choses que je sais d'elle,*" *On Film* (1980), in press.

Sequence 2

1   Mussman, p. 278: I find no evidence that what Godard claims here is so. Aron's book is translated by M. K. Bottomore as *18 Lectures on Industrial Society* (London: Weidenfeld and Nicolson, 1967).

2   *Godard: Three Films* (London: Lorrimer; New York: Harper and Row, 1975), p. 9.

3   "*Muriel* as Text," *Film Reader,* no. 3, 263.

4   Seuil/Avant-Scène script, pp. 11–12.

5   This shot seems to me an allusion to and correction of the confident, expository tone of the many high-angle long shots of Chris Marker's *Le joli mai* and of the corresponding perspective of its voice-over commentary: "From the tops of its towers and its surrounding hills, Paris can see the Paris of the future rise on the same hills where St. Genevieve saw the barbarians appear," and so on. Juliette answers this commentary in 6.3: "No one today can know what the city of tomorrow will be," and in shot 4.4, as I will try to show, Godard alludes to Marker's film even more specifically.

Sequence 3

1   There is no internal evidence to identify these references as what they probably are: the time of the fictional action versus the date of the filming. It is worth remarking that the date Juliette names is four days earlier than the appointment of Paul Delouvrier, which Commentary 2 gives as August 21 (in Mussman, p. 277, Godard gives the date as August 17).

2   *Pierrot le fou,* trans. Peter Whitehead (London: Lorrimer; New York: Simon and Schuster, 1969), p. 63.

3   In an interview Godard acknowledges as much, though in a backhanded way: "Writers have always wanted to use the cinema as a blank page: to arrange all the elements and to let the mind circulate from one to the other. But this is so easy to do in the cinema. Contrary to what Belmondo says in *Pierrot,* Joyce is of no interest to the cinema" (*Godard on Godard,* p. 234).

Sequence 4

1   *Le nouvel observateur,* no. 71 (March 23, 1966), 18. The translation is mine. H.L.M. stands for Habitations à Loyer Modéré (low-rent housing).

2   How much does the censor have to do with this? We know that in *Une femme mariée* the sequence on the monokini was censored, but in *British Sounds* (1969) and *Numéro deux* (1975) genitals are shown.

Sequence 5

1   William Rothman observes that these posters all advertise countries with which the United States has a special relationship: Thailand, Israel, India, Japan, and Spain.

2   This may remind us that Monsieur Gérard's business is illegal; Laurence Wylie points out that in France both prostitution and daycare require state licenses.

3   *L'avant-scène du cinéma,* no. 19 (October 1962), 9. *Poule* means "hen" or, in slang, "tart."

4   *Le nouvel observateur,* no. 71 (March 23, 1966) 19. *Vivre sa vie* has a comparable factual basis in the sociological study *Où en est la prostitution?* by Marcel Sacotte (Corréa: Buchet/Chastel, 1959). Some material in the film is taken directly from this book, notably the text of the "lettre classique" Nana writes in Tableau 7 and the facts reported in Tableau 8.

Sequence 6

1   After 1968 Godard, as Serge Daney suggests, associates photography with the nineteenth century, film with the twentieth, and television with the twenty-first. "The T(h)errorized (Godardian Pedagogy)," *Thousand Eyes,* no. 2 (1977), 38.

2   Richard Roud, in *Jean-Luc Godard,* 2nd ed. (London: Thames and Hudson, in association with the British Film Institute, 1970), p. 73, writes:

> Godard's use of colour points up this insistence on the real. True, it developed gradually. For *Une Femme est une Femme,* he says, "I had a décor and I chose my colours." For *Le*

Mépris, he looked for locations; as for the colours, well, they came as they were. "I didn't paint a grey wall white because I preferred white; instead I looked for a white wall, whereas for *Une Femme est une Femme,* I would have painted the wall white. In *Une Femme est une Femme,* I tried to use colour dramatically. In *Le Mépris,* no. *Une Femme est une Femme* was the first time for me; with such a wonderful toy as colour, you play with it as much as you can. But in *Le Mépris,* the more natural, less fabricated, Italian colours corresponded perfectly to what I wanted, so I didn't do any painting or arranging."

"The big difference between the cinema and literature," as he told the novelist Jean-Marie Le Clézio, "is that in the cinema the sky is there. One never has to say, is the sky blue or grey? It's just *there* . . . I never have the feeling I am differentiating between life and creation. On the other hand, for someone like Flaubert, it was a great problem whether to describe the sky or the sea as blue or grey or blue-grey. If the sky is blue, I film it blue."

3   *Sense and Non-Sense,* tr. Hubert L. and Patricia Allen Dreyfus (Evanston, Illinois: Northwestern University Press, 1964), pp. 52–53. In a diary entry published in November 1966 (Mussman, p. 298), Godard notes: "We talk with emotion and tenderness, she of Ivitch, I of the confined one of Venice, she of the *Phenomenology of Perception,* I of the study of Cezanne and of the cinema in *Sense and Non-Sense.*"

Sequence 7

1   The latter metaphor is evidently important to Godard, for he repeats it at the beginning of his *Nouvel observateur* article (Mussman, p. 274): "Yes, I'm making two films at the same time. The first is *Deux ou trois choses que je sais d'elle,* starring Marina Vlady; the other, *Made in U.S.A.,* with Anna Karina. They are completely different in style, and have nothing to do with each other, except perhaps that they let me indulge my passion for analyzing what is called modern living, for dissecting it like a biologist to see what goes on underneath." In an interview of March 1967 (quoted in Roud, p. 83), Godard said: "When I was a *lycée* student, I wanted to study mathematics, or at least thought I wanted to. I liked the idea of pure research . . . pure ideas."

2   A similar, but more convincing, metaphor appears in *Numéro deux,* where the reproduction performed by film and videotape is compared to biological reproduction as represented by a drawing of the intertwined helices of the DNA molecule.

3   The aspiration Godard states of attacking "the problems of social pathology" probably alludes to a pair of high-angle shots of an old quarter of Paris in *Le joli mai,* followed by shots of modern apartment buildings, over which the narrator says: "Even if what is described as 'project pathology' does not succeed in making us regret the former slums, we know at least that there there was room for happiness, and here we're not sure." I infer that "project pathology" is the name for a slum-clearance project.

Sequence 8

1   *Le nouvel observateur,* no. 77 (May 4, 1966), 16. My translation.

2   The young woman never reappears in the film, though her pimp does. The scene resembles Tableau 6 of *Vivre sa vie,* Nana's meeting with Yvette and her pimp in the café. There Nana's speech, "I am responsible," addressed as much to the camera as to Yvette, is also prompted by a track in on her.

3   There is some support in the scene for a more detailed comparison. Since there are "images" both in the magazine and on the film, an analogy exists between the pages and the frames. Curiously, shot 8.9, the second insert of the magazine, shows a page that appears toward the *beginning* of the action in 8.7; by the end of that shot the young woman has got well past this page. Indeed, the two remaining inserts, 8.11 and 8.13, confirm that what follows 8.7 is a *replay* of its action. This may help to account for why Godard specifies, apparently gratuitously, that the object we are seeing is called "une revue," a word that, as in English, means a *re-view* as well as a magazine. In shots 8.9–8.13, the film is indeed a re-view, though not the kind talked about "dans le langage journalistique." (This arcane joke has a

counterpart in a line from *Une femme mariée:* " 'Re-garder' . . . ça veut dire garder deux fois.") An opposition is thus established between the unfolding of fictional time onward from 3:37 P.M. and the image track, for "one hundred fifty frames further along" is not, as we see, further beyond 3:37 P.M.—in fact it is just the reverse; it is a replay from another point of view. Godard expands on this notion in Commentary 23 when he speculates on the power of film to trap a moment and preserve it.

4   This argument points, in passing, to a radical difference between image and voice in film. We accept the recording of a voice as the testimony of a subject. The shot cannot have comparable status in itself but only by its position in a chain of images—and there only by convention. Shots that signify point of view, the human vision of a subject, occur, as it were, within quotation marks. Film styles can, I think, be defined in some degree by how they account for this contradiction between the status of voice and image.

5   I am struck by the way in which the issues raised in this segment anticipate by almost ten years those of Christian Metz's essay "The Imaginary Signifier" (*Screen,* Summer 1975, 14–76). Metz's argument is that the screen is like the mirror of Lacan's mirror-stage, during which the child's ego is formed, except that the screen does not reflect the spectator. Although here it is the director who is absent from this "reflection," Godard is at pains to show that in some respects the director is himself a spectator.

6   *Sense and Non-Sense,* pp. 160–161.

7   In an interview originally published in 1962 (*Godard on Godard,* p. 181), Godard said: "The cinema is the only art which, as Cocteau says (in *Orphée,* I believe) 'films death at work.' Whoever one films is growing older and will die. So one is filming a moment of death at work. Painting is static: the cinema is interesting because it seizes life and the mortal side of life."

8   Voices other than Godard's which occur over the image include the secretary's of 10.2–10.12, the Algerian boy's of 13.6–13.9, the old woman's of 16.10–16.11, and the children's of 16.13–16.18. None of these, however, appears even at first to be in a controlling relationship to the accompanying shots.

Sequence 9

1   Sequence 9 closely parallels both Tableau 5 of *Vivre sa vie,* "The First Client—The Room," and Tableau 8, which rehearses a list of facts mostly taken from Marcel Sacotte's *Où en est la prostitution?*

2   "Ugetsu Monogatari is Kenji Mizoguchi's masterpiece, and one which ranks him on equal terms with Griffith, Eisenstein and Renoir . . . It is *Don Quixote, The Odyssey* and *Jude the Obscure* rolled into one." The difference in tone between these sentences, which Godard wrote in 1958 (*Godard on Godard,* p. 71) and that of the allusion in *2 ou 3 choses* reflects, perhaps, not so much on Mizoguchi as on the cinema itself. As Serge Daney puts it in the opening sentences of "The T(h)errorized (Godardian Pedagogy)": "We know that May '68 confirmed Jean-Luc Godard in a suspicion he had had; that the movie theater is, in every sense of the word, a *bad place,* at once immoral and inadequate. A place for easy hysteria, sleazy visual pickups, voyeurism and magic."

3   The first three shots of *Vivre sa vie* show Nana in left profile, full face, and right profile respectively. They are followed by an entire sequence, seven shots, in which she is seen only from behind.

Sequence 11

1   *Masculine Feminine: A Film by Jean-Luc Godard,* pp. 226–227.

2   Similarly, it is implausible—most especially in 17.1 and 17.2—that Christophe is a working-class child. Indeed, in 17.5 Godard allows us to hear Solange crying "Where is papa?" while Robert is holding her.

Sequence 12

1   It is worth noting that Godard, unlike Resnais and Antonioni, never expresses doubt about "what happened." In this case, what happened is roughly equivalent to what is written in the scenario. Godard's account of directing in these commentaries is consistent with his description of his work on *A Woman Is a Woman* (*Godard on Godard*, p. 182): "Of all my films, it sticks closest to the scenario. I followed it word for word, down to the last comma. I based myself on it in writing the shooting script. I read, 'She leaves the house.' I asked myself, 'What does she do, what does she see? Old people in the street. All right, that's my day's work.' " As Godard says, this instance is atypical; accordingly, the director persona in Sequence 12 is somewhat fictionalized.

2   Obviously there is something personal in this. Michel Vianey (*En attendant Godard*, Paris: B. Grasset, 1966) in several passages describes the care with which Godard crosses the street. Members of his immediate family died in automobile accidents and several of his films, notably *Contempt* and *Weekend*, include spectacular collisions.

3   In *Vivre sa vie*, Brice Parain makes the parallel argument that the road to truth is paved with error. One of Godard's preoccupations as a director, I think, has been to find ways of admitting error—error as a sign for the process of searching for the truth—into film. I would cite in this connection the jump cuts in *Breathless*, the overlapped action in *Vivre sa vie* and *2 ou 3 choses*, the obviously accidental pratfall in *Le petit soldat*, the multiple takes of the same action in *Pierrot* and *2 ou 3 choses*, the narrator's false starts in *British Sounds*, the clapboard in *La chinoise*, and the titles that label *Une femme mariée* "fragments of a film" and *Weekend* "a film found on the scrap heap."

4   *The Wild Palms* appears to have had a much more formidable reputation in the French film world of this period than it did, or does, in America. Jean Seberg reads from it in *Breathless*; Agnes Varda patterned her first film, *Le point court*, on it; Astruc talks of it as an influence on *Une vie*. Its attractiveness, I think, consists in a structure in which chapters of two entirely independent novellas alternate. It is a structure with such striking cinematic affinities that it is cited (although not by name) as a paradigm case of "Interférences entre langages" in Metz's *Language and Cinema* (pp. 213–214). Jacques Rivette, in *Rivette: Texts and Interviews*, ed. Jonathan Rosenbaum (London: British Film Institute, 1977), pp. 40–41, mentions the influence on him of films such as *About Something Else*, which comprises two parallel, nonintersecting stories. Richard Roud confirms that *The Wild Palms* is one of Godard's favorite novels (*Jean-Luc Godard*, pp. 49–51), "but he doesn't want to make a film out of it. Rather, he said he would like to have his last two films shown, first a reel of *Made in U.S.A.*, then a reel of *Deux ou Trois Choses que je sais d'elle*, then a reel of *Made in U.S.A.*, etc., just as Faulkner mixed two stories in *The Wild Palms*. *That* would be his adaptation of the novel."

5   Godard stresses the importance of this fact in the credits, where he identifies the film stock as "Kodak XX." We are especially aware of it during the reading of Poe's sentences about the colors of the portrait, during which Nana puts on lipstick. The person who has drained the color from her face is, of course, the man who chose Kodak XX as the medium in which to do his wife's portrait.

6   It always rains after you wash a car.

7   "Carwash," like "made in U.S.A.," "weekend," and "friction proofing," testifies to the American invasion of French culture. Godard makes use of the opposition of the two languages to call attention to this fact at several points: his apostrophe to George Washington in Commentary 4 is in English; and because Marianne speaks English on the phone in Sequence 11, we infer in Sequence 14 that she was speaking to the "American," John Faubus.

8   In the terms of film theory, such assent to the implicit organization of the visible is what underlies André Bazin's aesthetics and politics and what aligns them in opposition to those of the Russian theorists of the twenties, who insist that the visible must be divided and reassembled according to a principle not implicit in it. Godard, who came to film in the shadow of Bazin, thus faces a special problem as his films become increasingly critical of the society they

picture. The essence of his originality, I believe, is that he attacks this problem not by resurrecting montage (as many Latin American and Eastern European filmmakers have done) but by cultivating the tensions between image and sound and the corollary tensions between image and language and image and narrative.

9 I take it that the attention Godard pays to things in Sequence 12 has a precedent not only in Ponge but in Resnais's *Le chant du styrène*, which I have not had the opportunity to see.

10 In "Defense and Desire: Reading Structures of Dis-Location in Godard's *2 ou 3 choses que je sais d'elle*," *On Film* (1980), in press, Nicholas Browne goes further. He argues that a struggle between male and female informs the whole scene and that in 12.29 the man is "cut in two, dismembered, by the slash of the windshield wiper blade."

11 "The Tutor-Code of Classical Cinema" by Daniel Dayan and "Against 'The System of the Suture'" by William Rothman are reprinted in *Movies and Methods,* ed. Bill Nichols (Berkeley and Los Angeles: University of California Press, 1976), pp. 438–459.

12 In *Focus on Godard,* ed. Royal S. Brown (Englewood Cliffs, New Jersey: Prentice-Hall, 1972), p. 48, Suzanne Schiffman says: "Obsessed by truth, Godard is annoyed by the fact that the film seen by the public is not the original but a copy. He is jealous of painters, because you can see their original paintings. He often says 'A film doesn't exist. A painting exists.'" He expressed similar sentiments to Michel Vianey apropos of *Masculine Feminine.*

13 Why October? The leaves in 12.33 are still green. According to the Seuil/Avant-Scène script, filming lasted from August 8 to September 8, 1966. Several people have suggested that October is the month of revolution and that this dating confirms the connotations of the red field in 12.31. A more likely explanation is that the date refers to the writing or recording of the commentary—the "present" that Godard mentions in 12.28. In this case, the phrase starting "en ce début de fin" would be the grammatical modifier of "disons." Yet if Godard in fact means to bring to our attention the temporal separation of the filming and the commentary, it is not clear what he gains by making the point so obscure, especially grammatically.

Digression

1 This is from one of the seven entries Godard wrote for a "Dictionary of American Filmmakers" in the December 1963–January 1964 issue of *Cahiers du cinéma.* The translation I quote differs slightly from that in *Godard on Godard,* pp. 202–203.

2 In *Breathless* Jean Seberg and Jean-Paul Belmondo catch a moment of a Western (which we hear but do not see). In *Vivre sa vie* Anna Karina goes to see Dreyer's *Passion of Joan of Arc.* In *Les carabiniers* Ulysses and Michelangelo watch parodies of Lumière's *Arrival of a Train at Ciotat Station* and *Le repas du bébé,* along with a short called *The Bath of a Woman of the World.* In *Une femme mariée* Charlotte and her lover see the beginning of *Night and Fog* at the Orly Airport cinema but do not stay for the feature announced on the marquee, Hitchcock's *Spellbound.* In *Pierrot le fou* Belmondo goes to the movies in Toulouse and after a newsreel on Vietnam sees Jean Seberg in Godard's *Le grand escroc.* In *Masculine Feminine,* Paul, Madeleine, and her two roommates watch a parody of Bergman's *The Silence,* filmed in Sweden by Godard himself.

Sequence 13

1 Stig Bjorkman, in *The Films of Jean-Luc Godard,* ed. Ian Cameron (New York: Praeger, 1969), p. 146, proposes that this boy is, or represents, the "Great Hope."

2 Laurence Wylie explains that "the civilization of the key rings" refers to the popularity in France in the sixties of key rings as novelty items.

Sequence 14

1 Michel Vianey, in *En attendant Godard* (p. 195), quotes this reminiscence of Anna Karina's: "I presented myself for a supporting part in his first film. He received me in his office, I mean his producer's office. He said nothing. O-la-la, I thought, what kind of guy is this? I remained standing while he walked around me, conscientiously, taking his time. Then he asked me if it would embarrass me to undress in his film. I was annoyed; I said: 'No, I don't undress.' " In *Anticipation,* shot just after *2 ou 3 choses,* Anna Karina plays a prostitute in the year 2000; Godard has her protest to her client: "Undressing is not my duty; millions of people have fought and given their lives for specialization" (hers is not physical but sentimental love, love expressed in language).

2 Nick and Samuel are Nicholas Ray and Samuel Fuller (*Godard on Godard,* p. 251). The ambivalence Godard expresses in Sequence 14 regarding American film is echoed in his diary: "Mystery and fascination of this American cinema. How can I . . . hate John Wayne upholding Goldwater and love him tenderly when abruptly he takes Natalie Wood into his arms in the next-to-the-last reel of *The Searchers?"* (Mussman, p. 293). In *Far from Vietnam* (1967) he resolves this ambivalence by promising that as "a filmmaker who shoots in France" he will "struggle against the American cinema." He makes this promise while standing next to an American-made Mitchell camera and accompanies it with the shot from *La chinoise* in which a toy American tank is bombarded with copies of *The Quotations of Chairman Mao.*

It is worth noting that when in 14.4 Lévy begins to speak French, he addresses his remarks for the first time directly to the camera. The resulting implication that the spectator is also French reflects in turn on the film, which thus acquires a tinge of nationalism that is, I think, absent in Godard's previous work. It is also worth noting that Godard defines himself in *Far from Vietnam* as "un cineaste qui tourne en France" rather than "un cineaste français." In *Breathless* Belmondo uses the Swiss words *huitante* and *nonante* in place of the French *quatre-vingts* and *quatre-vingt-dix.*

Sequence 15

1 "Interview with Suzanne Schiffman" in *Focus on Godard,* p. 46. Godard himself admits to this fear: see *Godard on Godard,* p. 182. Why do all published sources give the length of *2 ou 3 choses* as 90 or 95 minutes, whereas the correct figure is 87?

2 *2 ou 3 choses* includes several references to *Orphée* besides these. Robert's earlier line about liking to talk "avec l'Inconnu" alludes to a moment in Cocteau's film when Orpheus, intently transcribing radio messages, tells his wife "I'm on the trail of the Unknown [*l'Inconnu*]." If Robert's choice of a stranger ("une inconnue") for the project of "parler vraiment . . . au cinéma" makes little sense in itself, it is more intelligible as a joke about *Orphée,* where people speak anything but "naturally" (for instance, "I'm on the trail of the Unknown"). Shot 12.29, Robert seen through the car windshield with the rear-view mirror at the top of the frame, pointedly recalls the moment in which Orpheus finally slips and catches the fatal glimpse of Eurydice in a rear-view mirror. Earlier, he sees a picture of her in a magazine and fears he has broken the prohibition against looking at her, but the chauffeur who is the emissary from the underworld explains: "Le portrait de votre femme n'est pas votre femme." Surely this stands behind the segment of Sequence 8 in which Juliette and the young woman look at the magazine, not to mention the passage in *Vivre sa vie* about "the man who does his wife's portrait." Finally, Godard's identification of himself in Sequence 12 as "écrivain" alludes to Orpheus's puzzling reply to the underworld judges concerning his profession: his identity card says he is "un écrivain"; he declares that he is a poet and explains that a poet is "almost a writer" but "doesn't write." Godard discusses *Orphée* and records his, to me, inexplicable admiration of it in a short essay reprinted in *Godard on Godard,* pp. 204–205.

3 Ivanoff's replies resemble those of the novelist Parvulesco (played by the film director Jean-Pierre Melville) in the press conference scene in *Breathless.* When asked about love and eroticism, Parvulesco says: "L'érotisme est une forme d'amour et . . . l'amour est une forme d'érotisme."

4 In *Jean-Luc Godard* (New York: Crown, 1970), p. 168, Jean Collet quotes the following reminiscence by Truffaut:

What struck me most about Godard at the time [1950] was the way he absorbed books. If we were at a friend's house, during one evening he would open easily forty books, and he always read the first and last pages.

He was always very nervous and impatient. He liked cinema as well as any of us, but he was capable of going to see fifteen minutes each of five different films in the same afternoon.

5 *Godard on Godard,* p. 173. Godard's remarks were published in the same year as an attack by Robert Benayoun on the New Wave, which Peter Graham reprints in *The New Wave,* p. 164:

There were quotation films, in which such and such a scene from Hitchcock, coupled with another one from Buñuel, leads up to a long Vigo sequence, shot in a Rossellini manner but rejuvenated by Chayefsky techniques. This more or less bulimic assimilation incidentally reflected a real fascination with the act of nutrition. Those who so admired the *pâté de foie* sequence in one of Becker's films lingered long in their own films over breakfasts, snacks, and banquets. But when the act of creation is replaced by the act of consumption, there arises a phenomenon well known in all cannibals: the eater thinks he has invented what he was eaten.

The cinema, when continually rehashed in this way, inevitably ends up by becoming insipid. The Nouvelle Vague film will give us an imitation, round a bistro table, of some fleeting gesture glimpsed in the third reel of the 1955 remake, in 'Scope, of an old 'B' Western. The height of subtlety consists of making one film in order to say one would like to have made another: 'I would like to dance as they do in Minnelli musicals,' declares Madame Karina, who fails precisely to do so.

Sequence 18

1 The repetition of the verb "oublie" again recalls the relation this film has to the work of Resnais. In *Une femme mariée,* after the intertitle "Memory," the husband tells of being at the Auschwitz trial where the accused "didn't remember a thing." Earlier in that film, Roger Leenhardt asks Charlotte whether she has heard of Auschwitz and she replies: "Oh yes. Thalidomide?" When she and her lover go to the Orly Airport cinema, they see, as I noted earlier, the beginning of Resnais's *Night and Fog.* Her husband's "memory" of Auschwitz is patently a memory of that film's last scene. *Far from Vietnam,* on which Resnais and Godard collaborated, begins with footage of the Vietnam War accompanied by Eisler's score for *Night and Fog.* The point made by this association, the Americans as the new Nazis, recurs throughout the film—which, however, takes care to distinguish the good American people from the bad American government. Godard makes the same rather meretricious analogy in Commentary 28 by pronouncing Esso "E.S.S.O.," emphasizing and grouping the consonants. This also accords with the rhetorical figure that transforms forgetting into remembering.

2 In this connection the man and woman are not unrelated to the protagonists of *Pierrot le fou,* whom Godard describes as "the last romantic couple." The red and blue they wear are also the components of a color *système,* which is, in turn, related to painting, specifically to an opposition between works of Renoir and Picasso. Given the evolution of Godard's thought in this period, the sense of renunciation in 18.4 plausibly includes these associations.